CW00798721

# Phew, Eh Readers?

## The Life and Writing of

# TOM HIBBERT

### Edited by

### Barney Hoskyns and Jasper Murison-Bowie

NINE
EIGHT
BOOKS

NINE
EIGHT
BOOKS

NEB 023

First published in the UK in 2024 by Nine Eight Books
An imprint of Black & White Publishing Group
A Bonnier Books UK company
4th Floor, Victoria House, Bloomsbury Square, London, WC1B 4DA
Owned by Bonnier Books, Sveavägen 56, Stockholm, Sweden

@nineeightbooks

@nineeightbooks

Hardback ISBN: 978-1-7887-0868-5
eBook ISBN: 978-1-7887-0869-2

All rights reserved. No part of this publication may be reproduced, stored in a retrieval system, or transmitted in any form or by any means, without the prior permission in writing of the publisher, nor be otherwise circulated in any form of binding or cover other than that in which it is published and without a similar condition including this condition being imposed on the subsequent purchaser.

A CIP catalogue record for this book is available from the British Library.

Publishing director: Pete Selby
Editor: James Lilford

Cover design by Caroline Grimshaw
Typeset by IDSUK (Data Connection) Ltd
Printed and bound in Great Britain by Clays Ltd, Elcograf S.p.A

1 3 5 7 9 10 8 6 4 2

Text copyright © Tom Hibbert, 2024

The right of Tom Hibbert to be identified as the author of this work has been asserted in accordance with the Copyright, Designs and Patents Act 1988.

Every reasonable effort has been made to trace copyright-holders of material reproduced in this book. If any have been inadvertently overlooked, the publisher would be glad to hear from them.

Nine Eight Books is an imprint of Bonnier Books UK
www.bonnierbooks.co.uk

MIX
Paper | Supporting
responsible forestry
FSC
www.fsc.org FSC® C018072

*In memory of the man himself, 1952–2011*

# My Top Five

1. Laura Debeque's Top 10 was the only thing worth reading in your mag. Her comment on Dillard and Clark's 'Train Leaves Here' was the only sane thing I've ever read about that sickly, over-produced, over-rated band the Eagles. Tell Laura I love her.
2. Has Chris Lightbown no humour? Seeing Charlie George dressed in drag was a fine laugh. It's only a game, Chris old man.
3. Michael Gray's review of those Motown records was right on, far out, power to the people, up against the wall, kill the pigs, too much. What a pseud! If you don't like the job, Michael, my mum's looking for a char.
4. Why does Tony Walton describe Jethro Tull's slagging over *Passion Play* in the press as 'the shit-heap of Critical Abuse'? – and then go on to be so unnecessarily rude about Home's *The Alchemist*! Perhaps he realises he's just a human turd after all.
5. 'The Letter' – by the Box Tops.

*Flowers in your hair,*
*Tom Hibbert*
*Henley-on-Thames, Oxon.*

Letter to *Let It Rock*, December 1973

# Contents

# Preface

# 'Don't laugh, it's true!'

## Barney Hoskyns

*'I've always considered rock journalists to occupy the least significant strata of a fundamentally useless conceptual sphere built entirely upon ego, sycophancy, defensive cynicism and perpetual financial/emotional insecurity. Do you – as purveyors of this ignoble practice – feel that yours is but a pitiful attempt to hold a mirror to the face of rock 'n' roll and disguise that its death-mask image is merely the eternal tombstone of a grave full of second-hand dreams?'*
Letter from Jon Lloyd-Webber (no relation), Oxford

The above letter isn't really a letter at all. At least, not in the strict sense of being an actual missive mailed to the offices of *New Music News*, in which it appeared in 1980. Indeed, it was penned by the very man to whom it had been sent – a fellow who called himself 'Boring Len' but was, in fact, the spindly, chain-smoking university dropout we know as Tom Hibbert.

Tom had composed the 'letter' from Mr Lloyd-Webber (no relation) for the simple reason that – as he informed his future champion and bandmate Mark Ellen – *New Music News* received 'no letters' and in fact had 'no readers'. It was one of many such items 'Hibbs' dashed off during his years as a music journalist, particularly as 'Black Type' in the rather better-selling *Smash Hits*.

Like many of Tom's epistles to himself, the Lloyd-Webber letter held a kernel of mournful truth within its verbose pomposity. Hands-down the funniest writer ever to apply his Wodehouse-on-amphetamine wit to the subject of popular music, he was as much an elegist for a lost rock era as he was a scourge of contemporary celebrities.

'I think he was at heart a satirist,' former *Q* editor Paul Du Noyer writes in this anthology-cum-*Festschrift*. 'From political braggards to show-biz buffoons, he regarded [his victims] as public figures who had let us down.'

In another wonderful tribute for this book, *Smash Hits* star Chris Heath writes that 'Tom came at everything less with negativity than with a sense of disappointment that the world and its inhabitants so often fell short of their wondrous potential . . .'

The 'disappointment' was the shadow side to Tom's revelling in rock's ridiculousness. The fever dream of jangly California cool that possessed him when he first heard the Byrds' 'Mr. Tambourine Man' in 1965 was already tarnished by the time he was trudging through the mud of moronic rock festivals in 1969. An innate and very specific snobbery meant that he rejected much of what was classed – in the definitions provided in his 1983 booklet, *Rockspeak!* – as 'ace' or 'tasty'. Everything from Led Zeppelin to 'the appalling Graham Nash' was eschewed in favour of a select group of damaged 'madcap grandees' that encompassed Arthur Lee, Alex Chilton, Vivian Stanshall and Roky Erickson.

Born in 1952, Tom Hibbert had come into '80s music journalism 'by mistake', following an invitation from his friend Mark Williams to contribute to the aforementioned *New Music News*. An opportunistic weekly launched to fill a void left by the temporary absence of *NME* and *Melody Maker* – whose writers had gone on strike – *New Music News* was a springboard for Tom's years at *Smash Hits* and then at *Q*, where his 'Who the hell . . . ?' interviews became the stuff of legend.

Even before 'Who the hell . . . ?' was properly under way at
*Q*, Tom's famous *Smash Hits* interview with Margaret Thatcher
was a perfect example of the way he cajoled famous people into
skewering themselves, the then Prime Minister obliviously parad-
ing the unctuous sanctimony that belied her bootstrap policies.
More telling, in some ways, was how Tom's legendary interviewing technique fashioned traps for icons such as Ringo Starr and
Gary Numan to reveal their prickly narcissism and bloated self-
regard. (*Not* included in this anthology – for reasons that require
no explanation – is the disturbingly prescient 1990 portrait of the
demonic Jimmy Savile.)

Some of the laugh-out-loud funniest things Tom ever wrote
followed his years as a jobbing pop journo. The '90s columns we've
included from the pages of the *Mail on Sunday* – like his Pendennis
diary entries for the *Observer* – give us Tom at his most gloriously
iconoclastic: the thoughts of a man constantly lamenting the decline
of music that meant anything at all. Pieces about rock T-shirts,
classic pop songs used in TV ads, and – in the internet Stone Age of
1995 – 'the super-information-highway computer "web" thingie' all
stand up remarkably well. Even something as slight and innocuous
as a review of John Denver's execrable autobiography, *Take Me
Home*, becomes a perfect puncturing of delusion:

> *'In a previous life, John Denver was a mountain lion. Don't laugh, it is
> true! Well, I'm sure it isn't true, actually, but that's not the point. The
> point is that he, Denver, believes it to be true. Yes, here again we have an
> American whose sense of reality has been drummed away, by celebrity and
> too much money, unto nothing.'*

Not long after the last of the Pendennis pieces was published, in
May 1997, Tom fell gravely ill with pneumonia and pancreatitis,
spending over three months in an induced coma. He was never the
same after emerging from Hammersmith's Charing Cross Hospital,

writing precious little in the final fourteen years of his life, but there will never be a funnier writer on pop music.

He lives on in these genius pieces, which lovingly mock the great, the good and the lamentable alike, exposing the irresistible self-delusions of pop entertainers for all to see. Get ready to cackle out loud at the joyous absurdity of it all – in Paul Du Noyer's words, 'the glorious stupidity of life'.

# Introduction

# Dear reader

## Jasper Murison-Bowie

Compiling this book, one is struck by Tom Hibbert's ready wit and dazzling/baffling turns of phrase, but most of all by his ability to care about his subject – to take the world seriously enough to fix it in his bemused gaze and either elevate it to the sublime or ridicule its absurdity.

It would be easy – indeed it's very tempting – to fill this introduction with pastiche Hibbert expressions and extraneous quotation marks. (You can bet a few will sneak their way through.) But though Tom's lexicon was hilarious, it's meaningless without his arched eyebrow to back it up and his sharpness to temper it. Occasionally, and particularly for the uninitiated, his unique patter requires a second look and a willingness to feel ever so slightly clueless. His great trick, however, is to welcome you into his world. By dint of being his 'dear reader', you are always on his side.

The literary jester is a fitting point of comparison. He mocks his subjects and in the process causes much mirth, but also represents frank honesty and remains unbowed before royalty – or in this case celebrity. Tom demonstrated clearly that popular culture's heroes weren't always as gallant as they might appear. He developed a cunning interview technique to tease out revelations other interviewers couldn't: having had a question answered, he'd refrain from posing another and instead just wait in silence. His unsuspecting victim would then feel compelled to fill that silence with something – *anything* – and in so doing come out with the most remarkable piffle, neatly hoisting them with their own petard.

Tom's elegant prose was deeply self-referential, replete with in-jokes and reflections; throughout the course of his career he was able to apply it to a number of different topics. This volume follows a loosely chronological structure, commencing with autobiographical pieces and then exploring some of his earliest published music writing before we get to a smattering of his *Smash Hits* and *Q* classics. It's a matter of personal disappointment that we were unable to locate the Hibbert guide to wiring your own home, supposedly published in a DIY home-improvement magazine in the late '70s – but perhaps it's for the best that it should remain forgotten, lest anyone mistake it for trustworthy guidance and electrocute themselves.

Once the magazine world had caught on to Tom's high ironies – i.e. by the time everyone was doing it, just not as well – he moved on to being a columnist for the *Observer* and the *Mail on Sunday*'s *Night & Day* magazine. If you weren't paying close attention at the time, you might have missed the marvellously preposterous event that was his swing-and-a-miss at running for political office in Henley-on-Thames, the constituency of his birth. Standing against incumbent Conservative MP Michael Heseltine for the long-defunct Whig Party, Tom recorded his campaign diary in the *Observer*'s Pendennis column, including references to an entirely fabricated wife, Celia, and three children with the splendidly Rees-Moggian names Benjy, Coriolanus and Griselda. We've gathered this sequence of columns so that you can follow along with the highs and lows of the politicking Hibbert.

It was always our intention for the book to be as much *about* Tom as by him. Thus it's been an honour and a pleasure to invite those who knew the man to reminisce about him. Throughout the book, you'll find a number of 'Hibbert and I' pieces that we hope will provide insight into what made Tom tick and what he might've been like to share an office or go to the pub with. The process of assembling the collection has been highly amusing as well as profoundly moving. Meeting Tom's delightful widow Allyce – whose recollections are gathered in her inevitably more personal 'Tom and me' piece – it's clear that for all his charm and humour, Tom wasn't always an easy person to be around, let alone married to. Nevertheless, the warmth of feeling towards him is plain to see in the pages that follow, expressed in such myriad ways by such a varied cast, that I'm left wishing I could have met him to experience his repartee first hand. (Though perhaps not as a guest in one of those fictional dinner party scenarios, given his penchant for out-of-the-box mashed potatoes.)

One suspects that, were he alive to see this publication reach the light of day, Tom would be slightly bemused by the gathering of his writings in this manner. There is something peculiar about plucking a handful of articles from the rest and bending them into a *post hoc* structure, given he was as much a cultural commentator as a music journalist. But his insights into the way things work, and his thoughts as to how they *should* work, crystallise through his writing into a lucid articulation of a worldview as meaningful now as it was when he was alive.

To those of you who knew Tom, personally or through his writing, we hope the book captures something of his magic and reminds you how the world appeared through his eyes. To those of you coming to him fresh: strap in tight, you're in for a treat. And now it's time to delve into that world of Hibbertiana and remember the singular genius of one of pop's great jesters.

Phew, eh readers?

# Part One

## Who the hell did Tom Hibbert think he was?

We set the scene with three long, semi-autobiographical
pieces that help to explain the Hibbert mindset
and worldview.

Tom in Henley, circa 1970, hoisted aloft by his friend Juggins
(courtesy of Allyce Hibbert).

*'I had my first letter published in* Melody Maker *in 1970. It was about Crosby, Stills & Nash and how crap Graham Nash was, which I think still stands up today.*

*'I remember reading [Nick Kent's* NME*] review of the first Television album and going out and buying it because the writing was so potent. I played the record and thought, "He's got it absolutely spot on."'*

Tom Hibbert, 2001[1]

---

[1] This and all subsequent epigraphs are taken from Paul Gorman's interview with Tom for the 2001 oral history *In Their Own Write: Adventures in the Music Press*. The quotes are also featured in Paul's wider-ranging 2022 book *Totally Wired: The Rise and Fall of the Music Press*.

# Just like Gene Autry: A foxtrot

From *Love is the Drug* (ed. John Aizlewood, Penguin, 1994)

It was, I suppose, the sunglasses that did it. My first term at a minor public school (Quaker, i.e. no corporal punishment so lots of mental torture by Latin masters instead), and while searching for cheap sweets in the high-street branch of F.W. Woolworth (contrary to popular belief, not *all* public schools had tuck shops in the mid-'60s), I came across the box of sunglasses.

Not any old sunglasses, you understand, but Ben Franklin-type sunglasses, all rectangular slits and all *cool* because they looked just like the glasses that *Jim McGuinn out of the Byrds wore*. There was no sign above the box saying *SUNGLASSES! AS WORN BY JIM McGUINN OUT OF THE BYRDS — AS SEEN ON TV!*, and goodness knows what these superb fashion accessories were doing in the crumby shop at all, but, of course, I had to have a pair, even though they cost a florin (that's 10p in modern money), which was quite a lot for a boy on an allowance of a bob (that's 5p in modern money) a week. Even though the blinkers were fashioned entirely from cheap plastics from the Orient, I *had* to have a pair. So I nicked them. My first ever brush with true crime. God, how scared I felt and how guilty but, you see, this theft was *essential* – 'It was a matter of life

3

and death, Your Honour, I throw myself upon the mercy of the Court' – for Jim McGuinn had been my lifetime hero, much much more than a schoolboy crush, for more than a week now.

You know that hoary old chestnut about everyone remembering where they were and exactly what they were doing when they heard that Kennedy had been shot. It's probably true. Sadly, I am old enough to remember. I was eleven years old and watching the exciting quiz show, *Take Your Pick*, downstairs while my parents were upstairs taking a bath. (They didn't quite approve of their children watching *Take Your Pick*, so I snuck it on while they were otherwise engaged.) Quite annoyed, I was, I can tell you, when my sinful entertainment was interrupted by a newsflash from Dallas just as Mr Miles was to open Box 13, wherein lay, quite possibly, a hilarious booby prize such as a floor-mop for one of the evening's common contestants. Yes, I remember it well, the death of the President: but the memory pales into monochrome insignificance when compared with the recollection of where I was and what I was doing when I first heard the Byrds' 'Mr. Tambourine Man'. *That* I can rewind and replay in all its Technicolor glory. It even comes with smells. The smells of schoolboy piss and schoolboy sweat and schoolboy cabbage and schoolboy liver dinners, the kind of liver that comes with grotesque tubes in and is only ever served to schoolboys, wafting in through the windows – for it was in the changing rooms, after my first ever experience of rugby football, that I heard the Byrds' 'Mr. Tambourine Man'.

I hated rugby and I still do. What a cloddish, graceless game. Some master had run around shouting at me (and *only* me, it seemed) to do things that I didn't understand because nobody had bothered to explain the rules of the cloddish, graceless game to me. I'd made a forward pass and my team 'mates' had laughed (Why? What was wrong with passing forward? That was what we had *tried* to do at my prep school, where we had played footer) and someone had stamped on my hand. It hurt, and here I was in the changing room, not wanting to take a shower and trying very hard not to blub when a muddy-booted, jock-strapped (what were jock-straps *for*?) sixth-former came in, took a transistor radio from his locker and switched it, loudly, on. '*Da-da-da-da-da-da-da-da-da-da-da . . . da-da-da . . . Hey, Mr. Tambourine Man, play a song for me . . .*' My mouth dropped open, I stopped my whimpering. My eyes dropped open. Suddenly, the world didn't seem such a disgracefully cruel and heartless place after all. With sweet music such as this playing in the world, there was hope for humanity. My courage knew no bounds. Throwing caution to the winds, I approached the swaggering sixth-former.

'I say, what is that you're listening to?' I chirped.

He turned on me, towered over me, with a withering sneer, 'What does it *look* like, you horrid little oik. It's a radio. Ever *heard* of a radio?'

Undeterred by his amazingly brilliant sarcasm, I pressed on. 'No, no, you see, I meant what group is it? It doesn't sound like the Beatles. I wondered if you, er . . .'

'What's your name?'

'Hibbert.'

'Well, *Hibbert*,' he sneered menacingly, snapping off the transistor just as the twelve-string guitar was starting to sing. 'You can take two marks for cheek!' (If you got six marks in any one week, you were 'gated', had to do detention, polish floors and stairs or other such delightful punishments.) Then he cuffed me round the ear and swaggered into the showers. That sixth-former is now a Conservative MP. Not a Byrds fan, I gather . . .

Fortunately, the school wasn't *quite* as *Tom Brown's Schooldays* as I have painted it. We were allowed to watch the telly sometimes – albeit sitting squashed up next to one another in our ties and blazers and shiny grey trousers on long benches that reeked of furniture polish. We were allowed to watch sports sometimes (*encouraged* to do so if the sport in question was bloody rugger), and, for some reason that, looking back on the atmosphere of the place, I cannot fathom, we were allowed to watch *Top of the Pops*. And that's where I saw them. The sunglasses of Jim McGuinn. His twelve-string guitar and non-Jaggeresque nonchalance. (Even at that age, I didn't like Jagger, silly fat-lipped show-off, and despite the fact that I'd seen *A Hard Day's Night* at Reading's Glendale Cinema – nowadays a church of foreign sorts – twice on the same day, the Beatles left much to be desired to my ears and sensibilities. The Byrds were simply *it* and life would never be the same again: Michael Clarke, the drummer, with longer hair even than Brian Jones; David Crosby, long before he turned to fat, looking thoroughly groovy in a cape; Gene Clark – who *was* that man with the tambourine, seemingly doing nothing? Obviously a brainbox and genius of sorts.

The sixth-formers on the whiffy benches tutted and said sixth-form things about this assortment of strummers looking like 'bloody girls'. But a majority of the little boys, the thirteen-year-olds, the chaps in my dorm who didn't much like rugger either, seemed to understand. John Patey, who was only a day boy (day boys went home after nine o'clock at night – how very odd this all seems now), got it. We were the class of 1965, and imagine John Patey's furious jealousy when I showed him my Ben Franklin sunglasses before Latin a few days later.

Patey (I'll never call him John: Christian names were always banned at public school for reasons only perverts and disciplinarians have ever understood) was taking guitar lessons. So was I. QED we would form a pop group just like the Byrds. It would take some time to save up for the equipment, but over the coming months, we were never diverted from our ultimate cause. He bought a useless electric guitar. I bought a useless electric guitar. I'd begged 'pater' for a twelve-string electric guitar for Christmas, but as these things cost more than £80 and Barnes & Avis had perfectly respectable models of the six-stringed variety (with impossibly high actions . . . cut your little fingers to pieces) for less than a fiver, we settled on that. Patey and Hibbert were joined by some spotty bloke whose

name now escapes me on the school drum kit and nobody at all
on the bass guitar, because we didn't quite understand how that
worked. A (liberal) sixth-former lent us a really crappy ten-watt
amplifier into which Patey and I would plug our crappy guitars.
We were fair set to change the world of popular music (just like the
Byrds had done) as sixth formers knew it. It didn't quite happen.

We'd had an enormous setback already when my housemaster, catching me in my fantastic sunglasses after lights out, doing
a splendid impersonation of Jim McGuinn performing 'All I
Really Want to Do', had confiscated the specs and, to add insult
to injury, ordered me to get my hair cut immediately. 'Bit shaggy,
Hibbert. You look like a *girl*.' Yes, yes, yes. What's *wrong* with
looking like a girl anyway, you frightful man? (With 'kindness',
the housemaster handed the spectacles back to me at the end of
term, but they were bent beyond all recognition and rendered
redundant. Whatever had he done with them? Weedily, I never
dared ask. Anyway, this setback worried us greatly. Who was
going to pretend to be McGuinn without the glasses?) The next
setback was that, when we plugged in our lousy instruments, we
didn't seem to sound anywhere *near* as good as the Byrds, for
some unaccountable reason.

The final setback was the name. There was a half-hour free
period after prep, when we'd rehearse; but after our first disastrous
attempt we didn't rehearse at all, we just argued about what to call
this band that would rival the Byrds in cool and quality. I wanted
to call it the Eagles – clearly years ahead of my time – because
the eagle is a brand of bird. Patey wanted to call it the Zambesi
Warriors because, or so he claimed, Zambesi warriors dress as birds
with feathers on their arms when in combat. I always got better
marks in history but, still, not having the relevant reference books
to hand, I could hardly put up an argument. The drummer didn't
care what it was called because he had a chance of being in the
house rugger team, which was far more exciting.

Funny how time slips away. Two or three years later, two of the members of this blistering trio would be smoking pot and dropping acid and doing, or attempting to do, things with girls. Additionally, I would still be listening to 'Eight Miles High' and still adoring the Byrds. I suppose I owe it all to Jim – by then Roger – McGuinn. But it was as the Zambesi Warriors that we took the stage, right there in front of the pipes of the school organ, at the school dance of 1966. Purple chiffon scarves and the most execrable version of 'Turn! Turn! Turn!' anyone had ever heard in their lives. How can you dance to 'Turn! Turn! Turn!', particularly when performed by an out-of-tune trio who can't play for toffee and who are 'singing' through microphones first pressed into service between the wars? You can't.

Before our appearance – we were, unsurprisingly, bottom of the bill (trad jazz band and folk troupe to follow) – the headmaster, who prided himself on being up-to-the-minute and conversant with all the current phraseology, had made an announcement: 'No snogging on the dance floor!' The girls from the school down the road had giggled and the sixth-formers had wiggled their eyebrows knowingly. But, to the sound of the Zambesi Warriors, 'snogging' was out of the question. Where had my clearly unhealthy obsession with pop music begun? And why was it always American stars rather than the home-grown variety that gripped me so? I don't know. Ask a shrink or somebody. All I do know is that from the moment I first heard Duane Eddy's 'Because They're Young' at the tender age of eight, I was hooked. For life. From that moment all pocket money and financial gifts from maiden aunts were saved up until the glorious moment when I could afford the four shillings and tenpence for the latest single by the twangy Mr Eddy. 'Shazam!', 'Kommotion', 'Pepe', 'Theme from Dixie', 'Ballad of Paladin'. All would be heard over and over in the listening booth of Hammants, Henley-on-Thames, a bicycle shop with a modest record department up some wooden stairs. The shop assistant, a Cliff Richard fan with an unfortunate complexion and very thick spectacles, was always very patient with me. She knew I'd buy the thing in the end. 'Don't know what you want this rubbish for,' she would mutter as she popped my proud purchase into a brown paper bag. I left the premises with an air of superiority, secure in the knowledge that as Duane Eddy came from Arizona that was somewhere probably exotic in America, he was, perforce, a million times better than Cliff's feeble Shadows.

'Some Kinda Earthquake', 'Ring of Fire', 'Deep in the Heart of Texas' followed. And, glory be, finally a Duane Eddy long-player, *$1,000,000 Worth of Twang*, which spent a happy term in my prep-school desk until the geography master found it there, had the effrontery to laugh at Duane's quiff and confiscated the miraculous thing (confiscation seems to be a recurring theme of my pop music childhood). I also got into quite a lot of trouble when I removed several boxes of Kellogg's Cornflakes from the school kitchens because they had a competition in which you could win a Burns electric guitar just like Hank B. Marvin's (not that I liked Hank B. Marvin, who could never twang like Duane, but I certainly wanted an electric guitar). I didn't win that guitar – goodness knows what the judges were thinking of because my tie-breaking phrase, 'I would like to win a Burns electric guitar because [in fifteen words or less] . . .THE TWANG'S THE THANG!' were words borrowed from the Great Guitar God D. Eddy himself; I won the right to clean the school van, inside and out, instead.

Listening to them now after all these years, Mr Duane Eddy's tunes all sound almost exactly the same and, alas, rather tiresomely jaunty, but my ears were different – wider? – then. But then, in 1962, my hero committed the mortal sin (to my way of thinking, anyway) of including *vocals* on a record. Worse than this, they were *female* vocals. With 'Dance With the Guitar Man', my first love affair came to a messy conclusion and I wouldn't feel the same about anything again – until I heard the Byrds. Now, there is no

9

discernible likeness between the music of Duane Eddy and the chimes of the Byrds, but then three years is a lifetime when you are so very young . . .

Although the Zambesi Warriors were to triumph in the rehearsal room (also known as the chemistry lab) when they managed, on one notable and triumphant occasion, to get all the way through '(So You Want To Be a) Rock and Roll Star' without breaking a single string or arguing once about what the next chord might be, they split up when a) John Patey traitorously switched his musical affiliations from the Byrds to the Jimi Hendrix Experience, and b) I managed to persuade my parents to take me away from the public school and send me to a grammar school, where they had things called girls.

This was the life. Here I would be able to impress the opposite sex with my growing collection of Byrds' LPs. I would show them the cover of *5th Dimension*, upon which McGuinn and Michael Clarke and Chris Hillman and Crosby were perched upon a colourful and mysterious carpet. I would lay out my theory: that the carpet was, in fact, a veiled reference to hashish and other exciting narcotics. Then I'd whip out *The Notorious Byrd Brothers*, upon which McGuinn and Hillman and Clarke were photographed alongside a horse, and tell the girls, who would be quite fascinated, that the horse was a veiled reference to David Crosby, who'd been thrown out of the band because his songs were stupid and McGuinn hated him. Then I would play them the Byrds' strange and beautiful 'Dolphin's Smile' and they would be mine for ever (or for a bit, at any rate). For some reason, however, the grammar girls of 1968 were more into the Beatles or the Herd or Marmalade than the Byrds, while all the boys were trying to grow moustaches (during holidays only) to make them feel more like Cream, the school heroes.

I smoked pot for the first time to the sound of Cream's 'Tales of Brave Ulysses' and I was very sick indeed. If it had been 'Eight Miles High' or 'Why' or 'Dolphin's Smile' or anything as lovely by my adored young men from California, it would have been all right, I know. And I first dropped acid while the 'friend' who had supplied it played his copy of Spooky Tooth's *Spooky Two* album over and over again. By the time Luther Grosvenor was playing the grinding guitar solo of 'Evil Woman' for what seemed like the millionth time, I was having something called a bad trip. I badly needed the twelve-stringed soothings of Roger McGuinn to bring me down, man. In the words of Vanilla Fudge (another group who tortured me as migraine rabbits scampered around my head that horrible night), 'I just hope the trip gets lighter', but my 'friend' didn't have any Byrds records because he thought the Byrds were nothing more than a 'pop' group.

To be a 'pop' group in the late '60s was a crime of staggering proportions. 'Pop' groups were for girls who appeared in school productions of *Antigone* and for boys who were still virgins. 'Pop' groups were for girls who did their homework in very neat handwriting and who dotted their 'i's with little circles and for boys who didn't smoke No. 6. I didn't smoke No. 6 and I was a virgin and I didn't like rock music very much at all. 'Pop' music, as purveyed by the Byrds, was the thing; if the philistines with the John Mayall's Bluesbreakers records and the John Mayall's Bluesbreakers fashion sense could but see it, the Byrds were far druggier, hence far more hip, than John Mayall's Bluesbreakers or Cream or the Nice. Indeed, I felt vastly superior to the common rock hordes. What on earth did they see in Led Zeppelin with that caterwauling twerp singing blues clichés rather badly when they *could* be wallowing in glorious harmonies and wondering why Roger McGuinn was so obsessed with outer space and the sea?

Nobody round here liked the Byrds at all and, really, I preferred it that way. The group were mine – my delight alone, and I imagined that this made me somehow special and strange. It certainly made me a snob. I longed to discover another American band, an American pop band more obscure than the Byrds and just as

11

splendid with which to annoy the Pink Floyd-dotty rabble. *That* would show them. While they were out on their army Cadet Force manoeuvres in their stupid khaki uniforms with their stupid bullet-free guns being barked at by a Sergeant-Major type, I (as one of only two boys at the school who refused to join the Cadet Force, being a 'Conscientious Objector', hem hem) would be in the sixth-form common-room listening to the magical sounds of this Mystery Group and everyone would think me odder than ever. I just *loved* being odd. God, I was odd, and God, I was witty, but nobody understood the jokes because nobody was clever enough. And everyone would hate my Mystery Group because everyone was so Dumb. They worshipped Cream and Cream's tedious drum solos and they didn't like the Byrds. Dumb, dumb, dumb. How they would *hate* my Mystery Group, hate them because they were *afraid* and didn't *understand*. Ha, ha. The poor, ignorant fools. *Fools!!!!*

The only drawback to this brilliant plan was that I couldn't seem to 'discover' this Mystery Group at all. The radio was no help. John Peel was no help. He played Quicksilver Messenger Service on the wireless once and, on the strength of that, I bought *Happy Trails*, which was jolly good but not quite *it*, not the stuff of which blind devotion is made. I tried the Velvet Underground because they came from New York and took lots of drugs, apparently, but try as I might to convince myself otherwise, they weren't my cup of tea at all, even though they had cool sunglasses. No, the Velvet Underground were too gloomy; they wouldn't do at all. Tried Frank Zappa. Hated him. Tried Jefferson Airplane. Liked them, but not nearly enough. Toyed with the idea of appointing Captain Beefheart & the Magic Band my Mystery Group but, no, the Captain was just too odd, too deliberately bonkers to serve my purposes – besides which the other grammar-school 'Conscientious Objector', a fine fellow called Basingstoke though that wasn't his name, had already discovered Captain Beefheart and had taken to coming to school in a battered top hat (soon confiscated, naturally).

It was, astonishingly enough, that most staid and conservative of record retailers, WH Smith, that came to my rescue. One day, while buying my weekly copy of *Melody Maker* (how I hated *Melody Maker*, it always contained pictures of Jimmy Page and, worse, Crosby, Stills & Nash. David Crosby had become a major hate figure since his bust-up with McGuinn and since he had severely marred the otherwise fabulous *Younger Than Yesterday* album with his pompous song 'Mind Gardens', where the fat one had quoted Shakespeare and sounded very silly indeed. I bought the publication anyway because, well, one just did), I noticed they had a record sale on. It was a rather strange sale: LPs, all on CBS, by people like the Electric Flag and Johnny Winter and my beloved Byrds (I'd already got *Dr Byrds and Mr Hyde*, thank you very much) for 13s 6d. And there were four LPs by some group I had never heard of called Moby Grape. 'What a foolish name,' was my first reaction (it came from the rib-tickling joke 'What's purple and lives at the bottom of the sea?' I later discovered).

Then two things happened. One: I realised, with a blinding flash of adolescent serendipity, that the initials of Moby Grape were the same as those of Mystery Group. Two: I studied the cover of one of these four LPs and noticed that the group looked achingly, smokingly cool. They were five men standing and sitting outside what looked like an olde American hardware store, as seen in countless western motion pictures and *Bonanza*. One of them (Alex 'Skip' Spence, I would soon learn) was wearing a brilliant fringed jacket and had brilliant hair and was next to an American flag and looked peculiar. Standing beside him was a fellow (Peter Lewis) in a blazer and a white polo neck, who looked as if he had just escaped from the Dave Clark Five: the contrast between these two at the back could not have been more striking. It got even better. Sitting at the front was a man (Jerry Miller) with a rifle propped between his legs. Next to him was another man (Don Stevenson), and between *his* legs was a washboard upon which he rested his right hand and formed the rude sign of the finger, the American equivalent of the British V sign. Next to *him* was a man (Bob Mosley) with brilliant boots, scowling and handsome. Best of all was the fact that this last person had a frying pan in his right hand. And even better than *this* was the fact that both he and the one in the middle were, with their left hands, holding up a spoon for no apparent reason whatsoever. Cool or what? Intrigued, beguiled, I bought the album.

It was with some trepidation that I put the record, *Moby Grape* by Moby Grape, on my parents' radiogram (we hadn't graduated to hi-fi yet; imagine my wonder when I heard the Byrds all over again in stereo a couple of years later). It was bound to be a crushing disappointment and I would have wasted 13s 6d on a dud. It was not to be. This was glorious. This was what I had been waiting for. They sang things like *'I got high this time around, this time round/ Everything is upside down, upside down,'* which to a boy flirting with drugs was just right, and the music was weird and spooky, but not *too* weird and spooky. This was pop – the longest song on the album was a mere four minutes, refreshingly brief by the standards of the day – but it was pop turned on its head, and the guitarists, of which there were three, played beautiful, dizzying pop/rock stuff, especially Jerry Miller, which had me thinking, 'Ha, ha, ha, eat your heart out, Eric Clapton, Jeff Beck and Jimmy bloody Page. These guys don't show off and monkey about with violin bows. They don't *need* to. Because they are strange and clever, you see. Ha, ha, ha.' I had discovered my Mystery Group. The Mystery Group even dealt in delicious five-part harmonies, unheard of in these progressive times. Yes, the prancing toy soldiers who were my classmates would really detest *this* lot. And so they did.

The next day, I managed to cadge a couple of quid off Basingstoke, who had a Saturday job in a plastic extrusions factory and was, therefore, rich beyond the dreams of avarice, and went to WH Smith. To my relief, but not to my surprise in this town of 'straights', the other three Moby Grape LPs were still there, waiting. I bought them. *Wow* had a strange cover with a huge bunch of grapes and an old ship on the front; on *Moby Grape 69*, they stood looking quite bored against a huge slab of rock, but there were only four of them now (no Spence). *Truly Fine Citizen* just had on its cover a stout and grinning policeman – what could it mean? Some anti-establishment message, no doubt. (Actually, it wasn't a cop at all but a security guard at Columbia's studio in Nashville whom the group had befriended and who had made sure no one got into the studio while the group were smoking dope, but I didn't know this at the time.)

'*Get out of my town!*' '*It's your town, I'll get out of it.*' '*Longhaired creep!*', ran a strange piece of dialogue on *Wow*'s 'Rose Colored Eyes'. This became a rallying cry for me and Basingstoke in the weeks to come, a secret message between two like-minded schoolboys soon bound for university and the world proper. There was a track on *Wow* called 'Just Like Gene Autry: A Foxtrot'. You had to play it at 78 rpm, and it had nothing whatsoever to do with pop or rock, being a thing written by Skip Spence featuring a genuine 1930s-style dance orchestra and 'starring Arthur Godfrey, banjo and ukulele'. This was such an unlikely joke, I could not contain my admiration. Skippy was clearly so cracked, I had found a new role model for life. I had fallen in love all over again and even the Byrds didn't get much airplay on our radiogram that summer.

By the time I discovered Moby Grape, the band had already split up. I found this out by buying old copies of *Rolling Stone* lurking in a hippie shop in Reading. Somehow, this made me even more of a fan. Moby Grape had split up and I had all their great albums, the entire collection. Moby Grape had split up so nothing could spoil them now. Moby Grape didn't exist. It was a perfect love affair. Nothing could ever come between us. And nothing ever did.

I lasted just one term at Leeds University. Freedom? In a ghastly hall of residence surrounded by Newcastle Brown-guzzling, rugger-buggering, mechanical-engineering types, I felt more imprisoned than I had at public school. It was worse than school. Everyone on my corridor was playing Santana, so I just cranked up the sound of Moby Grape on my cheapest of non-stereo systems as loud as possible. Still, 'Soul Sacrifice' or *Abraxas* or whatever it was called came sneaking in, swamping the soft bits of 'Indifference' and 'Motorcycle Irene' and 'Seeing' (probably the most gorgeous pop song ever). I couldn't stay here. I would 'drop out', that's what I would do.

I was supposed to be studying history at university. And that's what I did. Unfortunately, it wasn't the history of medieval communications and agricultural systems, as it was supposed to be, but the history of Moby Grape. As they were almost entirely unknown in this country, never mentioned in *Melody Maker* or anywhere like that, this was a time-consuming task, one which I set about with passion. I should have got a degree anyway, if you ask me. The more I discovered about the group, the more I became infatuated with them, the more I absorbed myself in the recordings. It was such a great pop story, the stuff of which legends are made.

They were signed up to Columbia just before the so-called Summer of Love. They were supposed to be a somewhat tardy answer to the Rolling Stones (because there were five of them and they all had what we now call 'attitude'), but it didn't quite work out like that. The *music* worked, for sure, but everything else went horribly wrong from the start. Apart from the fact that the group's bizarre take on pop sat uneasily beside all the other San Franciscan peace-vibe stuff of the era – Airplane, Grateful Dead et al. – the marketing of the debut LP put off potential buyers from the start. It was hyped in days when hype was simply not on. Five singles from that first album were released on the very same day: 'Omaha', 'Hey Grandma', '8:05', 'Fall On You' and 'Sitting By the Window'. What was the point of that? Only 'Omaha' got anywhere near the hit parade (No. 88). There were lavish launch parties for the record featuring, among other things, purple balloons and orchid petals dropping down from the ceiling on to the floor, where party-goers promptly slipped on them. For the launch party at the Avalon Ball-room there were 700 bottles of wine with Moby Grape labels – but somebody had forgotten to provide any corkscrews. They even had a purple elephant walking down LA's Sunset Boulevard. Moby Grape. Never knowingly undersold. The PR wheezes only served to make them seriously unhip, all credibility blown before they'd even started.

It got worse. Miller, Lewis and Spence were charged with con-tributing to the delinquency of minors. Miller was charged with marijuana possession. The debut LP cover was censored, air-brushed to remove Stevenson's rude finger and the American flag as well (they didn't bother with this censorship in Britain because nobody apart from me bought the damned record anyway). The band were thrown out of hotels everywhere in time-honoured tra-dition. Spence was taking too many hallucinogenics and hacked down Stevenson's hotel-room door with a fire axe, suffering from the delusion that Stevenson was the Devil. For that, Skippy ended up in Bellevue Hospital, an institution we used to call a loony bin. Finally, Bob Mosley quit to join the Marines because he wanted to go to Vietnam. What??!!! When I learned *that* fact, I was a little bit shocked. Wanting to go to Vietnam wasn't on the rock 'n' roll agenda at all, but, in retrospect, just *because* it's so non-rock 'n' roll, this seems the coolest crack-up manoeuvre of all. Particularly as Mosley was soon thrown out of the Marines for making a nuisance of himself.

So Moby Grape, a band that should have ruled the world, had split up before we'd even been introduced. 'It took some strange kind of genius to screw it up and screw it up so bad,' said Jerry Miller. How right he was. Genius, it is.

Yes, they fucked up royally, on a gargantuan scale, did my music idols. Cruel and callous as it may seem, I like my pop stars to fuck up; it shows they are (or were) of the human scale. I can't tell you much about Duane Eddy, probably doing okay, but at the time of writing, which is May 1994, the roll call of casualty looks like this . . .

Michael Clarke. Dead.

Gene Clark. Dead.

David Crosby. *Should* be dead, the shotgun-toting, drug/drunk-driving, rehab-recovery buffoon, but somehow he survives.

Alex 'Skip' Spence. Living in a residential-care house in San Jose, diagnosed schizophrenic. Panhandles for loose change. Promptly gives his takings away.

Bob Mosley. Itinerant.

Don Stevenson. Sells double-glazing or something.

Six down. Four to go. I choose my heroes well.

It is 1991 and I am on holiday in California with my wife, my sister and my friend William. In Fort Bragg, a small industrial town just to the north of the plush hippie enclave of Mendocino, I am despatched from the hire car into a package store for some more beer. When I return with my purchases in a brown paper bag, there's a strange atmosphere in the car. William seems to be hiding something under the passenger seat and there's some tense whispering going on.

'What's the matter?' I ask. 'Is everything alright?'

'Yes,' says my wife.

'Yes,' says my sister.

'Um,' says William.

I am not convinced and I make this clear.

'You'd better tell him,' says my wife with a sigh, and William digs the local newspaper from its hiding place and shows me the small ad he's found therein. Moby Grape, on one of their sporadic reunions, are playing in some sleazy club in Fort Bragg, it says here. What? No! No. It was last night. It has come to this. I missed them. I am plunged into a dark gloom, just as my travel-mates feared.

And that's my interesting story of how I never got to see Moby Grape, not on stage, not on telly, not anywhere. I saw the Byrds a few times but not the proper Byrds, just the McGuinn/Skip Battin/ Clarence White/Gene Parsons Byrds who made *(Untitled)*. They were *all right*, but I longed for Gene Clark (no longer with us) and short songs and proper harmonies and no bloody bass guitar solos.

I met McGuinn once in 1978 at the BBC and, overcome with horrid hospitality wine, plucked up the courage to tell him he was my hero. He was singularly unimpressed, downright rude if I remember right. I met him again a couple of years ago when, now a journalist, I interviewed him. It was a less than lovely experience. He was a surly old cuss, short on smiles and charm. This was the man who had driven me to crime, forcing me to shoplift from Woolies because I fancied his spectacles, and he could hardly be bothered to give me the time of day. So, really, I suppose I am quite glad that my path has never crossed with those of the men of Moby Grape. It might just spoil everything. Here is a love affair that has lasted for a quarter of a century – think of it! – a love that endures. It's all rather silly, isn't it?

# Bath 1970: Confessions of a festival-goer

## *The History of Rock*, Volume 6, Issue 63, 1983

The Bath Festival of Blues and Progressive Music, held on Saturday 26 and Sunday 27 June 1970, wasn't in Bath at all. It was in Shepton Mallet – a good fifteen miles from the city – and I suppose we should have taken a map because we got hopelessly lost trying to track down the village. Not that it made all that much difference, however, for when we *did* hit the right road, it was jam-packed with vehicles in a similar dilapidated condition to our own, and the traffic was progressing at a considerably slower rate than the thousands of rucksacked pedestrians trudging indefatigably towards the site in sandals and filthy, patched jeans.

At last we heard the strains of 'progressive' music wafting through the morning's warm air and knew we must be close. At this point – as if signalling a (not unwarranted) dislike of the Keef Hartley Band – the car spluttered and died. We got out and pushed; the trundling hordes ignored our plight.

### Hot dog horror

Two and a half miles later we parked, pitched the tent, stowed a gallon of best Somerset cider plus other assorted provisions (beans, nasty-looking tins of Irish stew, cheese and onion-flavoured crisps, chocolate digestives) beneath the sleeping bags and wandered down to the playing fields. At the gates, burly figures with armbands saying 'Steward' stood beside a large, ominous sign saying 'Beware of Adders. If bitten . . .'. We queued up with our tickets (£2.10s for the weekend). The queue did not move. At the front, a long-haired youth in a tie-dye shirt held the hand of a very-pregnant girl in grimy Paisley smock and pebble specs. The youth was involved in a lengthy discussion with the stewards: 'Look, man, me and my chick have hitched all the way from Northampton 'cause we thought this was, you know, like a *free* festival, not a rip-off festival, and we've got no bread . . .' ran the gist of his argument. The authorities' response: 'Push off, John.'

Once inside the grassy arena, we selected a few square feet of turf and settled down with our other gallon of cider. Some 150 yards away was a gigantic stage; on the right, portly, bearded roadies bumbled about with bits of wire while on the left, Joe Jammer made a horrible racket with lots of guitars. The group stopped, the crowd booed, the Maynard Ferguson Big Band came on to play some sort of jazz music, the crowd booed.

'Hey, people, like there's gonna be a few announcements while, er, the crew shift some gear around,' said the MC to the assembled multitude. 'Like firstly if anyone gets bummed out on a bad trip, the Release tent is to the right – that's *your* left, right, heh heh – of the stage. Right. Er, actually, you know, keep it cool with the dope 'cause we have got fuzz out there.' The crowd hissed and booed. 'No, listen, cool it – they're just doing a gig, right? Don't hassle them and they won't hassle you, okay.'

When the MC finally approached the end of this seemingly interminable 'rap', he announced that before the scheduled appearance of Fairport Convention, 'a very special friend would like to come on and sing some songs for free'. To loud groans around the field, Donovan took to the stage.

Two hours into Donovan's enervating set, I realised that I was uncomfortable; the crowd had swelled and my body was now restricted to mere inches of ground. To make matters worse, a stout American person to my rear kept kicking me – accidentally – in the back. He seemed to be under the influence of something, for he was fidgeting about, waving a bent steel coat-hanger in the air. 'What is this *wire*, man?' he kept asking himself loudly. My left leg had gone to sleep so I stood up. 'Hey, sit down, man. I mean, what is this *wire*?' squealed the American. I set off in search of toilet facilities.

Walking across a crowded festival site is a delicate art; the ground is all but obscured by bodies, heads and limbs so one must select one's footing with care. My progress to the latrines was slow and not aided by a lengthy period spent in a queue which, as it turned out, was not for the lavatories at all, but for a hot-dog stand. I got there in the end to find a trench in the ground awash with muck and already stenching furiously. I grappled with mounting nausea.

My trip back to my sacred clump of earth was even slower than the outward journey. I had lost my bearings, such as they were (there are few landmarks among a seething mass of humanity), but once re-united with my party, I swigged cider and attempted to enjoy the late afternoon's talent parade – Fairport Convention, John Mayall, It's a Beautiful Day, Colosseum – with little success. Then, as Steppenwolf were crunching their way through their anti-US establishment epic, 'Monster', a bleary-eyed hippie stumbled in the dusk, landing on my legs. The pain made me swear. Hippie sat up and blinked. 'Hey, I'm really sorry, man. This festival's got really bad vibes.' He shuffled off in his foul-smelling Afghan coat and his search for who-knows-what.

## A psychedelic breakfast

Immense TV screens were beaming the face and guitar of Johnny Winter through the darkness and it was getting cold. Shivering and tired, dirty and bored, I embarked on another tricky trek, to tent and bed. Once inside the welcoming canvas, I found that someone had made off with the cider, the beans, the crisps and the biscuits (but had left the cans of stew – a vegetarian thief, obviously). I was too weary to care and so, to the strains of Pink Floyd playing 'Alan's Psychedelic Breakfast' in the distance, I dropped into a deep slumber.

The campsite was a hive of activity as we breakfasted on cold Irish stew – we couldn't get the gas stove to work – the next morning. An evil-looking Hell's Angel stalked the grass, shouting, 'Has anyone got any change?' in a menacing tone. The snotty child from the neighbouring tent was playing a game with our guy-ropes while his mother sat cross-legged on an Indian blanket singing Leonard Cohen's 'Suzanne' very badly to the accompaniment of an out-of-tune Spanish guitar. The brat's game reached its conclusion with the collapse of our tent; 'Bilbo's going through a really destructive stage,' murmured the inept folk-singer.

On our way to the fest field, we passed the Pink Fairies, who were holding an alternative *free* festival on the back of a lorry before a minuscule audience. Meanwhile, on the official stage, Flock were hard at work trying to impress a much larger one with their hideous brand of jazz-rock. Our vantage point this day was even further from the stages than before and just as cramped, but at least I didn't have the feet of the mad coat-hanger fetishist to contend with. Flock made way for Santana made way for Frank Zappa and the Mothers of Invention, but if one had not been paying attention to the MC's announcements, one would not have noticed the changes. For a gusty breeze had blown up to whip the sound around like some celestial phasing unit: the music of successive acts had become indistinguishable.

Then appeared the band almost everyone appeared to have been waiting for – Led Zeppelin. The crowd rose to their feet to greet the hard-rock heroes and for the first time the festival turned festive as the throng bounced around and flailed their arms in praise of the heavy-metal din. Which was fine if one *liked* Led Zeppelin – for the minority that did not, however, it was hell. All around me people jerked their limbs, turning their bodies into potentially lethal weapons; there was no escape – I gritted my teeth and tried to ignore the buffets of the idiot dancers.

## Low-flying Byrds

Zeppelin screeched through their umpteenth encore – 'Communication Breakdown', I think – and left. So did a sizeable proportion of the crowd; at last I could stretch out on the ground and attain a modicum of comfort. Until, that is, the rains came – just as the band *I* had really come to see were about to begin. Instead of the electric excursions of 'Eight Miles High', 'So You Want to be a Rock 'n' Roll Star' *et al.*, the Byrds, through fear of electrocution, performed an acoustic set – better than nothing but a disappointment nonetheless. The water trickled down my neck, seeped through my jeans and into my shoes. I felt damp and miserable. Everyone else felt damp and miserable. Dr. John the Night Tripper came on and claimed responsibility – through his voodoo powers – for bringing on the rain. 'Thanks a lot, Doc,' we thought and waded back through the mud to base camp, leaving Jefferson Airplane and the droning MC to their own devices.

Grimy, damp and hungry, more dead than alive, we had braved the elements, endured the discomfort and listened to hours and hours of horrid noisy music we hated for the sake of a couple of enjoyable hours. 'Was it all worth it?' we asked ourselves. 'No,' we replied, 'never again!' But at least the car started: homeward bound, past the tireless Pink Fairies and into the night.

# Geroff!

*Mojo*, May 1994

Some youths had their testosterone rattling around to the sound of 'Sexual Healing' by Marvin Gaye, others to 'I Want to Hold Your Hand' by the Beatles. But for me, and people of my age, the testes started yearning at exactly the same time that *Ceremony* by Spooky Tooth and Pierre Henry came out. The front cover showed a man having a nail banged into his head with a hammer. The music was the yowlings of mankind played out upon a paraffin stove. A cacophony on the Island label. That was the ticket back then . . . and people ask me: 'Why haven't you got any children?'

1969. It was the best of times, it was the worst of times. Actually, that's not quite true because, looking back on it all, it was definitely the worst of times, full stop and the end. I cannot recall the names of many of the bands; they've been expunged from the memory like terrible Freudian nightmares of childhood and/or adolescence. There was that frightful, so-called group at the Lyceum one night which consisted of two girls 'playing' Fenders and droning on about sun and trees forever and ever in their Laura Ashley smocks. I can't remember what *they* were called, but I know they were 'name-checked' – alongside footballing phenomenon Frank Worthington – on the back cover of Family's third LP, *A Song For Me*, but I dare not look this up lest the private demons of a quarter-of-a-century ago

25

come scuttling out of the closet and force me to admit to myself: 'What a sad life it's been.'

Anyway, watching those caterwauling girls all those years ago, my friend turned to me as we sprawled upon the Lyceum's dirty wooden floor waiting for the next awful rock turn to come on, and said, in a manner which would now be considered 'sexist', but sexism hadn't been properly invented yet: 'I don't know about you, but I reckon there's something not quite right about a lady playing an electric guitar.' Despite this early example of political incorrectness, you saw what he meant. In 1969, that twilight zone of British rock music – splodged down between beat and psychedelia and whatever came next in the early '70s – there was something not quite right about *anybody* playing the electric guitar. What a racket everybody made as rock attempted to get all 'progressive' (Wowie Zowie! – as a Decca sampler of the time trumpeted it) and 'come of age' . . .

The worst 'concert' I ever attended (we didn't call them 'gigs' in that terrible era, we called them 'concerts', presumably to invest the proceedings with a dignity they scarcely ever warranted) took place at, of all places, Eton College – that seat of learning for nobs and toffs with funny collars and weals upon their bottoms. God alone knows how it all happened, but I suppose this was a time when education was letting its hair down, and so the housemasters turned blind eyes when they caught the Dry Bobs puffing pot in the 'pav'. Or something. Anyway, it was 1969, as it always seemed to be in those days, and the Pink Fairies were playing. This was always a ghastly mistake (the Fairies were often wont to set up camp and generator on the outskirts of rock festivals and do their own 'free' thing as a protest against the fact that they weren't on the proper bill, and against civilisation in general; nobody ever took any notice because the Fairies were so useless).

Anyway, the Fairies, these sonic terrorists, were doing a 'concert' at Eton and I, grammar school git from down the Home Counties road, got a ticket, and Lindsay Anderson's anti-public school film *if* . . . had just come out, so Twink, drummer of the Fairies and another cove out of that enterprise, spent the entire evening rather pathetically re-enacting the cane-thrashing sequence from the film, while the other blokes conjured up unlistenable items on their instruments in the background. It was hideous. We weren't even allowed to sprawl upon the floor – the normal posture for 'appreciating' rock in those times. Instead, we sat in churchlike pews while prefects in waistcoats roared and guffawed at the cheek and impudence of the inept wastrels on stage, haw haw. Blimey.

On second thoughts, I can remember an even worse concert I went to in my prime: Deep Purple at the Albert Hall (early 1970), subsequently 'captured' on the hideous disc *Concerto for Group and Orchestra*. Oh dear. And the worst group I ever saw was Aardvark. The Lyceum again. A catalogue of nasty sounds and nasty sights (man wigging away at an out-of-tune-organ with tea cosy on head and avec obligatory strobe light . . . flash, flash, flash, ooh, who'd be an epileptic at that point in history?). But you've got to hand it to us fellows, the 'concert'-attending class of 1969 and thereabouts. We never booed, never cried 'Geroff', and only occasionally (when there was a drum solo in progress) yelled 'Do "Toad"!'

We were quite polite as we sat or sprawled upon the floors of the Lyceum or Klooks Kleek or the Country Club in West Hampstead or the Nag's Head in High Wycombe. Even bands low on the bill (rarely noted: in the listings it was always Captain Beefheart '+ support', or '+ friends' – as if the dreadful Freedom, who always seemed to be in attendance on these occasions, had an incredibly close relationship with the top attraction you'd *really* paid your eight bob to see – or even '+ heavy friends' which usually meant the very, very dire Sam Apple Pie) were met with a polite-ish silence.

We never applauded very much when a 'set' by Hard Meat or somesuch came, finally, to a close. 1) We were *much* too 'cool' for that kind of nonsense. 2) The bloke in front having a 'bad trip' and being 'talked down' by a smelly chum had spilled his cider all over the floor and we were busy shuffling, caterpillar-wise, away from the ensuing deluge. 3) We didn't want to encourage the Meat; there was always the possibility that, Gawd forbid, the unspeakable Oirish 'outfit' might return for an encore of 'The World's Going to Blow Up and We Are All Mad', or whatever their absurd centrepiece 'crowd-pleaser' was called . . .

Pity the ones born in the mid-'50s. We missed all the musical fun: tots at the 'dawn' of rock 'n' roll and mere things with training wheels upon our bicycles when proceedings got going properly with the Beatles and the Kinks and the Dave Clark Five. And by the time the next exciting 'movement', i.e. punk, came along, we were in our twenties and viewed with suspicion – 'yer boring old farts' – by the bondage boys dahn the Vortex and the Roxy.

By a whim of fate, we just missed everything, even that short burst of British psychedelia. By the time we were sprouting facial hair and nipping back behind the bike sheds for a No. 6, wondering if we'd ever grow up to be like Noel Redding or somebody fantastically, irrefutably great like that, the burning question on the English rock scene had become: 'Can white men sing the blues?' (Or, as the Bonzo Dog Doo-Dah Band so tellingly put it: 'Can blue men sing the whites?') What a thoroughly dull question this was . . .

And what a thoroughly dull enterprise the British Blues Boom was altogether. The first group I ever saw (without my dad, who'd taken me to see the Shadows at Oxford's New Theatre some time in the early '60s, and the Shadows weren't much good, either – didn't play 'Apache', which, at the age of eight, I considered a massive swizz) was the Aynsley Dunbar Retaliation, London School of Economics, 1968: entrance fee a hefty 4s/6d, which is nearly 23p in new money.

And, in case you're wondering, the answer is no, the white man could not sing the blues. Well, Victor Brox, of the Aynsley Dunbar Retaliation – a broad man torn between puffing upon his cornet, tonkling upon his organ, or groaning through his billy-gruff beard about how he woke up this morning and found himself in the Mississippi Delta (which was quite surprising seeing as he was actually in central London in a dingy student 'refec' that reeked of elderly cabbage and 'best' bitter) – certainly couldn't.

Somehow the blues turned severely weedy in the hands of Dr K's Blues Band, the Spirit of John Morgan, the Keef Hartley Band (featuring Spit James and Miller Anderson in alarmingly futile 'twin axe' brouhaha), Chicken Shack (whose feisty guitar-meister had the longest lead in rock, which he'd use to stultifying effect by wandering into the audience and playing a wiggly-wiggly solo *at the same time!* I saw him do this at the Bath Festival in, yes, 1969: imagine the curly topped one's surprise when the crowd parted like the Red Sea and nipped off to the latrines, leaving our hero looking somewhat foolish) and all those crappy people . . .

I went to see Mason, Capaldi, Wood & Frogg, supported by Blossom Toes and Blonde on Blonde (whose debut vinyl waxing, *Contrasts*, has to be heard to be believed, as in 'Do you believe that people actually used to *listen* to music like this?') at the Top Rank Suite in Reading. Most fortunately, I wasn't wearing a tie so they wouldn't let me in.

We didn't believe in ties, man, straight cat. We were into freedom and stripy rugby shirts, as pioneered by Alex Dmochowski and John Moorshead out of the Aynsley Dunbar Retaliation. If we were particularly sartorially gifted, we had a grandmother who'd died and we'd wear her moth-eaten old fur coat. Animal Rights hadn't been invented yet. My friend Basingstoke (I don't know why we called him that; seemed funny at the time) had a splendid, battered top hat of which we were all profoundly jealous.

His favourite band was East of Eden – featuring the annoying violin scratchings 'n' squawkings of Dave Arbus – because he was mad. And he used to walk around clutching his prized copy of Juicy Lucy's first album (on the 'gatefold' cover was a plump lady covered in fruit – very tasteful). I don't know why he did this, but he did. At the Bath Festival of 1970, held in a huge field in Shepton Mallet, Basingstoke turned up in furs and topper with a plastic parrot on the end of a stick, which he insisted on waving at the lead singer of the truly abysmal Joe Jammer; Basingstoke simply *adored* Joe Jammer. That's how crackers he was.

Anyway, by '69/'70 the question about whether white men could sing the blues had been replaced by an even greater topic of discussion, i.e.: 'Who is faster? Alvin Lee out of Ten Years After or Dave "Clem" Clempson out of Bakerloo Blues Line, or somebody else who plays the guitar quite fast?' You see, it wasn't the notes played that were important, it was how fast you strung them together, as in 'twiddly-widdly-widdly-widdly going home see my baby twiddly-twaddly-ssszpraang!'

Well, Alvin was the fastest, definitely. His group was rubbish, for sure, especially on that night in, ahem, 1969, at the Country Club when I first 'caught' them and I first noticed that poor old Chick Churchill, the keyboard player, always found himself with so little to do at his mighty organ that he resorted to clambering upon the Marshall 'stacks' and clapping his hands in the air. This was the only way he could draw attention to the fact that he was in this tawdry group, too . . .

Oh, actually, on further contemplation I remember, with a certain sinking feeling, that the worst group I ever saw was Principal Edwards Magic Theatre, a combine of about twenty-six ex-students who strummed acoustic guitars and performed flirty dances and pretended to be flowers of the forest and told us the end of the world was nigh (to which we could only reply: 'If only it *were*').

There again, perhaps the worst group I ever saw was Pete Brown's Battered Ornaments – or was it Storyteller (featuring a man with a tree stump which he'd bang on the stage and call for silence because 'this next track [sic] we're going to do is heavily sensitive so *listen!*')?

Oh, yes, I saw them all, the musical frights of the late '60s and early '70s. I saw Blodwyn Pig and the Third Ear Band and Edgar

Broughton (who'd always turn up where he was least wanted with his noxious cries of 'Out Demons Out') and Savoy Brown (whose singer, Chris Youlden, was always going on about how he wished he was a duck so he could drink dry a river made out of whisky, or something, while madcap guitar player Lonesome Dave droned away in the background) and Arthur Brown, in various claptrap incarnations. I saw Atomic Rooster's first ever 'concert'. The sound system broke down and so did the light show, something of a relief on both counts. I saw Mighty Baby! Engrave it on my tombstone: 'He saw Mighty Baby! (And rather a lot of other crap bands as well).'

Oh dear, scars upon the memory. What a sad and turbulent 'rite of passage' it was for me and my contemporaries. And, you know, I don't get out much these days . . .

# Tom and me

*Allyce Hibbert*

Tom and Allyce, circa 1992 (courtesy of Caroline Grimshaw).

My first encounter with Tom was in 1980. I'd gone to Hay-on-Wye for a weekend with my friend Kate. We were staying in an old farmhouse belonging to a guy called Charlie Janson. Tom was there and so was his friend Mark Williams, who was in charge of the pigs or something. I think it was from the early '70s hippie-living days in Wales.

The weekend was unremarkable, except that Tom and I were the only guests going into withdrawal from the news. Neither of us could go two days without newspapers, in case something was happening in the world that we should be monitoring.

When we got back to London I went into Asterix on the King's Road, where I was waitressing illegally – and where Kate worked too. The phone rang and Kate said, 'It's Tom.' I said, *'No, don't!'*, because I had a boyfriend who was working in Nairobi on a TV programme. But she wore me down and insisted. Tom took me to see the Soft Boys, and he even got up onstage and sang a song with them. I got the distinct feeling that he was like, *'You're a girl, you're supposed to be really impressed with this stuff!'* I was obsessed with Bob Dylan and Leonard Cohen, but not with the pop world. But he did ask me who my favourite band was. And when I remembered Paul Revere & the Raiders from the '60s, he was *so* impressed. I think that's why he wanted to marry me.

After I'd had my visa taken away, Tom started coming to America to visit me. I still remember the first time he came to my parents' house in Massachusetts. I parked the car just before we arrived there and said to him, 'Okay, so the story is that the airline lost your luggage – and that's why you look like this.' His specs were one glass and one shade, and he had these awful black shoes he used to wear. I always thought that if all the mirrors in the world were destroyed, Tom would have been the last person to notice. Truly, there was nothing affected about it. It took me a while to work through his idiosyncrasies, and in the back of my mind I always suspected that they were slight affectations. But no, he genuinely preferred having packet mashed potatoes to having real food.

Tom said, 'We have to get married!' And I said, 'No, I'm too young!' I was twenty-three and he was twenty-nine. But we really were in love, and this was the only way we could be together. Tom had to be in London, so in 1982 I agreed to it. But then I had to appease my parents, since I was leaving America for ever. They wanted to have the classic American wedding, which was ridiculous and hilarious. And then we were off, a year and a half after we'd first met.

When we first met, I think Tom had just left Mark Williams' *New Music News* and hadn't started anywhere else. When I agreed to marry him, he took a job at *The History of Rock*, because he knew we'd need a mortgage. I remember him being quite well-paid. I was impressed!

Tom was friends with Mark Ellen: I think they were sharing a house in Leytonstone when I met him. And later they played together in a band called the Love Trousers. They played a few gigs around London, but the bass player was a set designer at the BBC, the drummer was an architect, and Mark was by then working at *Smash Hits*. So it wasn't a completely commercial thing. Tom really liked his friends, and they really liked him. That was one of the things I really liked about him – I thought it was a really good sign of mental health for a boy to have lots of different friends from all the different times of his life.

Tom tried to get fired from *The History of Rock* so that he'd get some money from them. But Orbis, the publishers, were fighting him tooth and nail and they put him to work on a magazine series called *Majesty*. In the end he just didn't turn up, so it all petered out. I remember being in the car one night with him and Mark, and Mark said to Tom, 'You should write something for *Smash Hits*.' That would have been about 1984.

The *Smash Hits* offices were such a great place to work. Tom was probably a playful deputy editor, he liked being a kid there. He was always bringing home new guys or girls from the office. He and Mark and Ian Birch and Neil Tennant were a bit older, but it didn't feel like there was much age difference. They were all pretty well integrated. I remember one night around Christmas 1984, we were walking in the West End somewhere and Tom introduced me to Neil, who was with Chris Lowe. They said, 'We've just recorded a demo,' and I thought, 'Oh dear, poor souls, doomed to disappointment.'

Pop stars played so little part in our lives. We only really knew *journalists*. Tom already had a pre-emptive disdain for writers who were too close to their subjects, the 'friends-of-the-stars' type. One of the only ones we knew was John Lydon, because he lived around the corner from us in Fulham. Tom admired him as a musician, but I think it was just because he lived a couple of streets away. I remember once John came in wearing ski clothes, having just got back from the Alps. I said, 'Hmmm. That's a bit un-rock 'n' roll!, isn't it?' He said, 'It's okay, I'm just taking the fight to the enemy!' I don't remember him and Tom sitting around talking about their feelings. It would have been factual, all about music and exchanging records. You would never call it a friendship.

I didn't like Robyn Hitchcock right away, because − as with Tom − I thought so much of Robyn must be an affectation, not realising it wasn't. We got really close afterwards and I remember the two of them playing guitar in the sitting room. Only occasionally would music break through to me, but I really loved the Soft Boys. I still thought Robyn was weird, but I gradually got to know him when we'd go over to Mark [Ellen]'s for supper.

When Tom was at *Smash Hits* and *Q*, he always knew everything about the person he was interviewing. He'd do a lot of work in advance. That was one of his disarming things: people would be flabbergasted. I remember Robert Redford ringing up one night to leave a message saying he'd so enjoyed the interview and been so charmed. I thought, 'Wow! You're really famous now!' I think Margaret Thatcher was the one person he *hadn't* actually boned up on. Because he was going to No. 10, *Smash Hits* gave him £20 to hire a suit, and Tom bought one off the rack at Mr Byrite. He thought that was such a brilliant name for a shop.

He was an utter pain in the ass about his writing. It was always last second, always some drama with magazine and newspaper editors ringing me up at the office, and me saying, 'Well, *I* can't do anything!' His father Christopher was a historian and a really disciplined writer, so I used to beg Tom: 'Can't you just be like your father, who gets up, writes for a few hours, has lunch, meets a friend for a walk, comes back, works a couple more hours and then at seven o'clock the bar opens? Can't you just have an orderly life?' His response was just to look at me as if to say, 'Are you *insane*?!'

By then he was doing a lot of stuff for broadsheets, and he used to write for the *Mail on Sunday* magazine, which I absolutely hated. You'd get those journalists who go into any situation and be ridiculous, and I always thought that was beneath him. But he did it so hilariously. He'd go and pretend to be a goat or something. I liked what he did for the *Guardian* – long pieces and reviews which I kept. He had a bunch of friends at the *Guardian*, so I guess that's how Pendennis came about. The *Observer* editors used to call me up and freak me out. Interviews would naturally have been on a tight deadline, because they were set up at the last minute, and it would have been going into the next available issue.

Tom's diet was insane. He used to eat tins of 'mixed grill in a tin'. It was a tin of baked beans and had one toy kidney, one toy sausage, and it was just so repulsive. We almost never ate the same thing, ever. I'd cook meat for him, but what he *really* liked was utterly creepy. Little jars of fish paste and things like that.

I'd have preferred that he didn't look *quite* so awful. He could have been himself but slightly more conventional. You'd have to hide every shirt, and only have 'Shirt A' hanging there. You couldn't talk him into it. He was stubborn. He had a great collection of T-shirts. He'd bought one in America: a guy in camouflage gear holding a machine gun. It said, 'Kill a commie for Mommy!' I was like, 'No, you can't go out in the subway wearing that! Someone might not see that you're being ironic!' I suppose his taste was for the comical;

he'd never wear something because it was comfortable. When we lived in Chiswick, there was this very skinny older woman down the street. One day I came home and she'd given Tom her Versace jeans because she couldn't fit into them. She said, 'Do you want them? They're too small for me.' Tom was the only person she could see who was skinnier than she was. Tom wore them with the huge chunky logo on the back and thought it was hilarious. He had no shame.

Tom loved travelling. We used to go to West Africa a lot. Those were our happiest holidays, in Gambia and Senegal, pretty much the poorest countries in the world. There was nothing intrusive about it. We felt really at home there. We used to go out to clubs that opened at midnight and stay in hotels that were actually whore-houses. Tom's whole thing of not really minding being hot or cold or hungry or thirsty really suited him well. We'd buy a package holiday and spend the first night at the hotel, then hire a car and be off after that – and then just go back for the last night. That was our secret, the secret package holiday. Just driving around. Many of those trips were with William Shaw, whom we met when Tom was deputy editor at *Smash Hits* and William was subbing.

When Tom got pancreatitis, it happened really quickly. He'd had it before, but obviously only a bore would eat well. That's the only thing I remember him acting superior about. Nutrition was for little people.

He was four months in an induced coma on a ventilator at Charing Cross Hospital. His sister Kate and I were at his bedside the entire time. We were so naïve. We didn't realise how it does a person's head in. The doctors would tell us: 'We don't really know about what happens to your brain, how much a person is thinking or feeling or taking in when they're on life support. The effect can be really profound.' I thought: 'Can't you just fix him and let him be alive again?'

When he came back home, I really expected him to come to, to snap out of it. But he never sprung back again. We had a flat for a few months in Coptic Street, just across from the British Museum, and we'd spend the days going around looking at houses in Blooms-bury. I basically said, 'These six months are the time when you don't have to get better, but you have to show me that you *want* to get better.' So I gave him six months. At the end of the six months, I remember talking to Mark Ellen. He said, 'You have to get out of this too.'

For a few months Tom was at his parents' house, and then he got a flat in Reading. I really think he just sat around with his old friend Juggins listening to music. But he'd still come to London once in a while. We still had such a bond. We used to watch *The Wire* reli-giously whenever he visited me. But it didn't amount to a whole person, if that doesn't sound too callous.

I was incredibly supportive for three years after he came home. Then I just couldn't bear to watch it anymore. I did what devoted wives do: took a job with *TIME* magazine in Hong Kong. I was happy to put up with all the horribleness of him being sick, and I would have given him a year or two to get over it, but it seemed like he had no will to get over it. He just basically fell apart, drank and didn't eat. I came back from Hong Kong in about 2007. I waited the time out and rented a friend's flat.

He was so lacklustre and lackadaisical. There was no life in him. Life wasn't rolling into his lap and he couldn't be bothered to get up. All his life he'd basically operated on the next thing coming up, and now he'd been out of it for too long. Mark Ellen was lovely. He used to come over and say, 'Let's go swimming, Tom!' He really tried for ages.

When he died, it was so horrible. Suddenly everything came flooding back. But then I could start liking him again, because I didn't have to deal with the reality of him.

I really like looking back on things, I always have – going over memories and pictures with people. So in a way it was like I had Tom back again.

# Part Two
# Writing by mistake

Tom gets his accidental start in music journalism courtesy of
Mark Williams' short-lived *New Music News* – plus selections
from the hilarious *Rockspeak!* and reminiscences of
Tom from Mark Williams and Mark Ellen.

The short-lived *New Music News*, 28 June 1980.

*'I didn't start writing until I was twenty-eight. I was a truck driver and all sorts of things. I wasted ten years of my life trying to be a pop star, among other things. I was in a band called One for My Baby, I was in the Sneaks with Jane Kennaway and I was in Elvis Costello's first band, Flip City, for two gigs. I was asked to interview him later, but I thought that would be too close to home. I'd like to do it now because he's gone completely mad.*

*'I got into writing about music by mistake via my friend Mark Williams. He started a magazine called* New Music News, *which was launched by Dennis Publishing during the strike which affected the IPC papers [in summer 1980], and asked me to write for it. I was working for Haymarket Publishing, doing stuff on how to improve your home. I'd written off to* Rolling Stone *but never written for the music press. I did my first interview with Alex Chilton on 28th May 1980. I'd never done an interview before, and it was very worrying, so I took loads of drugs in preparation for it, and he'd obviously done the same. Then we did some together and got on very well.*

*'*New Music News *was great fun, £100 a week. We thought we were offering something more humorous and scabrous than the others. It was much more* Private Eye *meets* NME. *The atmosphere in the office was barmy, psychotic. It was in a tiny office and everyone was on masses of speed. Then you'd have the most extraordinary people like Brotherhood of Man dropping by and David Van Day from Dollar and Adam Ant. They used to come in and take loads of drugs with us. But* New Music News *only lasted about a year, because the* NME *and* Melody Maker *came back and finished it off.'*

Tom Hibbert, 2001

# Hibbert and I

## 'Ziggy Byfield is going to be a star'

*Mark Williams*

Among several other things, Tom Hibbert was that rarity – a rock journalist of astonishing originality who was also a damned fine musician. It was as the latter that I first met him when, like me, he was a part-time member of a post-hippie diaspora who'd gone to 'get it together in the country' in rural mid-Wales.

Charlie Janson, Tom's friend from Henley, owned a farmhouse that became Party Central for those of us living nearby. When Tom turned up in the summer of 1975, he impressed us all with his guitaring and as the invariable winner of the late-night 'pop quiz' that revealed an exhaustive knowledge of numerous gen-res, especially such left-field psychedelicatessens as the 13th Floor Elevators and insipid UK chart-fodder – he could effortlessly recite Pinkerton's Assorted Colours' discography, for example.

At the time, Tom was earning a crust writing for a home DIY magazine and I was freelancing for *Melody Maker*. In May 1980, when IPC locked out its *MM* and *NME* journos over an NUJ pay dispute, I hatched the mad idea of launching a replacement weekly under the wing of Felix Dennis's mischievous little publishing company – for which, as a co-director, I'd launched several cheesy poster mags, one-shots and a motorbike magazine a few years earlier.

41

I'd already hired Tom to scribble some wonderfully tongue-in-cheek, almost parodical stuff for the likes of *Crossroads Monthly*. Hence hiring him as features editor for my idiot brainchild *New Music News* was, I thought, inspired. *NMN* required a monumental effort from a small and already lean staff, plus various preposterously pseudonymed IPC refuseniks working virtually round the clock, with desks erected on landings and the ingestion of various substances which Tom and I had fondly embraced during our rock 'n' roll-infused rural idylls, especially amphetamine sulphate, aka 'whizz', aka 'billy', washed down with copious draughts of Special Brew. However, since Tom was still double-timing for the DIY mag, this made for a serious deadline evasion: many was the time I sent dispatch riders banging on the door of his Fulham flat pleading for copy hours before we were due to go to press.

However, with his taped-together NHS specs, his undersized cricket blazer and carrier bag full of Carlsberg's finest, Tom was an elemental and much-valued figure in establishing *NMN*'s poptastic irreverence. This included loosely themed issues, including a 'moral issue' that had Tom allegedly persuading the Pope to reveal his favourite pop platters – notably Demis Roussos' 'Sorry' – and bigging up little-known pretenders such as Ziggy Byfield: 'Out of confusion comes chaos . . . into the spotlight strides a figure dressed in motorpsychobilia, crushing the be-kippered, simpering gaggle underfoot . . . Ziggy Byfield is going to be a star.'

Tom also made up the hilarious Letters page because, as he later admitted, if erroneously, 'we don't *have* any readers'. Typical example: 'I'm a 22-year-old Flying Saucers fan from Richmond, always dressed in studded black leather, smell of Brut, free with my dole money and into the usual rockabilly scenes, corporal punishment, dog muzzles, eating dog biscuits, nicking stuff from washing lines and Civil War torture.'

Not simply because of the physical toll on those producing it, *NMN* couldn't last long. When IPC settled its scores with the NUJ, their pop weeklies returned. The readers, and especially the record company advertising we'd crucially relied on, abandoned us. *NMN* struggled on for a few weeks, then quietly bellied up.

However, in the shape of Orbis Publishing's partwork, *The History of Rock*, Tom applied his encyclopaedic pop knowledge to something rather more appropriate than home improvement. This occasioned long and agreeable lunches in various Covent Garden pubs, deadlines remaining anathema to young Hibbo. And it wouldn't be long before his talents were recognised by Mark Ellen, who welcomed him aboard the hugely successful and influential *Smash Hits*.

By this point, Tom had further established his plank-spanking prowess, reuniting with mid-Wales cronies Charlie Janson and Paddy Poltock – bassist and drummer respectively – to form the Weeds, a thinly disguised paean to Sky Saxon & the Seeds, of whom he was a huge fan. The Weeds played gigs in Henley, Devizes and the yard outside Charlie's farmhouse, producing a merry racket which a nearby farmer complained had upset his sheep.

Tom was also involved in another, somewhat more conventional, rock outfit fronted by singer-guitarist Pete Mustill and named Tired of Living?, their name grimly prophetic after rhythm guitarist (and sometime Chris Jagger sideman) Angus Wood was killed in a car crash returning from a gig. But before that sorry event, the band cut a single co-produced by a tambourine-bashing Tom and I, celebrating Prince Chuck's recent engagement to Lady Diana. Sadly, 'Kiss a Lotta Frogs'' impudent subtext and bob-a-long beat decisively failed to dent the charts, thereby voiding my woefully unprincipled financial investment.

Clearly not sufficiently chastened by the experience, and their expectations of stardom undiminished, Tom, Mustill, Janson and ToL?'s sax player Tim Clarke somehow embarked on an American tour. Afraid their name might cause problems at Drug-Free

America's border controls, they re-christened themselves the Crabbers. Sadly, this incarnation *also* failed to set the musical world alight: after a few West Coast club gigs, Tom hightailed it back to Blighty, soon to wed tough-talking American picture researcher Allyce Tessier. Shortly afterwards he began his tenure and burgeoning fame at *Smash Hits*, *Q* and *Empire*. In the mid-'90s he went sort-of straight as author of the *Observer*'s Pendennis column, penning 'witty and bone-dry conceits from the perspective of a smoke-fugged barstool', as the *Guardian*'s obituary noted in August 2011.

And that epitaph came at the end of a life cut tragically short by diabetes at the age of just fifty-nine. By then Tom's ongoing ill-health following pancreatitis and pneumonia in 1997 – and his consequent unreliability – had outweighed the affection and respect he'd enjoyed and deserved in the industry. Eventually even when I shouted through the letterbox that I'd brought along a bottle of his favourite cheap Scotch – the improbably named Hankey Bannister – he wouldn't answer the door of the last flat he shared with Allyce in Turnham Green. The booze, the billy, upwards of thirty Marlboro a day and a junk-food diet had got the better of his pancreas and his lungs. When Paddy Poltock finally persuaded him to open the door to his tiny Reading flat that spring, a skeletal Hibbo could only apologise for the sordid surroundings and beg him to leave. He died a few months later and – like very few other truly original rock scribes; Lester Bangs and Nick Kent spring to mind – we shall not see his like again.

1981's Tired of Living? single, 'Kiss a Lotta Frogs'.

# Ziggy — Byfield, of course

*New Music News*, 28 June 1980

'You walk up, you see, you take the mike off the stand and hold it in your left hand and you put your right elbow on the stand and you say, "So I come in the other night and I says to the wife, 'Listen, I'm homesick.' She says, 'What do you mean, you're homesick? This *is* your home.' 'Yeah,' I says, 'and I'm sick of it.'"'

For a rock 'n' roll contender, Ziggy Byfield has had a less-than-orthodox upbringing. His parents were soldiers in the Salvation Army, but Trevor (for that was his name) soon forsook the war cry for the call of beat music and changed his name. Deke Reynolds & the Strangers failed to crack it, so Deke decided to try his luck as a stand-up comic on the northern working men's club circuit.

'I used to listen to other guys doing their act and make a few notes and then bomb around the next week doing the same gags with different names. But one night I was doing the act down in South Wales and I told a very unfortunate gag. I told it in sheer innocence, thinking I was going to go down a bomb and I very nearly did. I had to climb out the dressing room window and run.'

And change his name.

'I thought of Ziggy before Bowie, you know. One night I was staggering past this record shop in Epsom and I saw this huge display of Ziggy Stardust stuff and I said, "What is this? Is this me?"'

ZIGGY

It was in this befuddled state that Trevor/Deke/Ziggy fell into
rock theatre, spending two years in the cast of *Hair* and five in *The
Rocky Horror Show*, tap dancing away for coachloads of grinning,
snapping Japanese tourists.

'Throughout all this time I was writing songs and all I wanted to
do was to front a good rock 'n' roll band. I did some tapes with the
Rocky Horror band, PVK records heard some of them and said,
"Do you want to do an album?"' So the Big Zig went into the stu-
dio with a group of backing musicians, going under the name the
Blackheart Band.

Like Ziggy himself, the Blacks are no spring chickens – guitarist
Dereck Griffiths' roots can be traced back to beyond the Artwoods,
while drummer Bob Henrit played behind Adam Faith in the
Roulettes – but on the recently released album, *Running*, the wrin-
kles hardly show. The music has the raw innocence of lipstick marks
on a television screen, the vitality of arms clawing the air as a body
drops from the thirty-first floor. Ziggy takes another whiff from his
Vicks Sinex as he explains:

'My idea was to get a band in the studio sounding like they're
playing live . . . a boogie-ing band on record. There's little bits
here and there that are slightly overproduced where my fantasies
swept me away on cloud nine and I turned into Phil Spector for
five minutes, but if you listen closely there's bum notes all over
the place.'

Sort of like, er, punk music?

'Well, musically, I liked the punk thing but it was all this pompous bullshit of street-level knowledge and all that crap that got a
bit up my nose. It was all based on a pocket-lining hype by a very
small number of people – in fact the smallest number of people
you can think of. The whole essence of the philosophy of punk was
that it was totally unproduced whereas the unproduction was the
production so it was really a contradiction in terms. I don't want to
start stirring the shit up or anything but I think a lot of people were

47

ripped off very badly by the punk thing, specially guys and birds and that in the street who really believed in what they thought punk was, but the guy that was running the movement was the shits. I'm not into politics and all that crap. I'm into getting up on stage and blowing my bollocks off.'

Ziggy is similarly unimpressed with modern music: 'I'm not knocking Gary Numan, but I do find that some of his stuff is a little bit synthetic. It's pleasant to listen to but then so is the deep breaths of a barmaid pulling a pint of finest ale.'

So far, *Running* has drawn little response from the public or press but the cover, on which Ziggy is pictured hanging malevolently atop a motorbike, has secured him a role in television's *The Professionals* as King Billy, the leader of a motorcycle gang. And he hopes to be taking the Blackheart Band on the road later in the year. Will he be injecting any theatrics into the stage show?

'I don't necessarily go along with the philosophy of "You've got to have lasers and a thousand dancing girls", but a band should put a show on. What I would like to do is use bikes somehow. I've done a bit of scrambling so I can do jumps and spins and all that rubbish. I haven't passed my test but if we do shows, it's on private land so it's not a public highway so I don't need a licence.'

The Z takes another pull at his Transylvanian Cocktail, leans back in his chair and says: 'The number of people who knock Gary Glitter. It really gets up my nose.'

The direction and purpose of Ziggy Byfield & the Blackheart Band are clear: just get out and *do it*. The sizzling throb of *Running* live is going to tear the kids' heads apart.

'Who are these nameless kids that everyone talks about?' asks Ziggy. 'Everybody says the kids this, the kids that, the kids have never been in a dressing room. This is the whole crap mystique that's built up, that there's some big deal about going into a dressing room. If I want to meet some bird that works in Boots and she says, "Cup of tea up the canteen", we go up the canteen. That's her job and I've got my job so I invite her down for a sip of wine in the dressing room – that's my job. It's all very confusing, isn't it? I mean I'm confused by it . . . I really am confused by it.'

But out of confusion comes chaos, the dressing-room door slams shut on the ghosts of Trevor and Deke, then swings open again on gilded rising butt hinges. Into the spotlight strides a figure dressed in motorpsychobilia, crushing the be-kippered, simpering gaggle underfoot. Ziggy Byfield is going to be a star.

# Alex Chilton: Like blood on mixing desks

*New Music News*, 31 May 1980

His third time in London and Alex Chilton still hadn't learned that we don't usually tip barmaids over here. 'Why did she act so surprised?' he asked. Alex was in something of a daze, having just flown in from Memphis. But this wasn't just rock star's jet lag. On arrival, he'd been picked up by immigration authorities for not having enough money for the flight home, and had been detained for several hours. 'Bill Haley was on the same plane and he wasn't even stopped!' he mock-protests.

But you see, Alex, Bill's face is indelibly primed on the memory of airport officialdom as he jets in and out, playing yet another series of neurostalgia dates for his soft core body of fans who think that Jerry Lee Lewis gave rock 'n' roll a bad name. Whereas Haley has spent the last twenty years sucking his five minutes of fame dry, Alex kicked his apportioned moments of stardom on the head before anyone could even put a name to the face and has devoted the last ten years to obscurity or to being a star, depending on where you've been.

The '76/'77 Spots implosion created some very strange kickback. Iggy, the New York Dolls and the MC5, derided in their time, were suddenly fashionable; then psychedelic sub-stars like Sky Saxon and Roky Erickson were rediscovered. And Alex Chilton. The Ork EP,

*The Singer Not The Song*, Chilton's first release since the 1974 Big Star album *Radio City*, was in there among all the other picture sleeves, and selling.

So it was that Alex got tagged as another great ha-ha-he's-really-gone-over-the-top-this-time, 'seminal' cult artist. But whereas Erickson and Saxon seem permanently under the control of lunatic demons, there's a method in Chilton's madness and he has as unique a vision of the essential ingredients of the bowels of rock 'n' roll as . . . (pretentious commentary slowly fades and the picture goes wavy. This is a flashback . . .).

Memphis in the mid-'60s was a scary place. As Alex recalls: 'It was full of these enormous macho guys and I was constantly in fear of my life.' The only way to protect oneself was to be in a rock 'n' roll band – if you're on stage, you can see them coming and run. The big local band was Ronnie and the De Villes and when Ronnie defected, the group called up the seventeen-year-old Memphis fly and offered him the post: 'I thought, "Wow! The Memphis big time. I can make $100 every weekend!" and three months later we did "The Letter".'

But despite hitting it so soon, Alex grew steadily disenchanted with the Box Tops.

*NMN*: How did you get on with Dan Penn and Spooner Oldham (the Box Tops' main writers and producers)?

A.C.: Well, they treated me like, 'You're just the artist. Just stand over there and sing what I tell you.' I never got to know Dan. He's kind of mysterious. After we got so successful, he built himself a studio and started doing lotsa druuugs . . .

*NMN*: The rest of the group?

A.C.: There was always a distance between me and them 'cos they were a lot older and I made more money than them. After 'The Letter', a session band took over so they were never let in the studio. There wasn't ever a whole lotta love between me and the rest of the group. And finally I'd just had it.

51

Alex stormed off stage during a show one night, never to return. He went to New York to become a solo artist in Greenwich Village, 'but mostly I just hung around with a lot of journalists at Max's.'

Memphis again. You've heard so much about Big Star, the band that Alex formed with old school friend Chris Bell, and how good they were, that you maybe don't believe it any more. Two albums, *#1 Record* and *Radio City*, were released on Terry Manning and John Fry's Memphis-based Ardent Records, but despite their intense commerciality, sold absolutely not at all.

A.C.: The record business is a very safe thing. If you can sell 200 records, which almost anybody can, you're gonna make your investmeht back and 60 per cent more or something. But Ardent had a distribution arrangement with Stax, which was insane. Ardent threw all this money into crazy promotion and then Stax couldn't distribute the records because they only knew how to deal with soul.

*NMN*: I've heard some graphic stories about the mixing desk during a Big Star recording session. In some versions it gets covered in blood and in others it gets destroyed in a frenzy . . .

A.C.: No, well . . . er . . . a girl one night was taking a bunch of Quaaludes and Mandies, and I think she was a little bit angry at me because she threw a gin bottle at me and I got out of the way. It did go all over the recording board and it took us hours to clean it up.

*NMN*: Chris Bell left just after the *Radio City* sessions started. Why?

A.C.: I think he might have been angry with the people at Ardent and I think he was angry with me too. He left in kind of a huff and then I assume he came here (to England) and told Max Bell a bunch of dirty stories about me, but if you ask me it was totally his paranoia. He was taking very heavy drugs and then he got into Jesus . . . His funeral was on my birthday.

*NMN*: Big Star packed it in in 1975, leaving Ardent a third album (which was finally released on Aura in 1978 after *Potatoland*-like pressure) and a pre-Big Star solo album.

A.C.: Nobody's ever heard it yet. It's not all that great. It's got the original version of 'Free Again' (later on *The Singer Not the Song*) with a steel guitar and a country arrangement. Manning's still got the album . . . BLACKMAIL!

New York part two. Alex now fell in with Charles Ball and Terry Ork, and Jon Tiven produced the aforementioned EP for Ork records. (In Japan, the EP made up one side of an album, *One Day In New York*, with Alex Chilton and the Cossacks, featuring Jon Tiven and Richard Rosebrough, playing at CBGB on the other. The live side features a staggering 'Holocaust'. 'We'd never done that song together before that night and we never did it that good again. Which is always the way.') He got into production for other people too, doing Chris Stamey's 'The Summer Sun/Where the Fin Is' for Ork and almost producing Peter Holsapple's 'Big Black Truck'/'Death Garage'/''96 Second Blowout'.

A.C.: That was a great record till they took it off me and re-did it.

*NMN*: Why did they re-do it?

A.C.: Oh, Peter sacked me. I fell asleep when I was supposed to be mixing it.

*NMN*: What about Chris Stamey?

A.C.: I produced that one single for him and after that he seemed to want to produce himself. Last time we were together was in Austin, Texas, when he came down for a gig. We were playing kinda raucous stuff and Chris, as well as half the audience, seemed to go, 'This isn't it! I don't wanna do this anymore,' and he disappeared. I figured he owed me an apology. But he never called, so we haven't spoken since.

*NMN*: Jon Tiven!

A.C.: He's got some band called the Yankees and he's still trying to steal records from people . . . mine mostly. But then again, I rip everybody off too so I don't complain about that kind of thing.

*NMN*: The Cramps?

A.C.: I don't know if I'll hear from them again or not. We had a rotten time doing the album. It just didn't work out as well as the early things we did. I like the Cramps but they seemed like a better band in the early days . . . in the bars.

The parting blow before leaving New York was the release of the superbly blighted 'Bangkok' on Charles Ball's Fun Records. On the B-side was a manic version of 'I Can't Seem to Make You Mine', originally by Sky Saxon's Seeds.

A.C.: That was something that I thought was outrageously horrible in 1967. But it's such an obsessive piece that I could never get it out of my mind.

(The picture goes wavy again, the colour returns like in *Summer Holiday*, the flashback is over and it's May 1980.)

Alex Chilton is in London, preparing for two gigs at Dingwalls, and he's very 'nervous and excited' about it. The record company, Aura, see it as a kind of belated promo for the recently released album (*Hey Little Child*). Alex sees it more as 'a promo for me'.

*NMN*: I found *Like Flies* . . . somewhat, how shall I put it, inaccessible.

A.C.: I don't really think that. I think that the songs are easily understood and that the production is a lot different. A lot of people talk about production mistakes, like to make a rock 'n' roll record it seems like most people try to get really meticulous about it and try to get each thing in its place. But with the album – it's Jim Dickinson's group mostly, playing behind me, called Mud Boy and the Neutrons – it's just 'Well, I know you don't know this song but here we go, one, two, three, four, wham.' I think we came up with a lot of good things.

*NMN*: But compared with something like *Radio City*, the new album is rather uncommercial.

A.C.: I think it's commercial. There's just not all the fancy guitar work on it that's on *Radio City*.

*NMN*: You do some country stuff on the album like 'Waltz Across Texas', which sounds like a bit of a piss-take.

A.C.: Well . . . that's true! I don't know what possessed us to do that song! But I remember it from when I was five or six years old, watching Ernest Tubb's TV show every day, and when we were starting the album a bar opened downtown in Memphis that had that song on the jukebox . . . There were no plans to the album. Maybe two songs I knew I was going to perform like 'No More the Moon Shines on Lorena', a Carter Family song from the 1930s. That's the pivotal piece of the album.

(But it's not on the English copy because Aura have kept it to stick on the B-side of the single.)

For the Dingwalls dates, Aura have scratched together a pick-up band, tentatively called the Scandells. I'm sworn to secrecy as to who's in it ('It could be a problem if we decide to kick 'em out') but I can reveal that it comprises some ageing English punks who Alex has never heard of. (You call that a revelation? – Ed.)

'What are these guys like?' he asks me.

A.C.: For Dingwalls, we're trying to keep the carefree tunes in and leave the heavy, oppressive ones out. I want to do things like 'Bangkok' and 'The Letter' and 'Stranded on a Dateless Night', which is an old rockabilly thing off the Panther Burns' record, but I think I can do it better. I want to do a lot of screech and screaming feedback sounds. I want the whole band to sound like that all the time. I figure if I play well here and if I can really be that good and that sensational, then I'll come back and play more.

(Panther Burns is a Memphis band that Alex has been playing guitar with. 'It's this guy Gustavo Falco's thing. He's not really a musician and we done a record. I didn't have a whole lot to do with producing it, but I steered us out of the wrong directions.')

## PHEW, EH READERS?

As I leave, Alex is toying with the idea of adding a synthesizer to the band: '. . . someone who can't really play and who'll sound like he's in a different band.'

Is this stunning genius at work or get-me-a-ticket-for-an-airplane time? We shall see. Heroes are growing thin on the ground.

# Dave Berry: Malice in Sunderland

## *New Music News*, 21 June 1980

On the slippy polished dance floor below me, Nabisco sales reps in open, wide-collared shirts and chunky gold pendants gazed through the new perms of their fiancées and move imperceptively to the synth drum beats of the disco music. The bleary swimming eyes of the large figure grasped for focus somewhere around my upper lip; the body swayed forward and I prepared myself for the wave of scampi and brown-ale-stained breath that I knew would accompany the slurred statement that he was about to repeat yet again.

'The thing about *Dave* . . . the thing about *Dave* is . . . well, he's a real *pro*,' he said, jerking his pint pot dangerously close to my head to emphasise his point. I nodded gently and politely and didn't say what I was thinking – which was that 'real pro' can usually be taken as a euphemism for has-beens, or never-really-weres, who just won't let go, driving from working men's club to reveille cabaret niterie in their Vauxhall Cavaliers and bending their lips into the same Eucryl Smokers' Toothpowder grin at the same moments as last night, the night before and ever back into the bookings Papermated in the desk diary. But who am I to knock graft and what am I doing here anyway, summoning *l'esprit de l'escalier* as a very mini-skirted waitress inches past me, giving me a flash of the '60s black rings around her eyes, and I hear, 'Reet, this is for June and Trev. Yay!

The ggggGibson Brothers with Cayoooobaaa!' from the disco and something like a twiglet snapping in the back of my head.

This is no time for a crack-up. After all, Dave Berry had warned me about north-east nightclubs.

'The other night this guy came up after the show and asked me why I'd changed my name from Chuck!', he'd told me, laughing. 'On a good night they think I'm the Rockin' Berries.'

And those are the knowledgeable punters. Years of the cab-club circuit have changed Dave's reaction from one of baffled horror to wry amusement as his tongue slips further into his cheek. He's realistic about it, happy to have his bread buttered on the right side; you can make more money in one night in this world than you can in an eternity of 'prestige' London club-crawling. But now, after playing support to Adam & the Ants at the Empire Ballroom a couple of weeks ago, he feels drawn back towards the inner limits and I am here in Sunderland to assess his comeback potential . . .

'I was always into the new wave thing. I try to keep aware of what's going on but I'd never played to a punk crowd before and I was shit-scared. It was the biggest thing I'd done in eight years and I felt just like a kid again. I thought we'd get laughed off stage or have things thrown at us. But they really enjoyed it . . . I even got gobbed on! Now I'd love to do the Nashville and places like that. I mean, that's where I started.'

This is the fresh enthusiasm of someone who's just played their first major gig and is up and excited like everyone else – except this is someone who has been through it all before.

Dave Berry formed the Cruisers in 1961 and, after working the London clubs, got signed to Decca, releasing 'Memphis, Tennessee' in 1963. The follow-up, 'My Baby Left Me', ranks among the finest examples of hard, English R&B, containing an unbelievably spikey guitar break from Jimmy Page (he drained himself on this one and could never play again). But after the minor success of these early records, the Cruisers (who'd never been allowed to play in the studio) got pensioned off when Decca decided to dilute Berry's sound and redesign him for star appeal. The kitchen sleep sob ballads, 'The Crying Game' (1964) and 'Little Things' (1965), both made the top ten, and 'This Strange Effect' (written by Ray Davies, who gave Berry a demo of the song when they were both appearing on *Ready, Steady, Go!*) became one of the biggest-selling singles ever in Holland.

But it was the image that made Berry a starlet – the bizarre serpentine gestures, the mike leads snaking round leather and the vacant, hollow stare were a trifle avant garde to say the least – repulsive to mums, dream pillow to the girlies. Strong though the image was, it couldn't carry the forgettability of the music and soon it was over. 1966 saw the release of the final hit, the lamentable 'Mama', and Dave's first and last screen appearance. Featuring Spencer Davis, Acker Bilk, the Lorne Gibson Trio, the Three Bells and the seminal M.6, *The Ghost Goes Gear* remains a classic flawed cinematic masterpiece.

'Christ! I've never even seen it! All I did was sit up a tree,' Dave recalls.

And so then it was fourteen years of doing 'The Crying Game' around clubland, here and on the continent, which you might expect to leave chips on shoulders, so let's probe the wounds.

How did you feel when Alvin Stardust started cleaning up with an act copped from yours?

'He's a mate of mine, so I didn't mind, really . . . the only time it did rankle a bit was when I went to see his show and he was even using my lights and two of my old lighting crew.'

What about these necrophiliac 'Liverpool Explosion' packages that crop up at the drop of a nostalgic hat?

'Don't do 'em . . . people like Wayne Fontana, Gerry (Pacemaker) and Billy J. Kramer make good money out of all that, so good luck to them. Herman's Hermits are making a fortune in America doing all their old stuff, even though Peter Noone isn't with them and they have to go out as Herman's Hits or something. You know, I feel like only the Searchers, the Troggs and myself have any real feeling for the music.'

But the music seems to take second place to Dave's ideas for visual projection: 'What I'd like to do is have an empty stage, a couple of spots, drapes in front of the band and me singing and not being there. It would be great to do that kind of thing on television . . . imagine singing a whole song with just your feet in the shot . . . everyone would think you were a loony.'

Such a comeback is, for the moment, a mere pipedream – no record company interest, nothing but the buzz of being appreciated by some young punks in Leicester Square.

'I think I'll give Malcolm McLaren a call . . . he'd know how to handle it . . .'

So here I am in Foster's Club. ('The North-East's newest club for the over-21s', which rules out most of the Cruisers from membership – these red-shirted, black-slacked boys must have been on Farleys when the original Cruisers started.) They take the stage and begin something on their keyboards which sounds like a Ray Anthony version of part of side two of the Fudge's 'The Beat Goes On'. Then they switch to guitars and start the intro to 'Memphis', a smoke flash explodes and the familiar, lazy voice of Dave Berry slips over it and he's not there. Then he is and so are the Hans and Lotte Hass underwater poses that shocked a generation.

Someone gets on to the floor to dance, but is prevented from so doing by the manager in the black bow-tie (this puzzles me a bit – at least twenty people were 'dancing' with impunity to Tavares not ten minutes ago). The manager later tells me that people are 'discouraged' from dancing in a 'cabaret situation' as it tends to distract the artistes from their act. Yes, it's all pretty up here.

Apart from the DB limbs, the only thing that moves is Virginia the photographer; she doesn't know where she is, I don't know where I am, the band think they're at home listening to *Tons of Sobs* and the only thing that causes any reaction among the audience is a name-check for Bobby Goldsboro, which draws patter-cake applause. The old hits are paraded alongside crowd-pleasing classics such as 'Bye Bye Love' and 'Peggy Sue'; the encore is 'Hi Ho Silver Lining' and then the disco voice says, 'Yeeeeahhh, let's hear it for Mister Dave Berry & the Crusaders. rrrrRight, here's the rrrrReal Thing.' Tonight's buff punter thinks that Dave is Jeff Beck; a girl at the bar asks him, in accusing tone, whether he's 'on drugs'; and I ask one of the band why they didn't do 'Street Life', which is supposed to be a joke but he looks at me as if I'm quite mad (which by now I probably am).

Let's not knock the real pros.

# Letters to *New Music News*

## Letterox, 12 July 1980

Hello readers, I am Boring Len. Last week I wrote a letter to Letterox, *New Music News*, 1–3 Mortimer Street, London W1 and they published it. The next day I was trying to cross the road and a man came up to me and offered me 10p to edit the letters. It was a bit of a surprise but why not, I thought, as I had nothing else on at the time. I never do have much on as it happens but I'm a bit tired now so I think I'll go and catch up on some kip. Cheers – Boring Len.

———

I'd just like to say that the quality of your letters column leaves something to be desired . . . I know you've only been going for a short time and all that, but there must be more interesting people who put pen to paper than 'Boring Len'. Firstly, I happen to quite like a lot of the groups he finds so 'uninteresting', and secondly, what right has he got to say what's interesting or not when he himself is such a patently tedious person. Is he serious?

*Fascinating, Felixstowe*

**Who's 'Boring Len'? – Boring Len.**

———

Can't say I was impressed with the 'Police Special' feature by Mark Ellen. His comments on their albums were just ridiculous and bitchy, and how inane to say Sting's voice is like Paul McCartney's, when, in fact, Sting's voice is not only amazing but incomparable. One more thing for the benefit of Robin of UB40 – I'm not aware that Sting sings 'de' for 'the' in 'Walking on the Moon', but as Robin does seem to appreciate the greatness of Sting's voice, he's pardoned.

*P. Bonner, Stratford*

**I agree. Sting doesn't sound anything like Paul McCartney unless you say Paul McCartney really fast and then it sounds like Paumarcny, which doesn't sound much like Sting either – Boring Len.**

———

I've always considered rock journalists to occupy the least significant strata of a fundamentally useless conceptual sphere built entirely upon ego, sycophancy, defensive cynicism and perpetual financial/emotional insecurity. Do you – as purveyors of this ignoble practice – feel that yours is but a pitiful attempt to hold a mirror to the face of rock 'n' roll and disguise that its death-mask image is merely the eternal tombstone of a grave full of second-hand dreams?

*Jon Lloyd-Webber (no relation), Oxford*

**Do you think this one's supposed to be here or is it foreign? – Boring Len.**

———

I bought my first (and last) copy of *NMN* yesterday, in order to read the Mick Jagger interview. However, I also read 'Live Jive' about Steve Harley's recent Venue gigs. Tom Hibbert was not very appreciative.

I wouldn't have objected had Hibbert backed up his trivial (and resulting hollow) condemnations with some sort of reasoning. The only reasoning apparent is that Hibbert (or perhaps the *NMN* in general) doesn't like Harley. Why? – because the current trend in rock journalism is to slag him off as out-of-date.

However, Hibbert doesn't quite pull it off – 'the lazy whine that, for some mystifying reason, his fans adore'. Here, Hibbert isolates people who enjoy Harley as some sort of strange sect ('fans' – a ridiculous term anyway) with distorted eardrums. So Hibbert doesn't like Harley's voice – why not say so instead of making a fool of himself by attempting a clever put-down?

Finally, Hibbert's incredibly original street hipness comes to light, as it inevitably would with a journalist of this calibre. He talks of Harley's 'tiresomely comic rap about the teen-outlaw Dino' – whether he's implying that Harley's rap was tiresome because of the quality of the humour, or because of the treatment of the subject matter, is not clear.

An epitaph of Hibbert's review: 'It was as smooth and unsatisfying as cottage cheese', in the journalist's own immortal phrase.

*Paddy Clark, Emsworth*

**What's wrong with cottage cheese? – Boring Len.**

—

What's this Tom Hibbert geezer got against Heavy Metal? In last week's (dreadful) singles write-ups he gave every HM entry a real thrashing, or else was really patronising or unfair. He says: 'Van Halen show English buffoons how to tackle a slow clichéd riff' as if all English HM bands were automatically buffoons. He says: 'Dave Lee Roth doesn't sound like a hairdresser' – as if he's expected to. I mean, does he even *look* like a hairdresser?

Stormtrooper's sticksman he calls 'another terrible thrashing drummer'. Quartz's he calls 'heavy-handed'. What does the berk expect? Some limp-wristed old fairy with a tambourine? This is HM, mate! Why's Tom Hibbert got it in for drummers, or buffoons, or even hairdressers? My theory is that he's a failed hairdresser and a total buffoon who wants to be an HM drummer but can't 'cos he's such a fairy – and I'm sticking to it.

*Johnny 'Greaseball' Watkins, Brum*

**I don't have many theories about anything myself but yours sounds reasonable as theories go – Boring Len.**

# Slangsville!

**Assorted definitions from *Rockspeak! The Dictionary of Rock Terms* (Omnibus, 1983).**

**ACE** *adj.* Extremely good; excellent. *Ex: 'Rex went to the Fat Mattress GIG and said it was really ACE.'*

**BIFFOE** *(derog.)* An unintelligent male person; an unpleasant or obnoxious person, usually employed by a record company or within the media [UK usage].

**BOOGIE 1.** *N.* A simplistic musical form, popular in southern states of America, where it is often performed by stout men with long beards and cowboy hats. **2.** *v.* To move the body to BOOGIE music. **3.** *int.* A rallying cry often heard at concerts, largely meaningless.

**BREAD HEAD** *(arch.)* One whose prime concern is money or BREAD; term often used in *Melody Maker* Musicians Wanted advertisements. *Ex: 'Conga player/flautist wanted for NAME BAND into Hendrix, Mahavishnu, Flock etc. No BREAD HEADS or TIME-WASTERS.'* [Late 1960s, 1970 MUSO usage]

**CAPITALIST PIG** *(arch.)* Any rich or affluent person (unless he/she is a ROCK star). [Radical FREAK usage from c. 1968]

**CHOPS** Technical ability on a musical instrument, usually guitar. *Ex: 'Since the Trems' last vinyl OUTING, Chip Hawkes has really got his CHOPS together.'*

**COCK-ROCK** Types of ROCK music in which the performance is an explicit expression of male sexuality. Performers of the genre stress their 'macho virility' by suggestive stage movements, song lyrics that boast of 'makin' lurve all night looong' etc., and by anti-social ROCK 'N' ROLL antics such as the destruction of hotel rooms. Most COCK ROCKERS have severe drinking problems.

**DIFFERENT** Pleasingly out of the ordinary: general expression of approval, often employed by music business personnel to disguise inarticulacy or ignorance. *Ex: 'What do you think of the new Haircut 100 single?' – 'Well, er, it's, er, really DIFFERENT.'*

**DOSH** Money.

**EXPERIMENTAL** Of music that abandons conventional forms and instrumentation, usually with disastrous results; of music that is incomprehensible and serves no apparent purpose.

**FILLER** A sub-standard song or TRACK included on an LP record to fill up a side that is short on material. Some LP records are comprised entirely of FILLERS.

**FUSION** The blending of two different musical forms, as in JAZZ-ROCK FUSION. Usually the separate forms prove to be quite incompatible.

**GARAGE BAND** A musical group whose enthusiasm far outweighs their technical ability. [From domestic garage intended for motor car storage . . .]

**GET ONE'S HEAD TOGETHER** To organise the thought processes; to liberate oneself of neuroses and HANG-UPS. An activity usually conducted in a cottage in the country, often Wales.

**GREATCOAT BRIGADE** HARD ROCK or HM devotees, c. 1972–76, identified by their dull-coloured, military-style coats of heavy material which reach to the calves and are strongly perfumed with Newcastle Brown Ale. [UK usage]

**H.** Heroin.

**HEADLINE** *v.* To top the BILL at a musical event; to be the main attraction at a concert; to have one's name printed in bigger letters than anyone else's on a poster advertising a GIG.

**HERBERT 1.** *(obs.)* A person who irritates by his superiority on the dance floor. [Late 1950s, early 1960s.] **2.** A stupid person of no redeeming merit. [UK usage]

**HOG WHIMPERING** Excessively drunk; in a state of such intoxication that unintelligible sounds emanate from the mouth.

**HOIST** To drink alcoholic beverages. *Ex: 'Me and Reg went down the Fossil & Cucumber and HOISTED a few pints. Reg got HOG WHIMPERING, needless to say.'*

**IDIOT DANCER** A person commonly seen at concerts and FESTIVALS of the late 1960s, early 1970s, who makes wild, unco-ordinated movements of the head, legs and arms, usually in celebration of the music being performed on stage but sometimes with no discernible motive whatever.

**JAZZ WOODBINE** A drug-filled cigarette. [UK usage]

**JUGGINS** A slow-witted, subservient person; a simpleton who does as he is told. [From 1930s UK slang *juggins* = idiot.]

**KARMA** Eastern mystic principle of reciprocal good and evil. Popular with HIPPIES as a justification for non-activity.

**KEYBOARD WIZARDRY** The playing of two or more keyboard instruments while standing up, usually wearing a cloak.

**LIVE ALBUM** An LP record, often a DOUBLE, which is recorded while the artiste or group concerned perform onstage before a paying audience. Such records usually contain little apart from loud whistling noises, distorted applause, cries of 'Thank you ta wow oh yeh ROCKNROLL wow ta thanks' and the echoing beat of spectators attempting to clap along in time to lengthy CROWD-PLEASERS.

**MUSO** An obsessive musician; a ROCK musician who spends much of his time discussing the relative merits of GEAR, peering through the back pages of *Melody Maker*, practising his CHOPS etc.

**NASTY** Rough and exciting; 'raw' and 'earthy', usually of RAUNCHY types of ROCK music performed by male persons with gruff, low-register voices.

**NATCH** Affirmative much favoured by music journalists who are English but wish they were American. [From *naturally*.]

**NOODLE** To play aimlessly upon a musical instrument; to perform an intricate but ultimately pointless and very dull solo on an instrument.

**-O** Suffix utilised as superlative for HIP effect, as in CHEAP*O*, BIZARR*O*, WEIRD*O* etc. *'Tom Robinson can promote an attitude to a specific issue . . . which is preferable to the type of received swinishness readily available in the UK to the Fleet Street TRASHOS.' (NME Book of Modern Music,* 1978)

**-OID** Suffix employed for HIP effect to emphasise the strangeness, sickness or stupidity of something, e.g. SICK*OID*, GONZ*OID*, VOID*OID*. *'[Doug Sahm]'s ill-fated Atlantic sessions were schmaltzed up by* *those New York SCHMUCKOIDS whose idea of SOUL is the bottom of a shoe.'* (*Creem*, July 1973)

**PATCHOULI** A popular HIPPIE and HELL'S ANGEL scent, reminiscent of mildewed figs.

**PINKO** A person who holds wishy-washy feminist/left-wing/ gay liberationist views; a *Guardian* reader.

**POST-INDUSTRIAL** Term applied to music of the late 1970s post-PUNK era, characterised by unmelodic clanking noises and general gloom.

**POWDER THE NOSE** To absorb cocaine via the nasal passages.

**QUID DEAL** *(obs.)* A portion of a narcotic substance, usually cannabis, costing one pound sterling, a *quid*. [UK drug culture usage, late 1960s to 1971.]

**RAVER** A person who is fashionably boisterous; a person who is WILD and WITH IT. *1968: 'Fred here's a fair drummer,' I went on. 'But he hasn't got the IMAGE of a RAVER.' 'He's right,' Fred nodded. 'If I could knock off two years, things'd be different.'* – Robin Squire, *The Big Scene.*

**RIFF** A particular group of notes that are repeated during a song or musical passage, often ad nauseam. *'McLaughlin and Cobham smiled ecstatically at one another as they batted syncopated RIFFS back and forth like birdies in some trans-galactic badminton game.'* (*Crawdaddy*, November 1973)

**ROADIE** A person in the employ of a ROCK group, or their management, who handles and maintains musical equipment, protects group members from stress, and caters to their whims. ROADIES are often seen in concert halls prodding AMPS with a screwdriver, saying, 'One two one two one one one' into microphones, usually with a large assortment of keys attached to the trousers and a T-shirt bearing the legend 'Styx World Tour 1978'.

**SHADES** Sunglasses, often worn for HIP effect in dark nightclubs.

**SMASH** An immensely successful SINGLE; sometimes a 'smasheroo' or even a 'smasheroonie' [DJ, low-brow journalist usage.]

**SPLIFF** A drug-infested cigarette.

**TASTY** Exceedingly pleasant. Term often used by journalists to describe guitar-based music that COOKS. *Ex: 'The twin fretwork of the band's AXE-men brewed up a veritable goulash of TASTY LICKS and home-fried fills.'*

**TEAPOT** A POTHEAD; one who ingests POT in such quantity that his/her brain will only function under the aural stimulus of a Steve Hillage album.

**UNPACK** To vomit. *Ex: 'Reg UNPACKED fourteen pints and a cheese and onion roll in the Fossil & Cucumber.'*

**-VILLE** Suffix employed as a superlative, as in Drags*VILLE*, Ends*VILLE*, Cools*VILLE*, Weirds*VILLE*, Spooks*VILLE*. Popularised by US actor Edd 'Kookie' Byrnes in Warner TV series *77 Sunset Strip*, 1958–63.

**WANKY** *(vulg.)* Pretentious; of music, films, books etc. that are tediously EXPERIMENTAL; of easily detected BULLSHIT and hypocrisy. [UK usage.]

**YOU BETCHA** Absolutely; quite right; I agree. [From *you bet, you bet your life* etc.]

**ZONKERS 1.** *adj.* Extremely enthusiastic; highly excited; BANANAS **2.** *v.* GO ZONKERS. To go mad; what happens to dictionary compilers.

# Hibbert and I

## 'Real music, my dear fellow!'

*Mark Ellen*

Mark Ellen and Tom Hibbert, London, mid-'90s (courtesy of Allyce Hibbert).

The day I met dear old Tom, he was sitting in a haze of cigarette smoke in a sweltering magazine office, making up readers' letters. I watched him for a while, prodding a typewriter with a mischievous smile, then stopping to read what he'd written and rubbing his hands with glee.

72

All around him was absolute chaos, sleep-deprived souls hammering out copy and slicing cardboard layouts with scalpels in a sea of ashtrays and clanking electric fans, the print deadline looming. It was the summer of 1980 and we'd joined the staff of *New Music News*, an underground weekly cobbled together to fill the gap while the *NME* and *Melody Maker* were on strike.

'I'm writing the readers' letters, dear chap,' he explained, 'because we don't have any letters. Or readers.'

Unfazed by what this said about the title's commercial prospects, I fed a sheet of paper into the machine beside him and began inventing hot-headed complaints about the recent reviews of the Stranglers and Doll By Doll. These must have met with his approval, since he suggested we go down to Oxford Street where there was a photo-booth – and then write the replies to this home-cooked correspondence in the imagined personality of the first person we could persuade to have their picture taken (to be billed as 'guest editor'). We then wrote a rock 'n' roll version of the Lord's Prayer with one line at the bottom of each page of the issue – 'Our Father which Art Garfunkel . . .' etc. – which we thought was *hilarious*.

At about four in the morning, all this old hokum was packed off to the printers.

I'd never met anyone like Tom in my life: wry, impossibly witty and confecting the maximum of amusement out of everything around him. He was intoxicating company. His speech was peppered with quaint phraseology with echoes of Ealing Comedies and P.G. Wodehouse. Cigarettes were 'snouts'. Food was 'tuck'. Booze – he loved a drink – was 'sauce', and if you had too much sauce you were 'in your cups' and, soon after, 'plum tuckered out' and 'fast a-kip'. He was such an instant hit in the place where I lived in Dalston that we offered him the spare room and soon discovered he'd sailed through life on his effortless facility with words, acquiring almost no practical skills along the way. His 'cooking' became the stuff of legend, a ruse he'd perfected over the years whereby he'd offer to do supper, secure in the knowledge that the results would be so catastrophically inedible he'd never be asked to do it again. Tom's signature dish was 'burgers' – instant sage and onion stuffing moistened with tap water and pan-fried in marge. He'd devised a dessert he called 'electric pancakes' – standard pancake mix but with Martini Bianco instead of milk – but was mercifully never allowed to construct it. He kept the winter fires topped up with a hopeless invention he called 'logs' – tightly rolled copies of *Time Out* bound with string.

Slowly, his background began to emerge: a charmed upbringing in Henley-on-Thames. The son of twinkle-eyed and delightful historian Christopher Hibbert, he'd dropped out of Leeds University in vague pursuit of a career as a rock star with his group the Weeds, a two-guitar-and-drums (no bass) strike-force with echoes of Crazy Horse. Then came a move into journalism. He was fiercely opinionated about music and considered my record collection 'abysmal'. He'd found a Squeeze album and was appalled. And one by Paul McCartney. And some reggae and soul and Kraftwerk. He didn't care for country music, since he didn't trust anyone in a cowboy hat. About 5 per cent of the landscape was raw and uncompromised and, hence, acceptable: 'Real music, my dear fellow!' This small sector comprised the Stooges, the early Kinks, Neil Young, the MC5, Roky Erickson, the Dead, Captain Beefheart, Big Star and, at a pinch, Julian Cope. Most other acts were too polished and proficient and, thus, laughably awful.

We stayed the closest of friends for the next thirty-one years. A lot of his screamingly funny and original pieces for *Smash Hits*, *Q* and *Mojo* over that time are included in this book. But my fondest memories were from the '90s when, for eight years in a row, he and his wife Allyce, and my wife Clare and I and our sons, went on Easter holidays together in blustery British coastal resorts where Tom – a true connoisseur of old tat – had a particularly keen eye for a touching gift: an 'I Love Yarmouth' Pac-a-Mac, or a gull-shaped, plaster ashtray from Butlin's Minehead. Hibbs' favourite leisure pursuit was Crazy Golf, which he played with the superbly maintained, straight-faced, *faux*-intensity of a defending champion at the Open. In fact, we had one of these jaunts in Calella in Spain just to tackle its famously challenging course – 'a Double-Bridge, dear boys! *And* a Windmill!' I remember him kneeling to gauge the incline towards a particularly taxing Water Hazard, squinting professionally down the length of his putter to work out the best line of approach.

Tom became very ill in 1997, a combination of pneumonia and acute pancreatitis that put him in hospital for four months, some of it in intensive care. Throughout this ordeal, he briefly lost a lot of his memory – he never got fully back up to speed – but traces of his old sense of humour were still firmly intact. For a while he couldn't recall his home address, but mention any of his favourite sitcom characters and he'd cheerfully reel off all the actors' names and catchphrases.

The whole family adored him and still miss him enormously. And there was a soft-centred tilt about the way he wrote which reminds you of an age before the vicious media world of today. The central gag in a lot of his writing was a cartoonish disapproval when things didn't meet his exacting standards: you could sense him sighing theatrically and rolling his eyes, but he always made his case with such gentle-natured wit and elegance that no one got hurt in the process.

And I miss that enormously too.

# Part Three

## Ver *Hits*

Tom hits his stride in the pages of *Smash Hits*, Mark Ellen's fortnightly and hugely successful pop mag. Here are classic Hibbert interviews with Billy Idol, Margaret Thatcher and more, plus reminiscences of Tom from William Shaw, Caroline Grimshaw, Sylvia Patterson, Paul Rider, Tom Doyle and cartoonist Kipper Williams.

Singles column, *Smash Hits*, 1 September 1983.

'I had worked at The History of Rock at Marshall Cavendish, which was awful, and Mark Ellen called me up and offered me work at Smash Hits. I like to think I brought the humour into Smash Hits. Before then, it was the lyrics and very dry interviews. I joined and started making up ridiculous things like the "Bitz" pages, taking the piss out of pop stars. In the Letters pages, we had lots of running jokes about the groups, and the readers picked up on the humour.

'The Smash Hits office was terribly cynical. They were all very young. I was the oldest person there and got them to be very cynical. I was horrible, actually. There was a girl called Maureen Rice who was very enthusiastic about pop, and we were really horrible to her. She'd come in with this fantastically bright and breezy copy and we'd sub it and rewrite it so that, instead of being really nice to Paul Weller, it would appear in the magazine as being quite nasty. Quite pathetic, really, but good fun.'

Tom Hibbert, 2001

# Eurovision: It's that time again!

*Smash Hits*, 26 April 1984

It was back in 1956 that certain bright sparks at the Eurovision TV network hit upon the gruesome wheeze of beaming a 'glamorous' song contest 'live' to the television sets across the continent.

Every spring since then, millions of innocent Europeans have stared aghast at their screens as persons – many in tasteless frocks – have pranced about with a hectic lack of grace, often grinning, sometimes winking and usually singing in some peculiar form of gibberish. The tunes are hardly ever any good and the words often border on the totally dotty, but viewers remain transfixed by this mad spectacle.

Back in 1956, however, the BBC were rather toffee-nosed about the whole affair. They declined to enter the first contest and, after the poor showing of Patricia Bredin's feeble ballad 'All' in '57, withdrew again. But, in '59, the trusty warbling twosome of Pearl Carr and Teddy Johnson entered with 'Sing Little Birdie' and won. Hurrah!

Already a Eurovision sound seemed to be evolving as most of the entries could be sorted into two simple song categories – A) bouncy, wholesome thigh-slappers; and B) drippy, moist-eyed ballads. In 1960 the UK's swaggering boomer Bryan Johnson plumped for

Type A with 'Looking High High High', which sounded almost identical to every other entry.

Next year, Britain ill-advisedly entered somebody *young* – the harmless teen duo The Allisons with 'Are You Sure?' The lads' snazzy haircuts and wobbly harmonies, modelled on the Everly Brothers, were just a bit too 'racey' for the old buffers on the voting panels so the BBC had to change tactics again.

Over the succeeding years, they were to wheel out a startling array of dependable squares – none of whom managed to lay hands on the coveted first prize. Ronnie Carroll, of the ample jaw and sturdy teeth, had consecutive cracks at it with 'Ring a Ding Girl' (in '62) and 'Say Wonderful Things' (in '63). Diminutive croaker Matt Monro tried with the simpering 'I Love the Little Things' in '64. Kathy Kirby, of the glistening lips and fiery lungs, had a stab with 'I Belong' ('65) and, in '66, the Tartan Tenor, Kenneth McKellar, had a bash with the appalling 'A Man Without Love'.

But it seemed high time the crooning duffers were put out to graze. Switching to the 'swinging, singing dolly bird' method pioneered in previous years by France and Luxembourg, the BBC recruited Sandie Shaw and kitted her out with a 'gentle' mini-skirt and a lethal song, 'Puppet on a String'. Extremely perky, relentlessly bouncy and overwhelmingly irritating, the number swept to an easy victory in the 1967 competition.

Britain was beginning to get the hang of this Eurovision lark. 'Congratulations', sung by pop trooper Cliff Richard the following year, was even more defiantly hearty and jolly than 'Puppet'. Cliff did his best, diddling around in his trim double-breasted job with frilly white necking, but he just couldn't quite swing it. No sour grapes, though, he just vowed to return another time. (And he did, in '73, with 'Power to All Our Friends', but came third. 'I think we've been cheated every time,' he said. 'Something's wrong somewhere. I had two zonking great hits out of the contest but I'd like to win it once.')

Meanwhile, all across Europe, composers of popular music were perfecting the art of trite, booming, jaunty rubbish while lyric writers were searching for the key to absolute banality, linking words that made no sense but would lodge in the listener's mind and drive him or her absolutely potty. Lulu's 'Boom Bang-a-Bang' ('69), Mary Hopkin's 'Knock Knock Who's There?' ('70) and Clodagh Rodgers' 'Jack in the Box' ('71) were among the gems of brainlessness to emerge from the UK.

In 1974, ABBA won the contest, proving that classy pop did sometimes get a look-in on Eurovision. Not that this made the slightest difference to future contests. Ghastly as it is to relate, the terrible dress sense of the four Swedes had infinitely more impact on subsequent entrants than did their music. Agnetha's tea-cosy hat and dumpy culottes, Björn's monstrous boots and misaligned hair-do, Benny's frilly cuffs and nasty shiny jacket . . . dear oh dear, they *did* look a sight. Throughout the '70s, the contests would be cursed by willing but weak ABBA impersonators jiggling about in unwieldy boot-like contraptions, decked out in sparkling costumes with bits sticking out at wild angles, and singing with gusto but seldom with accuracy.

And then there were the awful stage 'antics' – Brotherhood of Man's soppy 'Save Your Kisses For Me' ('76) was accompanied by equally soppy little dance steps. And worse! – as a breathtaking finale to the victorious 'Making Your Mind Up' (in '81) — the Bucks Fizz boys grasped the girls' skirts and whipped them off.

Few have emerged with any dignity from the Eurovision Song Contest, but there are a few entrants that, for one reason or other, will go down in history forever. I speak of people like Finland's Kojo, whose nonsensical nuclear 'work-out' received a complete zero rating from the judges in '82. And Holland's astonishing duo, Mouth and MacNeal, who, in '74, succeeded in turning the dreary 'I See a Star' into something quite repellent by pulling idiotic faces and 'acting the goat' for no apparent reason. And the unidentified

Spanish judge who, during the 1973 contest, suddenly leapt to his feet and stormed out of the jury room crying: 'No! No! No! No more of these dismal tunes!'

Will our very own Belle and the Devotions rise above all this when they warble for Britain on 5 May? We can but wait and see!

# Prince: 'Detroit! My name is Prince and I've come to play with you!'

## *Smash Hits*, 22 November 1984

Arriving at my rather swanky Detroit hotel, I am engaged in idle chit-chat by the doorman. He asks me what the weather is 'doing at this time' in London and I ask him who he thinks will win the US Presidential Election, which is now just two days away.

'I figure that Prince guy'll win by a landslide.'

This is the doorman's little joke, the point being that in Detroit 'at this time' (American for 'now'), the Election is trailing a very poor second 'event-wise' to tomorrow's concert at the Joe Louis Arena. Reagan? Mondale? Who are they? The name on everyone's lips is Prince.

It is here in Detroit that Prince Rogers Nelson, the pouting pop 'n' sex bomb, has chosen to begin his Purple Rain World Tour and, in return, Detroit has gone Prince-crazy. On every street corner, you see gatherings of Prince clones, posing and sulking silently in purple, and the doorman seems quite tickled by all the hoo-hah. The clones have been hanging around the hotel all day, hoping for a glimpse of Prince (who is staying here – Prince's hotel room and *my* hotel room are only fifty-eight floors apart!). But, according to the doorman, fans won't get *close* to the star. Why, Ronald *Reagan* don't have security as tight as Prince does, he says.

He's got a point about the security, as I soon discover. Burly men looking mean 'n' nasty and sporting 'Prince – Purple Rain' badges on their massive chests are lurking all over the place. There are Prince fans everywhere too, but they're not doing much apart from looking sheepish and trying to avoid the attention of the bruisers.

'You've come all the way from *England* just to see *Prince?*' the girl on the check-in desk shrieks with amazement. 'I can *not believe* that! Prince is such a *sleaze*ball!' Her voice is piercing in the extreme and I *do* wish she would keep it down – for just a couple of yards away stands what must be the *largest* member of Prince's entire retinue. At a guess, I'd say he was 7 feet across and 22 feet tall. He is *dauntingly* beefy, he's probably got a short temper and will very likely crush the check-in girl to death if he hears her 'blasphemy'. And then he'll proceed to 'remove' all witnesses – e.g. me.

'Prince *rilly* grosses me *out!*' whines the girl; the hulk takes one giant step forward and hovers directly overhead. 'I *love* Luther Vandross,' the girl tells me at about 20,000 decibels. 'Prince is like *yeuuchh* but don't you *love* Luther Vandross?' Before I have time to try and snivel out of this by saying something like 'Luther Vandross is a load of old rubbish and not fit to lick the boots of Prince, who is the absolute tops, don't you agree, Mr Security Man, sir?', the hulk booms: 'Hey! I *dig* Luther Vandross!'

As I make my escape, he and the check-in girl are deep in conversation and about to fall head-over-heels in love – Prince's security man and the only girl in Detroit who thinks that Prince is a 'sleazeball'. Love is a strange thing . . .

'DETROIT! My name is Prince and I've come to play with you!' booms a voice over the largest speaker set-up ever used for an arena rock concert. And there he is, Prince, on a raised platform, in a shiny purple jacket and about to slide down a fireman's pole to squeals of ecstasy. Smoke bombs explode, fabulously exciting multi-coloured confetti rains down from the rafters, the Revolution are playing 'Let's Go Crazy' and Prince is twirling round and round. The Purple Rain World Tour is under way and Detroit is going mildly bananas.

There are 19,000 people packed into the Joe Louis Arena, a gigantic modern sports stadium. They're mostly dressed in purple – purple stockings, purple shades, purple mini-skirts, purple leather, lots of purple lipstick – and they have been patient. Throughout Sheila E's remarkably entertaining opening act – all boisterous percussion and not many clothes – they sat politely and, during the interval, they entertained themselves by chanting, 'We want Prince! We want Prince!' over and over, and indulging in the age-old American football stunt of standing up and sitting down in rapid succession, thus setting up a human wave round the vast auditorium. After forty-five minutes of this, the casual observer began to feel quite seasick. Then the lights went down and the roar of expectation was deafening. As David Coleman might say, the tension was 'electric' . . .

But despite the ultra-flashy lightshow, the slickly structured set, the noise, all the right songs – 'Delirious', 'Little Red Corvette', 'God', the almost totally brilliant 'When Doves Cry' etc. – I fear that something's not quite right tonight. The Revolution's principal function seems to be to play v. extended introductions – the intro to 'Purple Rain' goes on for *eight* minutes – to allow Prince to effect his numerous changes of costume. Why does he always take so *long* to slip into a fresh outfit? And why, after passing lilies to the crowd during '1999' and going into one of his twirly spins, does he *fall over*? Michael Jackson would *never* do this.

A purple bathtub hovers into view. Detroit cheers madly. Prince lies down and does a spot of moaning. Detroit screams. 'As you know, I'm not one for words,' he announces while showing off his ivory-tickling technique during 'Father's Song', 'and that's why we chose to have the first party right here in Detroit.' This rather odd statement creates general euphoria – roars, whistles, cigarette lighters in the air, much swooning etc. Civic pride and 'rawk 'n' roooll' together in perfect harmony as ever.

Now he's in nifty black leatherine, now he's in white. Now he's clutching a knife, and now – eeeeekk! – he's coming out into the audience with a torch. No, he's not. That was just a prank played with lighting and a lookalike. Now he's making twiddly-widdly noises and the feedback with one of his umpteen guitars, now he's got a hat just like the 'late, great geetar legend' Jimi Hendrix. Now he's climbing up one of the gantries and strapping on *another* guitar. But it's *not* a guitar – it's a water pistol! Now the lights have gone out. Now he's gone.

At the reception afterwards, comments such as 'calculated', 'over-rehearsed', 'too slick' and 'why didn't he take his clothes off?' fill the air. The man from the *Detroit Free Press* is cheesed off because Prince came on so late, he almost failed to meet his deadline. A radio journalist from Toronto is miffed because he missed most of the show due to a nasty altercation with one of the many armed policemen. A fellow with a beard from LA (man) is blabbering on to a writer from Japan about the 'negative vibe' of it all – Prince is on a 'bread trip', apparently, 'consumed with formula and ego'. The chap from *Smash Hits* in London keeps saying, 'Well, I thought Sheila E. was utterly fabulous,' but no one's paying much attention to me.

Oh, by the way, when I left the hotel, I ran into the check-in girl again and she engaged me in further idle chit-chat. She had been to the Prince concert, courtesy of the hulk, and 'Wow! How could I have thought he was a *sleazeball?* He was just totally something *else*, y'know?'

Which is American for utterly fabulous.

# Hibbert and I

# 'Are you the most boring group in the world?'

## William Shaw

Tom and William in Hackney, circa 1999 (courtesy of Allyce Hibbert).

In the *Smash Hits* office every writer took a space around a rectangle of desks, our typewriters fighting for room with enormous piles of vinyl, press releases, books, cuttings and letters. Ashtrays were full. Tipp-Ex was spilt on the carpet tiles. Dust gathered. It was disgusting.

Tom Hibbert was older than us. It was as though he'd been left behind there by the previous generation – which in some ways he had. He always seemed to be on the opposite side from me, a stick-thin figure, dressed – whatever the weather – in fur-lined leather bomber jacket, black jeans and black suede shoes, a packet of Marlboro at his side.

Most days he said little. On the surface, his presence was frequently negative. He often gave the impression of someone who found it painful to be in our company. At our frequent editorial meetings, he often said little beyond an exasperated 'Oh, *fuck* off'.

His influence, though, infected everyone around that table. Part of it was his language. Tom's words were beautiful. His most obvious legacy on the magazine was the absurd neologisms that became part of the magazine's identity. He loved juvenile words and the power they held. A pop group's PR gloss would be steamrollered aside by Tom's description of them as a 'British twangster combo' or similar. And of course, over the following decades, *everyone* copied Tom's language. In other people's less capable mouths, Tom's language became the default ironic voice of pop commentary. (Not just words. Tom's best sentences always had incredible shape and timing.) But more importantly for that era, Tom had very little respect for anything that landed on his desk beyond the occasional Bangles album.

I started writing for the *Smash Hits* around the time Tom interviewed Morrissey about vegetarianism. At the height of his fame, when he was idolised by most of us music writers, Morrissey in Tom's hands became the bickering idiot from a Beckett play that we now know him to be.

Like other great word-lovers P.G. Wodehouse or Geoffrey Willans, Tom created his own universe and others had to deal with it on his terms. Readers were in awe of him. For them he invented a cast of Flann O'Brien-type characters like Black Type, Uncle Disgusting and Sir Barbara Castle. They wrote him sack-loads of letters, desperate to be included in his beautiful strange world.

As more junior writers, we worshipped him, not just for his power as a journalist but for the power he gave us. In the mid-'80s, when the magazine's circulation soared and the great writer Chris Heath provided both its intellectual drive and its purest love of pop music, it was Tom who allowed us to be ourselves. *Smash Hits* would never be the functionary of '80s pop's massive and shiny PR machine. Why? Because of Tom Hibbert. (First question in Foreigner interview, January 1985: 'Are you the most boring group in the world?')

*Smash Hits* wasn't a reflection of pop culture, it was a thing in itself. So when it was clear young people were turning away from Thatcher's conservatism, it made sense for her to turn to *Smash Hits* for an interview. Again, the genius prose:

'As I walk into the drawing room of No. 10 Downing Street, the figure in the matronly maroon outfit and pearly necklace shoots up from a golden armchair, proffers a hand, and enquires in a treacly tone, "How do you do?"'

We were all in awe. So I was surprised to find out that he was also an amazing friend. He and his clever wife Allyce – who was working at the time as the picture editor for *Time Out* – took me under their wings.

Journalism was hard work and grievously underpaid, even then. Tom and Allyce's trick was to book the cheapest package holiday they could find, then sit in the shade, resentfully drinking cheap hotel booze and playing declaration whist. I started joining them on these holidays. On the first, I suggested we leave the hotel by hiring a car. To them, this seemed an interesting innovation and they indulged me.

On that occasion, we escaped Tangier for Fez and Meknes. A string of further holidays followed. We travelled back to Africa twice, went to Mexico, drove along the West Coast of America, and even motored around Ireland. It was always as a foursome: Tom, me, Allyce and one assorted other – one being my future wife, Jane.

They were insanely happy adventures, stupidly dangerous, fuelled by a diet of local beer and Marlboros.

In Africa, people pointed and laughed because Tom's legs were so thin. In your thirties, when you have an endless appetite for alcohol, you don't see what alcohol is doing to you. Tom was a great drunk. He was tremendous fun. Everything became an adventure.

Once we awoke with hangovers in an army camp in Senegal. Unwittingly we had driven into a war zone and, too late to make it back to anywhere more sensible, we accepted the soldiers' offer of cheap accommodation in the tourist mud huts they had commandeered. They invited us to eat and drink with them under a huge tree, full of copulating monkeys.

'What do you do for work?' the soldiers asked. Realising how dangerous it would be to admit we were journalists, Tom, Allyce and I all declared we were librarians. We emptied a bottle of gin and Allyce explained that being a librarian could be a very stressful occupation.

In the morning, we did our best to sneak away. Naturally it was Tom who put his hand under his bed to retrieve his black suede shoes and instead pulled out a hand grenade. We drove away fast.

When Jane and I married, Tom invited himself to be Jane's and my best man. It was one of the sweetest things he did. He was like that.

I think about him a lot. I wonder if he carried some trauma. I genuinely don't know. For all the time I spent with him, I have no idea what it was, or why someone who seemed so talented, so lucky in love, so charismatic, should also have such self-destruction in him.

Like all friends of people who love alcohol too much for their own good, I feel guilty about how much I drank in his company. I remember sitting with him on a beach in Spain as he rather embarrassedly explained that his doctor had told him he wasn't supposed to drink anything stronger than beer anymore. At the time we were drinking Metaxa.

Part of the darkness was that he felt unrecognised. He was intensely frustrated. He could become angry about it at times. Reading the newspapers in his company could be difficult. He was writing for teen-agers while more 'serious' people were writing for more adult media. But newspapers and grown-up publications weren't yet ready for the looser, anarchic voice of the magazine revolution of the 1980s – that voice that despised obsequiousness and championed individuality. And when they were finally ready, those spaces were being taken by newspaper journalists like Lynn Barber.

Like many who were ahead of his time, Tom had been left behind. Although opportunities started to arrive – with his great friend Mark Ellen's invitation to write the 'Who the hell . . . ?' column for *Q* magazine, and his later arrival at the *Observer* as a columnist – I think they were maybe too late.

I think Tom was becoming tired of it all, just as he was being offered the most. As someone who sat on the table opposite him at *Smash Hits*, I believe his greatest work was done there, often uncred-ited but recognised by its millions of fans.

Tom with William and his wife Jane, making new friends on a beach in Senegal, circa 1994 (courtesy of Allyce Hibbert).

# Morrissey: 'Meat is murder!'

## *Smash Hits*, 31 January 1985

*Are you feeling better?*
It's quite a struggle.

*What's the matter with you?*
Oh, just a general mental decay – so many things, the list is fascinatingly long. I *look* ill, don't I?

*Yes, you look terrible, actually. Are you under the doctor?*
I don't believe in doctors, I believe in self-cure. I've seen very threadbare GPs and I've seen very expensive doctors and I find that they're all relatively useless.

*How long have you not been eating meat?*
For almost a decade.

*Can you remember the last time you ate meat?*
I can't really – but I didn't like it the last time. I'm quite sure it was bacon because I had a moderate bacon fetish. And I can remember as it came to the end of my bacon period, I thought – oh, I don't like the taste of this anymore. It was simply the realisation of the horrific treatment of animals – I had never been aware of

it before. I suppose that I knew vaguely that animals died, but I didn't know how and I didn't know why. I think generally that people think that meat doesn't have anything to do with animals. It's like potatoes or something – it hasn't got a cow's face and it doesn't moo, so people don't think it's animals. But of course it is – as I'm sure you've recently realised.

*Yes, I did twig. Did you approve of the Animal Liberation Front's Mars Bars hoax?*
I wholeheartedly believe in hoaxes.

*But would you approve if it weren't a hoax?*
Oh, yes. Completely. Yes, I would because I think we have to take these measures now because polite demonstration is pointless. You have to get angry, you have to be violent otherwise what's the point? There's no point in demonstrating if you don't get any national press, TV or radio, or nobody listens to you or you get beaten up by the police. So I do believe in these animal groups but I think they should be more forceful and I think what they need now is a national figure, a national face – sounds like an ice lolly – I think they need some very forthright figurehead.

*Vegetarian pop stars don't tend to be very militant types – Paul McCartney, Limahl, etc . . .*
Yes, very effete figures, non-political figures who would never raise their voices which, of course, is pointless. Whenever vegetarianism has been covered in the popular press, it's been whispered, nothing ever very forceful. Nobody really concentrates on the reasons why people don't eat meat, instead this person eats blah blah blah . . .

*Yes. Brown rice and here's how to cook a nut cutlet in your Habitat kitchen . . .*
Yes, so the brown rice becomes the centrepiece of this person's stand – when, of course, it isn't.

*Why do you think being vegetarian is almost considered effeminate? Ozzy Osbourne, Ted Nugent, so-called 'macho' people like that have to be real red-blooded meat-eaters.*
Yes, I've never really thought about that. I can't think of any reason why vegetarians should be considered effeminate. Why? Because you care about animals? Is that effeminate? Is that a weak trait? It shouldn't be and I think it's a very sad reflection on the human race that it often is.

*What about your heroes? I'm sure Oscar Wilde enjoyed a nice leg of mutton.*
Or a big rump steak. Yes. He was a hideously fat person so I'm sure he did indulge quite often – in fact he did, but he is forgiven.

*And James Dean probably enjoyed a tasty hamburger.*
I'm sure he did. But we all have our weaknesses.

*So it's alright, is it?*
No, it isn't. Certainly not.

*How far can you take this? What do you want to achieve?*
Well, I'm very nervous about it because I'm deadly serious. It isn't, you know, catchphrase of the month. It isn't this year's hysteria. I'm madly serious about it.

*Did you have any pets when you were young?*
Yes, I had a pet which I still have, in fact. I have a cat that is twenty-three years old, which makes him something like a thousand in cat years. He's actually older than the other members of the Smiths, which is remarkable.

*What's his name?*
His name – and I'm not responsible – is Tibby. It could be worse but I think that was a very popular cat name in the early '60s. It's

quite extraordinary, because we have family photographs of me when I was a day old and I'm clutching this cat and there he is today, still hobbling around the house.

*What do you feed him on?*
Regrettably, cat meat. Sad as it is, he eats meat but nothing can be done now because he won't eat anything else. Certainly if I bought a pet today, I'd feed it on non-meat products like Smarties and baked beans. It's a shame that Tibby is glued to meat, as it were, because – in effect – he's eating other cats.

*But cats are natural carnivores. Wouldn't it be a bit selfish to impose your views on a cat and turn it into a vegetarian?*
No, because cat food is an animal. It's a horse or it's a cat or it's a dog or whatever. So how can I be selfish by not allowing an animal to eat another animal? I'm simply looking after it. Animals can live without meat. We get violently upset when animals eat human beings, it's horrific, it's dreadful. So why shouldn't we feel horror when human beings eat animals?

*I do.*
You do what? Eat humans?

*No, eat animals. Which human would you most like to eat?*
Well, now. This is tricky because I spent the last eighteen months criticising people, putting them down, destroying them, and I've reached the point where I realise that there's not any point. Because you meet these people and you find that some of them are really quite affable. Some of them are quite nauseating.

*Is Limahl affable?*
No, he's certainly not in that category. But I've got a new policy. I'm not going to drag people down anymore. Everybody within this

curious profession has to do their own thing, however obnoxious that may be. And nothing I can say is going to change that. Besides, I've too many enemies. It's quite distressing. It's a bit of a strain because one is welcome almost nowhere. I don't want to go to parties or go skiing with Spandau Ballet or anything but still it's become quite tiresome, this constant barrier of hate. Silence is the safest thing.

*What do you eat?*
I have a daily intake of yoghurt and bread.

*Do you think that this might be responsible for your present state of ill-health? A good McDonald's quarter-pounder would put you back on your feet in no time.*
I sincerely doubt it.

*If you died tomorrow, went up to heaven and met Colonel Sanders of Kentucky Fried Chicken fame, what would you say to him?*
Words would just be useless. I think I'd resort to the old physical knee in the groin – 'this is on behalf of all those poor animals who died simply because of you.'

*That was a trick question. You should have said Colonel Sanders wouldn't be in heaven.*
Oh.

*Okay. That's the end.*
Of what?

*Of the interview.*
Thank heavens for that. You didn't ask me about Band Aid.

*What about Band Aid?*
Band Aid is the undiscussable, I'm afraid.

*You brought it up!*
Yes, and *I* finished the sentence. Full stop.

# Phil Collins (of *course!*)

*Smash Hits*, 11 April 1985

With his pinched features and rapidly thinning locks, he looks more like a geezer you might bump into down the greengrocer's than a *bona fide* pop star. But don't be fooled by appearances. This man is *actually* one of the most successful singers of recent years, a 'crucial' record producer, sought out for his services by the rich and famous, and the singing drummer in one of the most popular left-over hippie bands ever invented. But apart from all that, who *is* this man they all call Phil Collins (for it is he!). Does anyone *really* know? Let us see . . .

Phil Collins was born in Chiswick, west London, on 30 January 1951 (Aquarius, astrology fans!). His full name is Philip David Charles Collins and he owes it all to his uncle Len, his uncle Reg and his toy train set:

'When I was five I was given a toy drum and my parents would hide it in the basement. It was a tin drum – so noisy – but I was really into it, so my uncles Reg and Len *made* me a drum kit and I used to sit and watch TV and listen to the tunes. There was this guy across the street who had a *real* set of drums so I exchanged my train set with him for them.'

As a youngster, Philip David Charles had quite a cherubic little face, an 'impish' sort of grin and hair of spun gold. He was a natural

97

for the world of child modelling and he was quickly snapped up by an agency who made him do things like romp about in meadows in woolly jumpers for knitting catalogues. The boy had a flair for acting too and he got tiny parts in TV and radio shows and, when he was eleven, was chosen from billions of candidates to play the role of the Artful Dodger in the West End production of Lionel Bart's hit musical *Oliver!*. Here, each night (and matinees too), he'd trill 'You've Got to Pick a Pocket or Two' in his youthful falsetto for the delight of all those American tourists in the circle.

But, even then, he realised that it was the old drum kit that truly held the key to his heart. He devoured drum tutor books, he polished his paradiddles and joined loads of entirely ropey schoolboy bands. Then, on leaving school, he became the 'sticksman' in Flaming Youth.

So, you ask, who the jiggins were Flaming Youth? A good question. Their music is buried neath the shifting sands of time and they were, according to Phil, a 'tacky group'.

And so, in September 1970, he answered an ad in *Melody Maker*. A 'name band' were looking for a new drummer and Collins turned up at a farmhouse in Farnham, along with billions of other candidates (well, fourteen actually) to audition. The group was Genesis and Phil Collins got the job. 'It didn't take me long to realise that Genesis was a very special thing,' he later commented, adding mysteriously, 'It was a great vibe going down.'

Genesis, fronted by eccentric and colourful singer Peter Gabriel, had been 'discovered' in 1967 by that mirthful master of melody Jonathan King and had already released two albums – *From Genesis to Revelation* and *Trespass* – by the time Phil joined. The LPs had only sold about nineteen copies between them, possibly because they weren't very nice to listen to, what with their 'concepts' and doomy songs about ice and bleeding bodies and wolves with dripping fangs eating up crowns and that sort of thing.

And the first Genesis album featuring Collins – *Nursery Cryme* – wasn't much of an improvement either unless one happened to be 'into' extended songs about boys getting decapitated during games of croquet. In Italy, apparently, people *were* into songs about boys getting decapitated during games of croquet, for the LP – a complete flop everywhere else – was a huge success there. 'Amazing!' said Phil. 'Italy really saved us.'

If not for the baffling musical tastes of the Italians, Genesis would have chucked it all in, but, mildly encouraged, they soldiered on with a fourth LP. And *Foxtrot* established the group finally within the hearts of junior hippies and serious, bespectacled students everywhere. By 1975, the band were absolutely ENORMOUS, riding on the crest of something HUGE.

And *then*, Peter Gabriel decided to leave . . .

Junior hippies and bespectacled students everywhere shook their heads in dismay. Their beloved Genesis were dead. For without the 'genius' that was Gabriel – who else in the rock world had the breadth of vision to stand on stage in a nun's habit, a spooky mask or with a gigantic pyramid stuck on his head? – what was left? The remaining members came up with a possible solution: Phil Collins would take over at the microphone and they'd get an extra drummer. It was a long shot, but it might just work . . .

It *did* work. 'He sounds more like Peter Gabriel than Peter Gabriel!!' exclaimed the boss of the group's record company with delighted relief. By 1977 Genesis were bigger than ever. On 1 February, the film *Genesis in Concert* premiered in London in the presence of no less a personage than Princess Anne, who was moved to comment: 'We found it most interesting.' Collins, meanwhile, was exhibiting his talent as a natural, dead-pan comic by saying things like 'I think the spirit of Genesis is more important than any one of the members, which is why we have survived. The music will continue to grow . . .'

But the spirit and growing music of Genesis had never been quite enough for Collins. He was the only group member who hadn't been to public school. He was the only one who felt the need to be a bit of a Busy Bee. In 1973 he'd started up an occasional band called Zox and the Radar Boys for a giggle and a lark. Two years later, he formed a jazz rock group with a lot of v. 'illustrious' musician wizards, called it Brand X and recorded three LPs of mind-boggling complexity and high yawn factors (one of which actually *got into the Top 40!!*). Then, in 1981, Phil Collins put out the dreaded SOLO ALBUM . . .

Solo albums by members of ancient progressive rock bands are, by tradition, gruesome horrors of self-indulgence, boring and unnecessary in general. So *Face Value* came as a bit of a shock. What a turn-up for the books! Here was a SOLO ALBUM with proper songs and tunes. It even had HIT SINGLES in 'In the Air Tonight' and 'I Missed Again'. What had gone wrong? Well, at the time Phil had just got divorced and was feeling rather miserable; the LP was therefore a trifle, erm, personal – but not so stupidly personal that no one could understand it. 'It wasn't a useful dictionary for people who are getting divorced,' quipped the singer. 'Most of the songs came about because I was very upset about it.' The public likes a good weepie. *Face Value* went to the top of the LP charts.

After this, Collins jetted off to Sweden to produce a tear-jerking album for ABBA's Frida, who had just gone through some traumatic divorce proceedings of her own; then he produced the sensational hit single 'Puss 'N Boots' for Adam Ant; then he did another album of his own. 'The new album's about not being divorced,' japed Phil, who had now found renewed happiness with girlfriend Jill. 'She didn't know who I was when we met, so it was totally honest.'

The second solo album, *Hello, I Must Be Going!*, was another glittering smash and Collins' version of the old Supremes' romp 'You Can't Hurry Love', complete with campy video, gave him his first number-one single. Collins was becoming Very Famous Indeed . . .

# PHIL COLLINS

In February 1984, Genesis performed at a charity concert at Birmingham's National Exhibition Centre in the presence of no less a personage than Princess Diana. Shy Di wore a bow tie and clapped her hands appreciatively to the group's big sound. Whether she was moved to comment 'We found it most interesting', history has not recorded . . .

# Hibbert and I

## 'We're VIPs!'

### *Caroline Grimshaw*

Tom and Caroline, circa 1991 (courtesy of Caroline Grimshaw).

The corridor is completely dark, just the reflections of streetlights on the floor. We sit propped up against the cold concrete wall: Tom Hibbert – legendary genius journalist wearing his trademark grin, clutching a half-smoked cigarette – and myself, in some kind of '80s pre-Acid House, post-pop Madonna pastiche.

'We are misfits, my dear, outsiders!' he proclaims – his insistent eye-contact intimate, drawing you into his Secret Club. The distant pulsating beat, bumping against the two of us, is a mere backdrop to our moment. Yet another EMAP Metro celebratory party seems irrelevant when you find yourself alone with Tom. Sales of *Smash Hits* may be scaling their way towards a million copies an issue, but so what? Let others receive the congratulatory handshake. As we huddle in the gloom, Tom tells me tales of those he loves and those he does not. His tone is sardonic; his stories unravel in elaborate detail as the cigarette ash dangles and falls – the only trace of our rendezvous.

Tom's was a club that every journalist and magazine designer wanted to be in, yet so often this self-effacing elf seemed to gravitate towards the shadowy corners of the glittery parties. When he professed to being an outsider, he adopted a flamboyant and devil-may-care tone, yet there was sometimes an underlying melancholy ring to his throwaway declarations.

Tom was a loner: slight, incredibly intelligent, charming, extremely charismatic. He invented a journalistic lexicon that so many still use today. Tom gave form to inanimate objects, encouraging the young readers of *Smash Hits* to believe that the personified typography on a magazine page could be a character you really wanted to have a conversation with. He encouraged us all to disregard rules that might annihilate creativity – and to just be the star of your own show.

My first encounter with Tom Hibbert was at *Smash Hits*; as the art editor of *ZigZag*, I was fortunate to work in a team of young, brilliant people. William Shaw, then deputy editor of *ZigZag*, was also a pop journalist for *Smash Hits*. My very first visit to the office introduced me to a world of insanity: people wailing, gesticulating, crouching beneath desks; others talking in rhymes behind tottering towers of LPs and 45s. Every other word spoken seemed

103

to be encased in Tom's 'inverted commas': a clear representation of Tom's mysterious inventive mind. *Smash Hits* appealed to the young and the not-so-young. Tom joined the staff in the early '80s, where, egged on by 'top pal' Mark Ellen, he took blank sheets of paper and filled them with outpourings of untried ideas and unbridled thoughts. By the time I'd become the art editor of *Smash Hits*, Tom had moved on, but the imaginary characters he developed to run the Letters page lived on. His stylistic devices and sense of the absurd were adopted by all – he was a legend that would never be forgotten.

At the time that Tom (again under the guiding gaze of Mark Ellen and David Hepworth) invented another innovative journalist-genre in *Q* magazine, I was fortunate to be in the office participating in the merriment. It was while employed as the launch art editor of *More!*, working with David Hepworth, that I found myself sharing the *Q* offices and witnessing Tom's infectious irreverence and exuberance for his pet project: 'Who the hell . . . ?' This infamous magazine strand was a masterstroke: interviews with celebrities so self-assured they could never imagine they'd be made to reveal their weaknesses, flaws and inadequacies. Yet every month they did just that, and the sounds of soft sniggering and then guffawing glee would emanate from the subs desk. Journalists and designers would gather to catch a glimpse of the latest feature. Sometimes the articles were unsettling. In the Jimmy Savile piece, Tom mused: 'But isn't there, perhaps, some oddness afoot? You hear tales, entirely uncorroborated, of course, whispered in sniggers at dinner parties . . .'

Tom lifted the lid on individuals by letting them rant and rave. The interviewee's speech, often seemingly typed up verbatim, became a personal confession of either stupidity or sometimes nastiness. Savile explaining his approach to relationships was monstrously disturbing: 'But I look down from my wise-owl perch and see some lady and go, "Eh, there's a nice one", so I hoist it up on the branch, keep it for

twenty-four hours, and then say, "You really have to go now" . . .
You can't be in a disco with 600 birds in Aberdeen and stopping
overnight and faithful to one fuck in Leeds.'

Meanwhile, the editor, Mark, would pace the office, checking
every minute detail. Tom would sit hunched with a cigarette, his pop-
themed T-shirt creased. He would wrap his arms around his rocking
frame, grinning, eyes glinting.

What do I remember the most? The way Tom chuckled to himself,
lost in a private world; his enormous love for his gorgeous wife Allyce;
his enduring friendships, especially with Mark, who championed and
cared for him right up to his death. I miss those unscripted moments,
when he'd join a dinner party gathering in my ramshackle Islington
home. I can hear him now, regaling his audience with stories, eyes
darting around the table, the candlelight flickering, as the laughter
turns to a roar.

And then, lurking outside the Garage on the Holloway Road.
Cold, dark – the queue is a snake. It's raining. Tom does not want
to queue for hours.

'We are VIPs,' he explains in his quiet way. That night, we were.
He was always Tom Hibbert – raconteur, friend, VIP.

# Pet Shop Boys: An ex-*Smash Hits* writer and the grandson of a nitwit

*Smash Hits*, 18 December 1985

Neil Tennant is speaking with the weary and deliberate tone of a man who's just been told some terrible news: 'I don't think *anyone* has faced up to this fact yet,' he says, 'but Madness *have* gone a bit boring, haven't they?' He sighs gloomily; it's as if Madness going boring was a tragedy fit for national mourning . . .

In response to a question about the 'state of pop', the Pet Shop Boys have been scanning the singles charts in a magazine and all is doom and despond.

'I *hate* Starship,' says Chris Lowe.

'Starship's an ab-so-lutely *wretched* record,' says Neil Tennant.

'I think Paul McCartney's record is atrocious,' says Chris.

'Paul McCartney's record is *tragic*,' says Neil.

'King's record isn't *particularly* bad.'

'Well, it's their best *one*, but I *hate* the way Paul King is like "Oh, hi gurls!" He makes me slightly nauseous.'

'Bryan Adams and Tina Turner's is terrible.'

'Tina Turner should be *ashamed* of herself . . .'

And so it goes . . .

'Oh *dear*.' Neil sighs an even gloomier sigh than the one for Madness. 'The charts are a *very* boring experience. That's the annoying thing about being in the charts at the moment – it sort of doesn't *count,* because they're all so *awful . . .'*

Gloom.

'Oh, look!' Chris has arrived at the chart slot that reads: '*WEST END GIRLS' – Pet Shop Boys.* 'We've got a little black spot next to us. I wonder what *that* means.' Deciding that it probably means something quite good, the Pet Shop Boys perk up . . .

Neil and Chris had never really thought too hard about making hit records before they met in 1981 and started writing songs. They'd both been in a group before, but nothing *serious*: Neil's group Dust (formed in Newcastle around 1970) had been a flitty Incredible String Band type folk thing with warbling girls called Pauline and Maureen, while Chris had been a teenage piano player in a little dance group called One Under the Eight (there were seven of them), who performed old-time popular favourites like 'Hello, Dolly!' and 'My Way' at places like the Conservative Club and the Masonic Lodge in Blackpool. Not very rock 'n' roll, was it? Chris didn't even *like* pop music very much until he started hearing disco stuff around the time of *Saturday Night Fever* – but at least he had a showbusiness family background of sorts: 'My grandfather was one of the Nitwits. They were a sort of comedy jazz group and he played the trombone. He had a beard and he used to wear a wig and he had this big gout bandage over his foot and people were always tripping over it . . .'

No such high jinks in the Tennant family: 'My family's always been in rubber,' Neil reveals. 'It always embarrassed me when I was at school because when we did French oral, I always used to have to say "*mon père est un représentative d'une firme de caoutchouc*", which means "my father works for a rubber company". In fact, he works for a *Swedish* rubber company, which was even *more* embarrassing.'

After leaving college, Neil went into publishing and journalism: he would eventually end up working for *Smash Hits,* doing exciting things like going 'on the road' with Big Country. Chris was studying for a career in architecture ('He built a staircase in Milton Keynes!' says Neil in the animated tone of a man who's been told some thrilling news) when they first met. It was in a shop on London's King's Road (not a pet shop, nor a hip boutique like the Sex Pistols, but a dull old hi-fi and electronics shop). And it was 19 August 1981.

Neil was 'a real kind of Elvis Costello fan' back then but Chris instantaneously converted him to disco and introduced him to the not-very-well-known work of an Italian New York writing-producing Svengali figure called Bobby O, who has made trillions of records out of thunderous disco backing tracks with girl groups like the Flirts and Teen Rock singing over the top. Bobby O became Neil's hero, Chris and Neil became the Pet Shop Boys . . . Then . . .

'*Smash Hits* forced me to go to New York for *one day* to interview the Police, who I'd never *ever* liked, so I thought, "Well, if I've got to go and see the Police play some *horrible* concert and then do a *fantastically* boring interview with Sir Stingford, I'm *also* going to have lunch with Bobby O."' And he did.

On 19 August (cosmic coincidence) 1983, Bobby O took Neil out for a cheeseburger. They had never met before but the flamboyant New York studio impresario (who looked like a cross between Bruce Springsteen and Woody Woodpecker) was flattered that this journalist from England had even *heard* of him. And when the journalist from England revealed that he wasn't *just* a journalist but had this little pop duo on the side, Bobby O put down his burger and boomed, 'Neil, *baby*! Let's make a *record!!!*' And so they did.

The Pet Shop Boys signed a production deal with Bobby O and in 1984 became a sort of cult new wave disco act in Europe with the original version of 'West End Girls'. In 1985, they lost the erratic Bobby O, chucked in their careers and – bang! – quick as you like, a *proper* hit record, a 'moody' video, breakfast TV, 'hunky' pin-ups and all the trimmings.

So, guys, tell us about your, like, 'musical manifesto'. Neil is stumped by the dreadful question . . . 'Oh dear, this feels a bit like when I interviewed Bonnie Tyler . . . When you're in my position of being an ex-pop journalist, it's simply an embarrassment trying to analyse and describe what you're doing, because you start saying all the really naff and ridiculous things pop stars used to say to *you* in interviews. I used to think about pop stars for eight hours a day because it was my job and so now, when we're on stage, I can't move my *hand* without thinking, "Oh, *no*, I've seen that *so* many times before; it looks just like so and so!" Chris has the same inhibitions, I think.'

As if to contradict this, Chris comes out with: 'I used to pretend that Tchaikovsky could compose through me, and it worked.'

*Well!* Neil does one of his eccentric English cackles – a noise that used to rip through the *Smash Hits* office persistently: 'I do miss the office atmosphere and making horrible jokes about pop stars,' he confesses. 'I must have made *hundreds* of horrible jokes about pop stars in the pages of "Bitz", but I think my enduring contribution to *Smash Hits* was that I was the first person to call Billy Idol "Sir William Idol" – now changed by yourself to Sir William "Billy" Idol. Oh, and might I add that my other big contribution was "pur*lease*"?'

The main difference between writing about pop and *doing* it, says Neil, is that when you're *doing* it, you 'have to look presentable. That's the real strain: you have to have a shave and everything.'

But, *actually*, the main difference between the two is *everything*: there's just no comparison and already it seems a very long time ago that he was writing unpleasant things about Culture Club: 'I did a review when they appeared at Heaven. They were fiercely trendy at the time, but they were *dreary* – white reggae with toasting. It just seemed very boring so I slagged them off – and the day the review came out, I bumped into them in the street and Boy George said, "Are you Neil Tennant? I thought your review was pathetic. You're really bitchy!" And they all stood around me and I thought there was going to be trouble because that old Mikey whatsisface is quite tough-looking. And Jon Moss is quite tough-looking . . . well, he was *then*. . .'

Ah, happy days!

'He is rather fab, Boy George, though; I have a history of liking pop stars when they go down the dumper. I didn't like Adam Ant until he went down the dumper, then I developed a kind of pathetic devotion to him. Gary Numan was never fantastically interesting until *he* went down the dumper, and now I love him to death. I always love them when they go on the slippery slope.'

So, will the Pet Shop Boys ever take a ride on the slippery slope themselves?

'Well, to go on the slippery slope – which is a very *steep* slope – you have to have climbed up very high, like Culture Club. And I don't think we'll ever climb high enough . . . We're a bit boring, really . . .'

Boring? The Pet Shop Boys *boring?* Coming from the man who once popularised the immortal phrase 'It's like punk never happened', this is a bit *thick!* 'Well,' says Neil, 'the classic fact is that the Bee Gees were a lot bloody better than the Sex Pistols. *And,* I might add, we've been told that Barry Gibb *loves* "West End Girls".'

And in the giddy firmament of pop, what greater honour is there than *that?*

# The BPI Awards

*Smash Hits*, 26 February 1986

Crushed up behind steel barricades outside the Grosvenor House Hotel, the massed hordes of pop star spotters are becoming distinctly disgruntled. For one thing, it's the coldest February night in London for forty years; for another, none of the smartly dressed nobs filing past and into the hotel foyer seem to be terribly famous. Look! Here comes Kenney Jones, drummer of the Who. Who? Look! Here comes celebrated actress Ms Rula Lenska! Who? Look! Here comes me! Who?? 'Huh!' tuts a cross girl from the crowd. 'And *that* ain't nobody *neither!*' Her autograph book remains empty . . .

Hard cheese – all the truly glistering guests have chosen to sneak in the back. This is indeed a wise decision – for stepping through the front doors, the very first thing one encounters is the probing microphone of Steve '*Knock Your Block Off*' Blacknell. Oh *no!* 'So, ladies, who have you got your money on tonight?' The 'zany' TV 'personality' has cornered Bananarama, poor things, so I move swiftly on upstairs, following in the footsteps of . . . good lord! Is it tousle-topped millionaire composer Andrew Lloyd Webber striding in front of me? No, it is *not*, as a matter of fact: it's his lesser-known brother Julian, who plays the cello a bit. 'Hallo, Julian,' I quip. 'Oh, hurm, aah, hello,' he replies plummily and sidles off to lose himself in the throng.

And *what* a throng! The bar is jam-packed with 'top' music industry persons – men with beards and cigars, ladies with 'glamorous' gowns and lashings of make-up and . . . I do not recognise these people. Hang on, though – *there's* a familiar face. Great heavens! It's Bryan Ferry in lustrous bib, tucker and suave bow tie. How resplendent he looks. He always does. 'Hallo, Bryan,' I quip. 'Oh, hurm, aah, hello,' he replies, casting his gaze about the room. 'Why is everyone dressed up like me?' It's wall-to-wall dinner jackets as far as the eye can see. There's salmon on the menu, there's a Conservative minister on the bill – cor, ain't it posh, Mum? Ain't it quaint? Come with me, won't you, into the ballroom, where the evening's pop festivities are about to commence . . .

Here we sit with all the super soaraway journalists at the press table in the balcony. We're a million miles away from the stage (on which people we can hardly see are making speeches we can hardly hear – was it any good on the telly?) and so instead of trying to follow the 'action', we scour the tables below for rich and famous household names. Let us see now . . . Corks! Who's that in the Australian bushwhacker's hat and most distasteful shirt ever conceived by man? Could it be? Yus, it's George Michael with his 'pal' Andrew, skulking and sulking in the darkness. Hoop-la – once they have collected their 'special' award from Tory skinhead Norman 'on-yer-bike' Tebbit, they'll be a-whooshing off into the night, never to be heard of again. Rorks! Who's that in the garish Harlequin two-piece and disgusting kipper tie? Could it be? Yus, it's Howard Jones. Huppity-hup – once he's delivered his weeny 'speech', he'll be away too – whisking the v. pregnant Jan home to bed. And who's that with the sparkling . . . oh, it's Elaine Page. Time, I think, to 'wash my hands . . .'

Imagine the scene. There you are in the gentleman's toilet minding your own business when this little chap comes in, stands next to you and starts telling you what a big swizzle everything is because he wanted to get Madonna's autograph but Madonna isn't *here* and . . . Crumbs! If it isn't world-famous choral super-star Aled Jones! Blimey! I wander out into the corridor to compose my thoughts and – bump! – straight into an aged, crag-faced gent in sober grey suit. Do my eyes deceive me, or is this world-famous croaker from the U.S. of A., Huey Lewis? The very same! Quite a matey geezer is Huey, as I soon discover. He seems a trifle bemused about tonight's proceedings – he's not too sure quite why he has won an award and he is *thoroughly puzzled* by Norman Tebbit: 'Who *was* that guy?' he asks huskily, 'He looked like Dracula . . .'

A tall, pallid fellow with startling raven hair strolls our way: 'Have you met my good friend Charlie Sexton?' enquires Huey and – boom! – I am shaking hands with the seventeen-year-old-boy-genius-and-future-of-rock 'n' roll in person! Blimey! 'These occasions are, well, they're okay,' says Charlie, 'but they kinda give awards to the wrong people, y'know?' Like Huey Lewis? I jest wittily. 'No, like Kate Bush – I think she is *great*. She should have got something but . . .' A slight, balding figure trundles past, distracting my attention – for it's not *any* old slight, balding figure trundling past, it's . . . Phil Collins, winner tonight of not one, not one-and-a-half, but *two* awards. Cripes! 'Hallo, Phil,' I quip. 'Ta-ra,' grunts our homely hero. And he is gone . . . 'Hey! I thought you were talking to ME!' snaps C. Sexton, placing his hands around my throat . . . Americans, eh? . . . Why, here comes another one – a tiny cove in a denim jacket – unless I'm greatly mistaken, it's Nils 'boing boing' Lofgren. Coo! Nils has just been on stage accepting an award on behalf of Bruce, 'who-sadly-can't-be-with-us-tonight' Springsteen; Nils feels pretty 'honoured' by this, actually; and, he tells me 'confidentially', he wants to go on playing guitar with Bruce forever and ever and *ever* because he thinks that Bruce is the absolute TOPS! Well, I'll be blowed! This calls for a drink, so come with me, won't you, to the 'exclusive' celebrity bar up on the 6th floor or thereabouts . . .

Making my way to the lifts, I am accosted by a couple of wizzly old blokes asking where the 'khazi' might be. Recognising them as Francis Rossi and Rick Parfitt of world-famous boogie team Status Quo, I send them off in the wrong direction – and next – swoosh! – who might this be wafting out of the elevator? Goodness! It's Alison Moyet, who greets me in chummy fashion and then relates some awful news about her chickens. They all died. 'Oh, I do miss them,' she says mournfully, 'so if you hear of any chickens going cheap, do let us know, won't you? Must fly – toodle-oo lover!' Shiver me timbers!

Moments later and here we are in the pop toffs' snug with Mike 'Smitty' Smith, Sarah Green and the gang. Glasses are chinking, conversation is 'buzzing' and there's rather a lot of kissing going on over there in the corner: 'Oooh, congratu*l*ations Richard kissykisskiss isn't it brilliant moi-*suuumack* congratu*l*ations Peter isn't it supah . . .' Winners of the Best British Newcomers award, Go West, are puckering up for their many well-wishers and, twixt smacks, they tell me their 'feelings' . . . Richard feels pretty 'thrilled', quite frankly, while Peter feels pretty 'chuffed', quite frankly. But 'at the end of the day' it's not awards, it's music that really counts and publicity is all very well but showbiz 'razzmatazz' is pretty meaningless, basically, because at the end of the day it's the music that really counts and . . . kissykisskiss *moi-suuuuuumackkk* . . . Mercy me! Recording artistes, eh? Here's Midge Ure nattering on about how the music industry's becoming like a 'global village' or something while Curt Smith's telling me in one ear how he just bumped into Norman Tebbit, who seems 'alright' and *Mrs* Curt Smith's confessing in the other that, on the whole, she'd prefer to be at home with the pussycats. 'Oh, hurm, aah, hello,' quips pop's Mr Loquacious, Paul Hardcastle, and blow me if I'm not being introduced to Charlie Sexton all over again . . .

. . . And who is *this* inching his way round the door, skew-wiff haircut and probing microphone at the ready? Could it be? Oh NO, it IS! It's Steve Blacknell . . . I'm off . . .

# Hibbert and I

# 'Crivvens!'

## Sylvia Patterson

It was all there in his blazing brown eyes, unmistakable through round, wire-framed glasses: the mirth, the mischief, the magic. In 1986 he sat next to me in the *Smash Hits* open-plan office, a slight, enigmatic figure in a battered brown 'Fonzie' jacket, his two index fingers rat-rat-tatting across an electric typewriter and a 'snout' (as he always called it) dangling from his permanently amused lips. I'd just turned twenty-one, a naïve, fright-wigged goth newly beamed down from Scotland, and Hibbs was the most brilliantly creative mind I'd ever encountered – the deputy ed. whose task, for the first few weeks of my rookie staff writer post, was to cast those merrie eyes across everything I wrote. So foamingly keen was I to add to the swingorilliant *Smash Hits* lexicon – the one Hibbs had pretty much invented – that I'd sprinkle the Celtic exclamations 'Jings!' and 'Crivvens!' throughout every breathless sentence. One day, he gently took me aside: 'Maybe a bit *less* of the old Jings, eh, Sylvia?' Crivvens!

From '86 through '87, Hibbs remained right next to me and remained an enigma, an ageless, classless, shaggy-haired presence who talked like a carousing comedy toff in the novels of P.G. Wodehouse. 'I say!' he'd declare, 'good laawrd!' Unknowably older than we pesky new kids on staff, his taste in music was also

115

unfathomable, enthusiastic serenades given as much to aristocratic popstrel Princess Stephanie of Monaco as hoary old hippie herberts Spooky Tooth. He barely socialised (much preferring the post-work company of his wife) and office parties were rare but, once, after a few 6 p.m. swigs of the rock 'n' roll mouthwash, Hibbs leapt onto his desk, on toothpick legs, playing wildly extravagant air guitar while bawling every word to Australian John Farnham's yodelsome soft rocker 'The Voice'.

Hibbs' lifetime collection of interviews, of course, became classics of the craft, all those quietly, deceptively merciless ribbings, but it was his hidden work I loved most, conceptual capers from our *Smash Hits* days which didn't even bear his name. As his news desk ('Bitz') commissioning ed. in '87, I'd hand him a press release on, say, the new single by jazzy R&B swingstrelle Natalie Cole and, thirty minutes later, a sheet of A4 would be ripped from his typewriter where he'd rat-tat-tatted a 'story', 'Things In Pop Called Cole', with a ludicrously described list: Natalie Cole, Nat King Cole, Lloyd Cole, Richard Coles, Pepsi-Cola, Newcastle, Arthur Scargill ('famous coalman, not much good at pop'). In summer '86 he invented the *Bitz Book of Life*, a 'cut out 'n' keep' mini feature in a corner of 'Bitz', which would (he advised the viewers), build up, fortnight by fortnight, into an 'encyclopaedia of life!' It was printed, deliberately, in almost illegibly tiny type, its topics anything but the soaraway hit parade, more portholes into his kaleidoscopic mind: from 'Aphids In Spinach' to 'Deimos (planet like a raisin)' to '*Love Is An Uphill Thing* (book by Jimmy Savile OBE)', to 'The History of Rock 'n' Roll Part Three: Elvis Presley' (which began: 'Born in a coal scuttle in Tucson, Arizona . . .').

The last time I saw Hibbs, at a book launch in 1999, he was still recovering from an illness so serious he'd died on the operating table, twice. 'Sylvia,' he chirped, 'I haven't seen you since I was dead!' He lived for another twelve years, finally succumbing aged fifty-nine to the dimension he always referred to as 'the hospital, for a very long time, i.e. forever'. At his funeral, his lifelong buddy Mark Ellen read out a passage not from any sacred text but from the *Bitz Book of Life*, as the congregation openly giggled: 'Born in a coal scuttle in Tucson, Arizona . . . debut vinyl outing "Blimey, Mum, You Should Hear My Pelvis Yodel" . . . box-office smashes in which he kissed a girl in a bikini on the lips and said, "Aw, shucks, ma'am!" quite a lot . . .' The music, meanwhile, was telling: the Kinks' 'Waterloo Sunset', the Byrds' 'Eight Miles High', the Electric Prunes' 'I Had Too Much to Dream Last Night', Moby Grape's 'Naked, If I Want To' (the Koffee 'n' Kreme version). Those songs told me all I ever needed to know about the mysterious Tom Hibbert, a man atomically built from the freedoms of the '60s counterculture.

Today, I still remember his eyes, brim-full of all that subversive surrealism he brought to a none-more-mainstream music publication obsessively adored by millions. I also remember, in summer '86, leafing through the latest issue of Ver *Hits* and finding, nestled without fanfare, in the forthcoming events page Happenings, yet another Hibbsian wheeze, rat-tat-tatted right next to me, snout as ever on the dangle. In among news of imminent tours from Amazulu, the Mission, Chris Rea and Castle Donington 1986 was something called the Upper Bubblington Village Fete:

*'Upper Bubblington Village Fete: 10 August (Tickets 20p from Ronnie and Madge, Cucumber and Spongebag public house, The Green, Lower Bubblington. Main Tent: Reg 'Reg' Snipton & His Banjo Gals; Twizzle; The Complete Bastards; The Yodelling Gondoliers; Pepe & Lord Alfred; Firecracker Sweet; Doom!; Reg 'Reg' Snipton & His Banjo Boys; Mad Goths; Herman In A Bucket; The Rita Gorm Experience; Virgin Prunes. Village Hall: Papier Maché for infants (a talk with slides by the Reverend Doris Toobody); Flower Arranging and the Feminist Experience (group activity orchestrated by Dame Margot Riviera); 'Skegness Observed' (exhibition by local artists Hector and Eunice Babbage); 'My Interesting Collection of Bits I Have Cut Out of*

*the Local Newspaper* The Bubblington Bugle *over the Years' (talk by Reg 'Reg' Snipton); 'Scotland The Brave' (caber tossing with your host, Jock E. Cranna). Stalls: Tombola; Guess the Cake; Raffle (sherry glasses and trifle); Strangle the Monkey; Throw a Coconut at Reg 'Reg' Snipton; Get Completely Ripped Off for Some Useless Homemade Flowerpots by Dame Margot Riviera etc. etc. (Note: This event has now been cancelled owing to lack of public interest.)* ('No, it hasn't. You just made the whole thing up to fill up some space because there are hardly any groups doing 'gigs' at this time of year' – Ed.) *('Bah! Rumbled!!'* – Happenings.)'

The spirit of Hibbs, I expect, will continue to make me laugh for a very long time, i.e. forever.

# Billy Idol: An Englishman abroad

*Smash Hits*, 8 October 1986

'Hibbs' with Billy 'Sir William' Idol and his mum Joan, Majorca, 1986
(courtesy of Allyce Hibbert).

Tuesday evening in Majorca. I am standing in the bar of my
Palma Nova hotel when I am approached by a genteel, respect-
able-looking couple in middle age with glowing sun tans. With
them is a non-genteel, non-respectable-looking young man. He

too has a glowing sun tan topped with a crop of blond spiked-up hair. He wears a dark shirt open to the midriff and around his neck he wears a jumbo metal cross. On his arm there's a tattoo of a woman with the wildest hair ever seen. The young man is none other than Billy 'Sir William' Idol and the couple at his side are his parents, Joan and Bill Broad. Can this *be*? The rock 'n' roll 'rebel', known for his menacing sneer and extravagant behaviour, on holiday in *Majorca*? With his *mum and dad*? Yes, it is *true*. Joan and Bill own a holiday apartment just around the corner overlooking the Mediterranean and Billy 'wild man of rock' Idol has joined them for a few weeks' sunbathing while he awaits the release of his first LP in absolutely ages, *Whiplash Smile*.

As we all saunter down a dusty track to a local restaurant, Billy tells me what a lark it is being in Majorca – apart from a spot of bother in a club the other evening: 'I went to this place with Stevie Stevens *(Billy's guitarist who joined the Broads in Palma Nova over the weekend)* and they tried to throw us out.' Why? 'The guy behind the bar got the idea that I was trying to nick the glasses.' And was he? Billy's only reply is a long, throaty cackle. He cackles quite a lot, does Billy. Does an awful lot of smiling, too. The famous sneer, it seems, is reserved strictly for photographs and performances.

Another illusion is rudely shattered as we sit down to dine. Billy Idol, who I had down as a raw steak and potatoes man, does not – gasp! – eat meat! (Though 'it's not because of animals – I mean, I wear leather all the time.') And when he was at university, he once cooked a nut cutlet for twelve people!! Whatever *next*?

We tuck into the *sole meunière* and Bill Broad chatters to me about his son's new LP. He is well-spoken, Mr Broad (i.e. he's a bit of a toff) and one can hardly imagine him hanging out in New York studios listening to 'rough mixes' of rock music albums. But that's just what he's been doing recently and he's got all his studio terminology spot on as well. 'The problem Billy had was finding the right musicians. These drummers think it is terribly easy to play Billy's music because Billy likes to keep it simple, but it really isn't, you see,' he says. 'Huey Lewis was making his single in the same studio and Billy was rather rude about it but I could tell the mix was just right and I said, "You know, Billy, this Huey Lewis song will be a hit."' Bill Broad senior was right, of course.

It seems rather extraordinary that Mr Broad should be taking such a keen interest in his son's career and even helping him to sort out his managerial problems. For previously one had been led to believe that the Broads, father and son, did not enjoy the warmest of family relationships. In fact, the last time Billy spoke to *Smash Hits*, he ranted on in a somewhat resentful fashion about his dad: 'He gave me hell when I wanted to be in a rock and roll band,' he said at the time. 'I want to give him hell for the fact that he didn't believe me!' And over the dinner table, the equally well-spoken Joan Broad confirms that things used to be pretty rocky between her husband and son. 'Bill refused to talk to Billy for two years when he was taking his A-levels,' she says. 'He did not approve of Billy's interests.' But the old wounds have healed, presumably, because now you couldn't find a matier pair than this tool-hire company director and this snarling rock 'n' roll 'maniac'. Maniac? Billy cackles: 'It was *Smash Hits* that had the cover headline "Billy Idol – Is He Bonkers?" Was that you? Yes? *Great!* Ha ha. I *loved* that! Is Billy bonkers? Ha ha ha!'

The wine flows, Bill Broad delivers a rather stern warning that if Billy has much more, he'll be good for nothing in the morning, and we stroll back along the dusty track, Billy locked arm in arm with his mum, nattering together sweetly. 'Isn't this great?' says Billy. 'Ha ha ha.' And then he goes to bed.

Wednesday morning in Majorca. Billy Idol is stretched out on the beach on a pink li-lo, lapping up the rays. Next to him on a blue li-lo, sunbathing topless, as is the fashion, is his mum. And next to her, the husband. The Broads on a totally orthodox British holiday, being offered nasty items of jewellery by Spanish beach sellers and shooing them away and then going for a brisk dip in the ocean. What could be more, um . . . unremarkable?

Some time later, Billy is sitting at a table outside the beach café in his black swimming trunks (which he had to buy here because he left his others in New York; oh, well – 600 pesetas – a snip!) and a punkily-torn T-shirt, sipping Coca-Cola. This is the 'interview', in which Billy tries to convince me that *Whiplash Smile* is a monumentally brilliant LP even though I don't need convincing.

So we talk about his parents.

'When I joined Generation X it was a break from what my parents wished me to do. I went to university for a year and I left to become a punk rocker and my dad saw that as some weird turnaround. My dad runs a tool hire business and I did get alienated from those things but now I'm in a position to show them *why*. The funny thing is that my parents have seen much more Generation X gigs than they've seen Billy Idol ones, so for them it was always the worst of me. But now I'm rediscovering them and they're rediscovering me and it's a great time. They're sixty and I'm thirty and I'm finding out who my dad is again. He's a much bigger man than I thought.'

We talk about his 'wild man of rock' image . . .

'I want to be a normal person but that's pretty hard in the States, where they've got this whole idea that life doesn't exist unless you're being seen all the time. They had this rumour in the *New York Post* one week about me being dead – and the next week they had to put in that I *wasn't* definitely dead. It went from dying of AIDS to having my blood changed somewhere. And I was at home all the time. People wanted to put out these rumours that I was on a drug binge but I was on a music binge. I can be more than just the old Rebel Yell with a sneer who wiggles his hips a bit and then pisses off. I want to show people that I'm not just a rock and roll *thing*, I'm a human being. They walk around outside my gigs with placards saying "Billy Idol Is A Satanist" and "Billy Idol Is The Next Anti-Christ", but my lyrics support love and beauty and gorgeousness. People would rather read about the wild man of rock but music isn't always crazy and wild, it's satisfying and gorgeous and luscious and a whole velvetness that makes you feel coddled . . .'

We talk about England . . .

'I've spent a little more time in England recently and I saw Ian Botham score the old 367th wicket and I was like fist in the air, screaming, "Fantastic!" And then we lost the Test so I was crying into my beer. That must freak everyone out: "He likes cricket? He must be crazy!" Ha ha. But I miss a lot of English things like that. And they have the best hair spray . . .'

We talk about America . . .

'I don't see myself as English *or* American, because I lived in the States when I was very young. When I was about three years old we moved to Long Island and Elvis was on the radio and it was all Walt Disney and huge fins on cars and colours and drive-ins. My dad was pursuing the American Dream, but he didn't find it so he came back home. But *I* still have this dream about America. It is a magical place . . .'

We talk about tattoos . . .

'On the Rebel Yell Tour there were all these nutcases who had their bodies covered in tattoos like mine. The worst thing was one person had a Generation X tattoo and he'd had to put "R.I.P." underneath it so I felt really bad about that. Let's hope he gets another one saying "Billy Idol – Live Long And Prosper". Ha ha ha . . .'

We talk about Sigue 'Sigue' Sputnik . . .

'I was going to buy advertising space on that for *Whiplash Smile* (*adopts deep American advertising-type drawl*). . . "Billy Idol, former Generation X, makes a neeeew al-buuuuuuum". Ha ha. I thought that would have been dead funny. But I don't need to slag off

Sigue Sigue Sputnik. Boy George once called me a head without a brain and John Lydon always called me the Perry Como of punk, but so what? Ha ha ha. I don't want to put anyone down. I'm a groover like Marc Bolan. I'm the Ronald Biggs of rock 'n' roll. Look at me, sitting here on the Costa Del Crime. Ha ha ha.'

And we ask the inevitable question that we asked once before: Billy Idol – Is He Bonkers?

'The thing about Billy Idol is . . . you're right. He IS bonkers – but he's bonkers about music! . . .'

Wednesday evening in Majorca. Mr and Mrs Broad had booked the table for 7.30, when we were all to dine with Mr and Mrs Broad's friends Bill (yet another one) and Hazel, who are permanent Majorcan residents (and very charming too; Hazel's favourite possession in the whole world, Joan Broad was telling me last night, is her signed copy of *Rebel Yell*. Well!). Anyway, the table was booked for 7.30, but due to some extended trundling about the island looking for suitable locations in which to snap Billy and his famously blue eyes, we arrive rather late. Bill Broad is fuming and gives me a severe ticking-off about 'unprofessional conduct'. Rather alarming. Billy arrives even *later* and doesn't get ticked off at all. It's jolly well not fair. Then just one bite of his *sole meunière* (again!) and Billy fwisks off with his dad to the nearby airport where they are going to pick up Billy's new girlfriend Anita (a budding popstress who was until recently in a group called the Cherry Bombz or, as Mr Broad puts it, the Cherry Bums). In their absence, Mrs Broad makes yet another startling revelation about her 'wayward' son. When Billy was about eleven, he used to – gasp! – caddy for his father, carting his clubs about the golf course for 50 pence a time! And 'he was really rather good at it'. Gosh.

The airport party returns. Anita greets the assembled company, sits herself next to Billy and the two of them proceed to spoon quite hectically – tongue sarnies, the whole shooting match – oblivious to the polite conversation around them. *What* a kiss up! I wouldn't do that in front of *my* parents, would you?

Thursday morning in Majorca, Mrs Broad has just been for another brisk splash in the sea and is drying herself off on the beach. She is alone. Bill has gone off for a round of golf and *goodness* knows when Billy and Anita will be up. 'Do you know,' says Joan Broad, 'they were so pleased to see one another that they stayed up with their videos until five o'clock and they were *rather* noisy. And they finished off all the vodka and all the brandy *and* all the wine. They didn't touch the whisky, though, which is probably quite a good thing . . .' Blimey! But wait! Who is this loping through the sand towards us, looking as chipper as anything? It is Sir William!

'Ello. Ha ha ha. We went swimming in the sea at three o'clock in the morning with our clothes on. I got me leather trousers all wet.'

Now, that's a bit more 'rock 'n' roll' isn't it? But hang on . . .

'Anyway, it's been great meeting you, chief, but we've got to go now. Lunch at the golf club . . .'

Lunch at the golf club? Whatever, whatever next? And with that, we bid farewell to this sunny isle and the family Broad . . .

# The Margaret Thatcher interview

*Smash Hits*, 25 March 1987

Tom with the Prime Minister, 10 Downing Street, 1987 (photo by Paul Rider).

As I walk into the drawing room of No. 10 Downing Street, the figure in the matronly maroon outfit and pearly necklace shoots up from a golden armchair, proffers a hand and enquires in a treacly tone, 'How do you do?'

'Sit down, sit down,' she urges, a 'radiant' smile playing across her famous features and, hitching up the trouser leggings of my *Mr Byrite* suit (£19.99 – a snip!), I do as I am told. 'Now, dear, would you like something innocuous to drink? Orange juice? Tea? Mineral water?' I plump for the water and she scuttles to the drinks cabinet, crying: 'It's Malvern Water. British. We only serve *British*.'

Quite.

Here I am being poured a glass of refreshing mineral water by the steady hand of Margaret Hilda Thatcher, Prime Minister of the universe. It's all *very* peculiar . . .

So what, might you ask, is Mrs Thatcher doing talking to *Smash Hits*? Simple, really: you see, pop goats, she wants *you*, the youth of the nation, batting on *her* team. Fancy that. So here we are, me, Mrs T and a couple of 'helpers' – a young press officer to lend support on taxing youth-oriented questions and a bloke with an impressive tape recording machine to record the conversation for posterity.

I present the PM with a token of your affection – a *Black Type* tea towel which she appears to mistake for a Fairy Liquid advertisement.

'Have you seen a Nanette Newman Fairy Liquid advertisement on television?' she asks. 'Lovely. *Lovely!*' she proclaims. And then we embark on the interview itself, during which she displays an eagerness to please combined with a skill in evasion (riding roughshod over interjections) that marks her out as the 'professional' she is. Margaret Thatcher is a serious politician and she wants *your* vote . . .

*Who were your heroes and heroines when you were growing up?*
'I think you've got to remember that I was growing up in wartime when things were very, *very* different. And indeed, if you were growing

up in wartime you really do appreciate peace. It was a time when the bomber force went out most nights and the fighters were about and there were battles and you were losing ships – you just imagine if the Falklands had gone on and on and on – so it was a very different time. But then you had to have all kinds of relaxation and I suppose really our heroes in those days because we had no television, we had radio and everyone listened to Winston Churchill and everyone listened, for example, to J.B. Priestley give his talks and Arthur Askey and Tommy Handley – all of those great variety things on radio were very much part of our lives. And then the other great entertainment in my generation, which one day I hope will come back, was to go to the cinema to see a film. And what did we see? Ginger Rogers, Fred Astaire – fantastic! And these great musical films: there was Jeanette MacDonald, Nelson Eddy, Anne Ziegler, Webster Booth, those marvellous . . . Jean Arthur in *The Plainsman,* all the Western things, and there was Carmen Miranda in *South of the Border* – but the point I'm making is that those stars meant as much to us, because it was a life that was a way beyond anything we ever imagined and we thought it was very glamorous. But I suppose things turn out to be less glamorous the closer you get to them: they were jolly hard working, *jolly* hard working. But we looked to them avidly because it was a kind of escapism from the lives that we led – humdrum lives, sometimes very difficult lives . . .'

*Was school difficult and humdrum?*
'Well, we had another school evacuated to us, so we went in the morning and they went in the afternoon and so it was very different. Things were much more formal in those days. At primary school we were taught in classes of forty but, my goodness *me*, by the time we were six or seven we all knew how to read and write and we knew our arithmetic . . .'

*Did you get up to any naughty tricks?*
'I don't think I was terribly naughty. I liked the work, I did a certain amount of sport, I tended to be rather serious because

I enjoyed . . . they were serious times in which we were living. I was the youngest of the family and I very much enjoyed listening to serious discussions – *very* much – and therefore I was thought to be rather a serious child. But it was because I was passionately interested in many of those things – I was interested in debating societies and I was interested in all kinds of things. I think sometimes, you know, parents try to give their children the things they didn't have. My father left school at the age of thirteen, although he was very intelligent, and therefore was quite determined that I should have a very good education. My father hadn't had it so he tried to give it to me – *very* much – therefore I did not have a great deal of parties or pleasure. So when I was bringing up my children I wanted them to have more fun times. They were taught to sail. They were taught nearly all of the sports and they had, I hope, a little bit more fun. So you try to compensate. Each generation rebels and then only when you become a parent do you realise the wisdom of some of the things your parents were saying.'

*Did your children rebel? Did Mark grow his hair long?*
'No. No, he didn't grow his hair long, but he liked motor racing, which worried me *enormously*. But Mark went for the motor racing and he also became a very good golfer. We took them away for holidays. We hired a house, I took them away and my husband came down at weekends so they learned to sail there. We went to the same place every year so that they had a lot of friends. Friends are the most important thing in life. They really are. I can't emphasise that enough. And people are friends because you have an interest in common – it may be photography, it may be music. Music gives you a lot of friends. Mark was certainly quite interested in music and Carol had very much her own ideas and still does and she's a journalist. Young people will have their own ideas as to what they want to do and I think it's a mistake to try to persuade them into a direction into which they don't want to go. On the other hand if

they want to do terribly glamorous things which aren't going to give them a living, you've got to say, "Now, look dear, don't you think it would be worthwhile taking some training which will give you a much better chance of earning a basic living?"'

*So would you have been fed up if your children had formed a pop group?*
'I wouldn't have been at all upset. I know a *number* of people who are very keen on pop music – jazz in my time – so I shouldn't have been upset at all. I'd have been much more concerned if they didn't do anything. I wouldn't have been at all concerned at a pop group because you meet a lot of people and you're often doing something together and Mark did, as a matter of fact, learn the guitar because he wanted an instrument that you could go around instantly and you could get people singing.'

*Was he any good?*
'Not particularly. But he had quite a musical sense and they all listened to – *heaven* knows we had *all* the latest pop records. There were the Beatles in our time, you see, and they're just coming back because their songs were tuneful. I remember "Telstar" – lovely song. I absolutely loved that. The Tornadoes, yes. And we had Dusty Springfield, the Beatles I remember most of all, Lulu, Dusty Springfield, Dusty Springfield . . . yes, but they had this thing on all day and it became a part of the background . . .'

*They didn't play it too loud?*
'Good Lord, yes! Ha ha ha! Turn that thing down! Of course they did. Of *course* they did. But far better to be interested in that than not to be interested in anything at all.'

*How do you react to today's left-wing pop acts – the Housemartins, the Style Council, Billy Bragg – who can't wait to get you out of No. 10?*
'Can't they? Ha ha ha! Well, I remember when I went down to Limehouse studios once, there was a pop group there who I was

told I wouldn't get on with at all well and I was absolutely fascinated because they were rehearsing for television and it is a highly professional business. *Highly* professional. Cameras have to come in on certain shots, they use a fantastic amount of energy and of course their voices . . . and I've watched Elton John, too, who was highly professional – but I'm so sad that he's having this difficulty – with his throat. *Highly* professional. I think it has become much, much more professional in the technique you use now. You just had echo chambers in our time but now it's *much* more professional. You've got to use technology. Don't be frightened of it. It's going to bring fantastic opportunities.'

*Yes, but about these pop groups that want to get Mrs Thatcher out of No. 10 . . .*
'I don't mind these . . . most young people rebel and then gradually they become more realistic. It's very much part of life, really. And when they want to get Mrs Thatcher out of No. 10 – I've usually not *met* most of them. Ha ha ha! And it really is lovely to have a chance to talk to them – and it's nice they know your name, ha ha ha! But you see, I'm not up to date with pop music at all though sometimes I'm told what's the latest thing in the charts and I'm fascinated that some of the older things are right up top – things from the '60s. That one, er, "Love a Woman"? "When a Man Loves a Woman"? Yes, that is *marvellous* and do you know why I think that? Because it's not just noise and rhythm – there's a theme to it and there's melody and also when you're young, so many of the things are either about rhythm or they're really about girl loves boy, boy loves girl. That is the perennial theme and that is absolutely lovely. It's a *lovely* song and I, I'm interested that they're coming back. The rhythm is easy but it's having a good tune that's the hard part.'

*How did you feel about Live Aid?*
'I thought it was *marvellous*. I watched some of it on the Wembley thing and it was absolutely terrific. It was the first time that we'd

131

been able to get a great body of young people not merely interested in something but actually *doing* something for it and loving doing it and I thought it was absolutely terrific. And I watched some of that, and one group after another came and they did a marvellous job. They did a *marvellous* job. I think young people do want to give something: they don't only want to take something, they're desperate to give something – particularly to other youngsters who just don't have a chance. *Please* believe me – our generation was the same. I wanted, when I was young, to go and work in India because helping people who are not well off or who are poverty-stricken is very good and let me say this: you can never judge anyone by their appearance ever. Some of the kindest people have the most strange appearance. You can't tell their politics by what they look like. You might be able to tell by what they've got printed on their T-shirt, but not by what they look like.'

*The government was widely criticised for not doing enough for Ethiopia, and Bob Geldof was rude to you on one occasion . . .*
'Was he rude to me? I met him. He wasn't *rude* to me. We did talk. Obviously he came up and talked to me about the things that most interested him. But what fascinated me was this: it was not "Why doesn't the government give more?" but "What can *I* do as a person?" *That* was his approach. And after all, if government took so much away from young people that they hadn't anything left to give, that wouldn't be much of a life. That would be government substituting their judgement for what people want to do with their own money and that's always been my point. If you want to take everything away from people in taxes, it's because you don't trust them. Well, I *do*, and I think they should have some say. Of *course* we have to have enough for defence, for law and order, for social services, but it's people's earnings and if you left them with nothing with which to give themselves, you'd have a very dull society. And a wrong society. Yes, *wrong. Wrong!* If government say the money you

earn is first mine and I'll decide only what you should have left, I would say that would be . . . *wrong*.'

*What would you say are the worst problems facing young people today? AIDS, unemployment and . . .*
'You always wonder what's going to happen to you in the future. I can remember as a teenager some young marrieds I knew . . . they knew who they'd married, they knew what their training was going to be, they knew the sort of job they'd got, and it is the tremendous uncertainty and it is both a problem and an excitement and a challenge (*???* — *Ed*). These days when it comes to training, there are far many more choices than we ever had: we've got the young youth training – YTS – and now we've got another one called Job Training Scheme. There are quite a lot of jobs available for which you can't get people because, in the midst of unemployment, you've got a shortage of people taking the requisite skills. It is problematic when they don't necessarily get the right advice, and that's why I feel that as well as talking to your contemporaries you should have some older people to talk to.'

*But the future must seem bleak for young people faced with AIDS ads and heroin ads on television . . .*
'Yes, I agree. You see, television tells you a lot of things you wouldn't otherwise know, but it stops a lot of things because it's too jolly easy to go home and do your homework and then sit down in front of the television and the family's sitting down in front of the television and you're not talking to one another. Television must not be a substitute for doing things you want to do. Alright, it may be going out and belonging to a pop group, it may be that you're keen on going and cheering a football team, it may be that you're keen on learning snooker, but do do *something*. Don't just be a spectator. And if families go and do things – they may be interested in model railways – and I think it's

marvellous to learn an instrument because music takes you right out of yourself, and we all have gramophones or disc playing things these days . . .'

*Um. Have you ever seen* Spitting Image?
'I did watch one, not with myself, but there were one or two things on about the Royal Family and I didn't like them very much. We are fair game, politicians, but there are certain things I don't like images of and one is the Royal Family because it is the monarchy and I think it's got to be protected. Also I'm told that *Spitting Image* would hurt very much, so I think it's better not to be hurt too much. Like when your youngsters say, "I want to get Mrs Thatcher out of No. 10", never having *met* Mrs T. However . . .'

*What do you like on TV?*
'I adore *Yes, Prime Minister*. It's great fun, isn't it? Sometimes I do watch some of the old films . . . now, I did watch yesterday one from the First World War called *Dawn Patrol*. It was a very telling film. It taught you a lot. I also watched because I loved it – I just happened to turn on for the news – Welsh male voice choir – 1,000 voices . . . And I *did* enjoy *Superstore*. I enjoyed it enormously. I didn't know there were things called . . . TV video? Pop videos? Fantastic! Paul Daniels, I watch. He's fantastic. Marvellous. Really so unbelievably skilled. And the *Eurovision Song Contest* . . . now, we haven't done terribly well recently but when we won, we had a group of four in it and it was a song about a little girl and because she's only three . . . Brotherhood of Man? Lovely! A fantastic young group, really professional, and they'd worked out all their actions because in my young day it was Cliff Richard and Adam Faith . . .'

*When are you going to knight Cliff Richard?*
'Cliff Richard has done wonders. It was he who got the movement going, really – moving to the music, and Adam Faith came

in with a slightly different technique – always melodious and still about . . . Cliff Richard more than Adam Faith . . .'

*So will you put in a word for Sir Clifford?*
'Always be serious! . . . Alright, ha ha ha!! . . .'

*You have been called a lot of things in your time, from 'Margaret Thatcher, Milk Snatcher' when you were education minister . . .*
'Yes, I remember that too, and it seemed to me one thing that people could purchase – milk for their own children. The important thing is for the state to do things which the state can do but to leave people with money to do things themselves. If people's talents are to develop to their fullest ability, they must have the freedom to do that, so good luck to your pop groups. They do very well for us in exports – they do a fantastic job and if some of them want to have yellow hair, punk hair, short hair, long hair, blue jeans, yellow jeans or, these days, my goodness *me* we've got some smart ones. Marvellous! When I go and look at some of the clothes for young people, gosh they *are* pricey but, really, I think that the sort of informal period has gone. You know, some of the rules are coming back and life is much better when you have rules to live by. I mean, it's really like playing football, isn't it? If you didn't have any rules, you wouldn't be able to play the game. Of course you'll have the whistle blown sometimes, but freedom requires some set of rules to live by to respect other people's freedom, so if we're remembered that way, I think we'll have done a reasonable job for people the world over.'

# Hibbert and I

## 'Travellers on rock's lost highway'

*Paul Rider*

I think Tom would have found this 'Tom Hibbert as I remember him' exercise very funny, since he refused to take anything, himself included, very seriously. But I do remember him often. And when I do, I think of his Dennis the Menace socks – Dennis was a definite 'influence' – and of travelling.

We spent a lot of time together during the '80s heyday of record-company-sponsored trips for *Smash Hits*. We visited all sorts of places. We had a memorable outing to Majorca for a few genuinely bizarre days with Billy Idol, who was staying with his mum and dad in their holiday flat. We even went to Blackpool with Black Lace, but generally we seemed to go to America.

Travelling with Tom was great – he was as funny as he was eccentric and we laughed a lot. Or I did. But there was a problem: we had to sit in Smoking. Tom was a keen smoker and it was a given that he had to smoke. I suppose I could have protested but I knew whatever my discomforts, being 6' 3" and crammed into the choking hell of the smoking bit at the back of Economy, they were nothing compared to the challenges of spending five, six or more hours confined with a nicotine-deprived Tom Hibbert. So in Smoking we sat.

Tom's metabolism seemed to run mainly on cigarettes and booze, punctuated with the odd coffee and the occasional snack. He had complete disdain for the notion of healthy eating; he was actually not a fan of food at all. If you went out for a curry with him, he'd head for the English dishes section at the back of the menu and order an omelette, which he probably wouldn't eat. He was comically amused – and I suspect rather revolted – by what he called my 'trencherman tendency' to tuck into gross American hotel breakfasts. He had a coffee. I blamed jet lag, but he had a point.

America and Tom had a complicated relationship, but he knew it well. His wife, Allyce, was American, and he'd spent a lot of time there. He was not keen on Florida. From what he said, he'd had difficult moments with his in-laws mainly to do with their Florida condo and swimming pool, and his failure to sport the correct 'leeesure' wear. Apparently Tom's all-black jeans, shoes and Ramones T-shirt outfit was deemed inappropriate for poolside living. Tom was outraged when his mother-in-law went out and bought him more suitable attire – a sports shirt and matching Bermuda shorts. Sadly, I do not think there are pictures of him in this get-up.

He liked New York a lot because it had great music and plenty of dark smoky bars that served serious drinks. He could tolerate Los Angeles if he did not have to go outside in the sun too much. He did not like Atlanta. He said it was a swizz – a favourite Tom word – because it sounded good in Little Feat songs, but in fact it was boring and a bit of a dump. And the other thing he disliked in Atlanta was the Ritz-Carlton Hotel.

As privileged, seasoned rock journos of the '80s, 'travellers on rock's lost highway' in Tomspeak, our natural habitats were airports and posh hotels. Unfortunately, in America these were also homes to a species of beaming minor officials and authoritarian flunkies who would really get Tom's goat. One such creature was the waiter at the door to the bar of the Ritz-Carlton.

We were in Atlanta to do Jon Bon Jovi for the cover of Ver *Hits*; everything had gone to plan. We'd seen the gig the night before, photos had been taken, Tom had done the interview. It was time to relax with a celebratory drink. But between us and the bar was the waiter, who smiled and informed us in a syrupy drawl that he could not serve us as our attire violated the bar's dress code.

Tom was incensed. His character, always a strange mix of Keith Richards and P.G. Wodehouse, went full-on Wodehouse with a splash of Vivian Stanshall.

'Now listen here, my good man!' He did not actually say that, but that was the tone of what he *did* say. 'My friend and I are here as guests of Mr Bon Jovi. And I am sure you would be happy to serve him *however* he was dressed!' (The Bon Jovi look at this time was sort of ripped and torn with scarves.)

The waiter stopped smiling and drawled back: 'Mr Bon Jovi dresses that way because he is a rock star, sir. And he is staying on the club floor, where there is no dress code.'

It was a fair point, but Tom was in no mood to give up. He had noticed that at the bar sat a group of very large men, certainly golfers, vividly dressed in what Americans call 'plaid'. The one stood closest to us had his huge behind covered in blue and yellow check, supported by a white belt.

'Frankly,' Tom said loudly, 'your dress code is a bit weird if you let in people dressed like that!' and waved his arm in the direction of the bar.

The waiter winced and a grumbling noise came from the golfers, from which you could pick out words like 'goddamn' and 'faggot'. An international incident loomed. But just as the golfers were about to make their move – slowly – the bar manager appeared, whisked us around a corner and sat us at a table behind a large plant.

'You can sit here!' he said and flounced off to placate the golfers.

'They're British!' we heard him say.

Tom was quietly triumphant and delighted when the drinks arrived; the evening was set fair. There was a slight hitch when the waitress tried to point out there was no smoking behind the plant, but direct eye contact with Tom was enough to send her off in search of an ashtray.

He was extraordinarily fearless at times. In another international incident in Dublin, a bored and lightly inebriated Tom nonchalantly enraged a large crowd of U2 fans by booing and shouting things like 'twaddle' every time Bono and his chums finished a song. He really did not like U2: they were far too earnest and self-important and 'wrote rubbish tunes'.

In spite of being one of the most contrary people on the planet, Tom could also be charming. Even when his interviewees were at first put off by his often-strange questions, and his habit of sitting in complete silence for minutes on end, they would still succumb. From Bananarama to Margaret Thatcher, it worked on such a wide range of people.

David Sullivan, the porn magnate and owner of the *Sunday Sport*, who Tom interviewed for *Q*'s 'Who the hell . . . ?' was so impressed that he offered Tom a job after fifteen minutes of chat. On the way back from Sullivan's Chigwell mansion, Tom seriously considered the idea: 'I bet it's better money than EMAP!' But in the end he decided it might be too much hassle.

The last time I worked with Tom, he was interviewing Dennis Potter for 'Who the hell . . . ?' It was a strange mission, because Tom knew *exactly* who the hell Potter was. He was a bit of a fan and respected him; the normal debunking did not happen. Potter was very publicly dying at the time, self-medicating with red wine and Fernet-Branca. The conversation, though often sharp and funny, was dark and fatalistic. At one point they cheerily competed with each other over who smoked the more toxic cigarette brand: Potter's Rothmans versus Tom's Marlboros. Potter claimed victory and status as the more serious fatalist – but only by a nose. It seems sadly prophetic now: both of them left us far too soon.

Tom (and Lola Borg, a *Smash Hits* designer) modelling for a *Smash Hits* 'Fashion' spread, 1984 (photos by Paul Rider).

# Jon Bon Jovi: 'I am Superman!'

## *Smash Hits*, 8 April 1987

The mayor of the city has declared it 'Bon Jovi Day' here in Atlanta, Georgia, USA; the place is *crawling* with 'moshin' muthas' in satin strides, and on the city's premier rock radio station, the DJ – a husky-voiced, ditsy number named Kate – is going Bon Jovi barmy. Between each track she blathers about the beauty of ver Bons and takes calls from listeners who say things like 'Hi, Kate! I've got a ticket to tonight's show and I'm sitting in row 110CC!' To which Kate replies, 'That is *gurrrrattte*! You'll see everythang from there and let me tell you, the show is *amaaaaaaazing*!!' Then she sticks on another cut from the Bon Jovi LP, *Slippery When Wet*, and we in the car speeding gigward go, 'Goodness!'

It's the third month of an eight-month-long tour; Bon Jovi have reached Atlanta, Georgia, for two sell-out shows in the 17,000 seater Omni arena; their LP has sold 7 million copies thus far – the fastest-selling album of all time, apparently – and they are big, big, big. BIG! And why not? But despite his superstar status, Jon Bon Jovi *still* can't get a meal in the hotel's restaurant because he doesn't conform to the dress code of sober slacks, sports coat and tie to be worn at all times in the outrageously snooty and pretentious Ritz-Carlton. 'Stupid!' is Jon's verdict on the hotel's rules for 'guest attire'. 'They just judge the book by looking at the cover; they don't open the cover and look inside.'

Quite right.

Not one of the 17,000 'folks' seething inside the Omni tonight would ever make it inside the portals of the Ritz-Carlton. There are stacks of girls in splendidly-ripped jeans sporting Heather Locklear-type bouffant hair-dos and wild southern accents, 'y'all', swooning at the very thought that soon – very soon – Jon Bon Jovi will be mounting the podium to kill them with his charms. There are stacks of boys – some as young as ten – in sneakers and Bon Jovi T-shirts just bursting to do some serious head-shaking and chant along in unison on their favourite choruses . . . And . . . And . . .

SPLOOOK! Some gigantic sparkler devices at the fore of the stage explode majestically to announce the arrival of Bon Jovi and the entire auditorium is on its feet – cigarette lighters aloft – squealing, scream-ing, cheering and going crazy apeshit in general. David Bryan in the spotlight strikes up some impressive, churchy organ. Richie Sambora splangs his guitar, Tico Torres and Alec John Such make a bit of a racket and – bong! – there he is in some slinky jeans and, believe it or not, a U2 T-shirt. Squeal. Squawl. And the first of the evening's many pairs of knickers flies through the air to land at the feet of Jon Bon Jovi.

Down in the audience, all is adulatory mayhem – fists punching the air to the very 'tight' hard rock beat, policemen feigning guitar solos on their night-sticks (American for 'truncheon'), and people clambering up on seats and falling off in an exultant mass. Jon stalks the stage, he prances the catwalks, he introduces 'You Give Love a Bad Name' with a lengthy, 'humorous' rap about falling in 'lurve' with a 'lady' who consequently betrays him in the arms of another. He poses, he pouts and he prattles with gusto – his every move greeted with a hail of further screamings.

And then the pièce de résistance: 'I can't hear you at the back,' says Jon. 'I guess I'll have to come and take a closer look.' Upon which ropes and handles come down from the ceiling and, holding on, Jon is winched slowly over the heads of the bawling throng to a mini-stage mid-auditorium, where he straps on an acoustic guitar to perform 'Silent Night'. Upon which the entire female population of Atlanta just faints away . . .

The next morning finds JBJ yawning into a cup of tea up on the 19th floor of his creepy hotel.

'There *were* a lot of knickers last night, weren't there?' he says sleepily. 'And someone threw a sheet. Ha! But knickers are better than bottles – you can bet your ass on *that.*'

You surely can.

Jon takes a delicate sip from his teacup. The sunshine wafts in through the window, trickling through his hair, and it becomes disgustingly evident that this man has *not* been beaten with the ugliness stick. He is simply *ravissant,* my dears – a fact that, perversely, dogs him. Jon Bon Jovi does *not* enjoy his status as a rock 'n' roll sex symbol:

'I *hate* it. I don't like it at *all.* I won't speak to the "teen" mags because all they want to talk about is hair spray and stuff and it's all just a crock of shit and I don't want to sell the band on that.'

But you're *such* a dreamboat, Jon . . .

'Well, I don't want to go out and run into a brick wall or nothing, but I don't want to play it up with hair spray neither. I'm trying desperately to grease my hair back – that's why I'm letting it grow. I'm just going to grease the whole thing back and get as low key as possible. I'm letting my hair grow to death because I don't want to be too cool for school.' *(??)*

Jon Bon Jovi is a *major* pop star – hit singles and regular TV exposure coast to coast testify to that; but he's not a *comfortable* pop star because he feels 'he only came to rock 'n' roll' and he wants to let his music and his shows do the talking. Yes, he's *that* kind of guy.

'We're just a rock 'n' roll band – that's all we ever claimed to be. We never set out to change the world – rock 'n' roll to me was always entertainment, it wasn't a place to be talking about politics or nuclear holocausts. As much as I love U2 and Little Steven's my idol, it's like *you* write about that stuff, *I* ain't concerned.

'This is just the beginning. I've fought hard to get to this plateau, so I'm not going to go down. There's Jagger and Bruce and Dylan to chase and Bowie and Genesis and about eighteen other bands. I ain't done yet. I'm not satisfied, not at all. I would give *anything*. I would sell my soul – that's a pretty sick thing to say but I've said some pretty weird stuff to myself, you know. Like I'd give a day of my life for every day I can sing good – that's pretty sick but I've said that to myself. *That's* how much I dig it. I dig it so much I'd give up everything and everyone I know. It is *bad*. I want it so bad that there ain't nothing I wouldn't do to get it. I love my family dearly, of course, but I'd kill my mother for rock 'n' roll and that's *sick*. It's the weirdest sensation.'

Indeed.

'We're the people's band. We're the kids' band and when I fly out over them there's a lot of smiling people out there – and they're having fun and no matter how tired I might be, I am Superman! I'm gonna *kill* somebody to put on the best show I can, because that is better than any drugs or any alcohol or any money – anything. I'd give up all my money for that sensation. Sick as it sounds, it's true.'

Such rare intensity of commitment has resulted in an awful lot of money for Jon Bon Jovi to give up if he should feel like it. Look at the record sales, look at the eight months of sold-out venues, look at the private plane that ferries the band from city to city, look at the huge Bon Jovi entourage that is – even as we speak – stalking the hotel in defiance of the dress code. Jon Bon Jovi is doing alright – 'and a few years ago I couldn't even buy beer' – though life on the road (man) is taking its toll:

'It drives you crazy and I'd be lying if I told you it didn't. It's really exciting to sneak over to a shopping mall and buy a new album and be a normal person again. Yesterday I snuck out and bought my 17th copy of *The Animals' Greatest Hits* and that was a good feeling.' *(??)*

Does he alleviate hotel boredom then *à la* Beastie Boys by indulging in destructive antics?

'I know absolutely nothing about the Beastie Boys, and it's great because they know all about us and so long as they keep reading those articles and watching us on TV, that's fine. Didn't they cut a hole out of the floor in the Holiday Inn? Well, that's great but I'm wondering how they could afford to *pay* for it. We can afford to pay for it but we don't do it anymore because of security.

'Once we used a blow torch to write our names on a desk, and when people would leave their shoes out in the hallway to get shined we'd mix them all up and throw the rest out the window. We've done all that, sure, and I've smashed a few things myself – it's just boredom. What did I smash? Oh, I smashed *people*. People in limousines. But I don't want to talk about it. If you get in a fight you get in a fight, but I'm not a fighting person. I'm a happy drunk.'

He is indeed a man who likes a drink but not, apparently, partying on down in clubs because 'all that Hollywood shit is boring and I can't be nice to people I don't like. I'm not a politician. I don't go to the clubs in LA. I don't go to the clubs in New York. I don't even go to the clubs in London. I've never been to the Limelight or the Hippodromes or whatever you call 'em.

'I'd rather . . . I was going to say I'd rather watch TV, but in England all they ever do on TV is play darts. It's true. And snooker. Hey, if I *want* to see snooker, I'll go down the pool hall and watch 'em play. Why do I want to sit there and listen to some guy whispering "and he's about to shoot the red ball into the side pocket"? Man, *really*! And TV shuts off there at midnight. Jesus, I go crazy in England with TV, but I love London. Why? Because you can go to the pub or something or you can go to McDonald's . . .' *(??!!!)*

The tea's all gone and it's almost time for Jon Bon Jovi to cruise down for the soundcheck at the Omni, where tonight, once more, he'll face the flying lingerie, trundle the stage decked in an American flag, provoke and tease the girlies even though he's not a sex symbol (hem hem). But before he slinks off, let us ask him one serious question: are Bon Jovi, or are they not, sexist fiends?

'Well, I've heard that we're sexist – probably because of the album cover *(the American cover of* Slippery When Wet *shows a foxette in a wet T-shirt; the British version, thankfully, is more refined)*, but that wasn't sexist at all. It was much better to put a picture of her on the cover than a picture of a *guy* on the cover, know what I mean? You'll never find *that* problem in *this* camp, you know? One thing we're *not* is Frankie Goes to Hollyweirdo or whatever . . .'

Indeed they are not. For they are Bon Jovi and they only came to rock 'n' roll . . .

# Kylie Minogue

*Smash Hits*, **20 April 1988**


An ugly old warehouse-type building in a very seedy south London back alley that is quite infested with puddles. This, believe it or not, viewers, is the nerve centre of the British pop industry – for this is the home of PWL, the Stock, Aitken & Waterman company, where almost every single hit of the last century and a half was concocted. And behind those squalid walls a wee girlie from 'down' 'under' (i.e. Australia) is recording a long-playing 'disc' even as we speak . . . Let us go in and meet her, shall we? . . .

As one enters the PWL portals, one is greeted by the figure of Lord Peter Waterman, forty-one, who proceeds to tell one at some length how completely brilliant he is and how completely brilliant Kylie Minogue is and how the 'twinning' of Kylie and Stock/Aitken/ Waterman is a completely brilliant thing for the development of popular music and how Pete has become so brilliantly rich through SAW's hits with Rick Astley and Mel and Kim and the 'Rams and Kylie and everybody else that he's bought a diesel train to run round his garden in Cheshire because he really likes trains and he used to be a stoker on the railways, which was a completely brilliant job and almost as brilliant as being one of the most brilliant songwriter/ producer types in the known universe etc. etc. Talks rather a lot does Pete Waterman, forty-one. And when he's finally finished, he takes you into a room where Ms Kylie Minogue is sitting on a chair, waiting to talk to you some more . . .

Good lord, but she's tiny, this wee girlie from 'down' 'under' (i.e. Australia) – about 3 inches tall and as plump as a Twiglet.

'You're not nearly as tall as you look on the telly!' I protest.

'I know! I know!,' she cries, covering her face with a dainty hand in shame. 'Don't tell them how short I am, will you?' she implores.

Heaven forfend! Kylie Minogue, readers, is very short indeed. But despite this 'handicap' she has managed to become absolutely massively successful in Australia for her stunning portrayal of Charlene Thingie on super-soap *Neighbours* and for her two enormous pop hits, 'Locomotion' and 'I Should Be So Lucky'. And now, of course, she's rather famous in Britain too, and what usually happens when you become famous in Britain is the so-called 'news' papers start writing horrible things about you. Kylie Minogue has not escaped the 'treatment' and she is, if the papers are to be believed, suffering from acute anorexia nervosa (i.e. she only weighs about 2 stone) and enormous depression all at the same time. Not much fun, is it?

'Yes, I'm anorexic,' Kylie confesses, 'And did you know that I'm having a fling with Greedy Smith *(beaming, slightly mad singer of Mental As Anything)* and I've broken up his marriage, which is odd because I've never actually met the man, and also I hear I didn't actually sing on "I Should Be So Lucky" because it was actually Rick Astley speeded up and I'm always taking my clothes off . . .'

Jonks!!

'. . . Well, none of that stuff is true . . .'

Bah!

'. . . Why do people want to write that sort of stuff? Why do people want to believe it? It's stupid!'

Kylie Minogue is nineteen years old – 'I'm Melbourne-born and bred. My mum's Welsh and my dad's fifth-generation Australian.

Is he descended from a convict? Oh, I don't know. I'd be really interested to find out my family tree, actually . . .' – and she's been on the telly 'down' 'under' for nearly half her life: 'The first thing I did was when I was ten, I appeared on one episode of something called *Skyways*, which was a series that didn't last too long because it was pretty dreadful and then when I was eleven, I was in *The Sullivans (useless Australian soap opera all about people with corks on their heads in the Second World War)* and I played a Dutch girl called Carla and I had to speak in a Dutch accent, which I wasn't much good at, and I didn't have any parents and I didn't really know what I was doing. It was good, though . . .'

Kylie's break into the glistening world of pop came last year when some of the cast of *Neighbours* got together to sing at a benefit concert at an Australian Rules Football Club ('Have you seen Australian Rules Football? It's really gory. I don't follow football, myself . . .') and Kylie ended up on stage singing 'Locomotion' (ancient hit of the '60s by Little Eva) because she was the only one who knew all the words, and so thoroughly stupendous was her performance that day that they decided to turn it into a record and, well, the rest, as they say, is history. She had never dreamt of being a popstrel before that:

'I never had any ambitions to be a pop star – except that when I was about eight or nine, I used to have pretend ABBA concerts in my bedroom with my friends. We'd put on dresses and dance to ABBA records and pretend to be ABBA and we'd prance about the bedroom or the lounge, singing into hairbrushes. I was always the blonde one.

'What's her name? Agnetha? Yes, I wanted to be Agnetha when I grew up but that's as far as my pop singing aspirations went.'

And when she wasn't bouncing about pretending to be ABBA with her playmates, she was, apparently, glued to her telly, which can't have been much fun because Australian television used to be quite hopeless and consisted mainly of *Skippy the Bush Kangaroo (stupid old* programme about a kangaroo who hops all over the shop, putting out forest fires and hiding top secret microfilms in his pouch) . . .

'Skippy? You remember Skippy? Teeheehee.' At this point Kylie launches into a fair impression of an episode of *Skippy the Bush Kangaroo:* 'Skippy!! Watch out, there's a forest fire, Skippy!! Hey, put out the forest fire, Skippy!! Teeheehee. Actually, Skippy was a bit before my time. I was brought up on *The Flintstones* – I always wanted to have a car like Fred Flintstone with the feet poking through the bottom – and *I Dream of Jeannie* and *Get Smart* and all those American shows they had on in the morning. I would have liked to have watched Australian shows on the TV but there weren't a great deal.'

These days, of course, you just cannot get away from Australian telly shows with *Neighbours ('Neigh-bours! Everybody needs good neighbours! Di di di di di di dee dee!'* etc. etc.) spearheading the fray. Kylie, as everybody knows, is Charlene, the feisty youngster who is always wobbling about with pom poms because she wants to be a cheerleader or something. So how closely does Ms Minogue resemble her on-screen character? Not very, it seems:

'Charlene is much more boisterous than I am. I don't like sports. I prefer making dresses and being quiet because I get very tired. I didn't like sports at school. What I liked at school was mainly arts and graphics and human development, not running round the yard with batons in my hand. But Charlene's the type of girl who *always* has a baton in her hand. Charlene just doesn't get tired. I think it would be great to have her strength and then I could bop those journalists who say I'm anorexic on the head. Yes, I'd really like to bop them one but I'm just not aggressive like Charlene . . .'

So. Is anything truly awful going to befall Charlene over the next few months? Is she going to break off with Scott and be beamed up by an alien spacecraft and have lots of nasty dreams or anything?

'Oh, I can't think of anything . . .'

i.e. she's not saying. Oh, well . . . And with that, viewers, I am ushered out of the centre of the British pop industry by Pete Waterman, forty-one, as Kylie has to get back in the studio and jolly it up on another bracing pop melody. As I leave there's this plaintive little Australian whisperette in my ear which begs 'You won't tell them how short I am, will you?' once more. Your secret's safe with me, little lady (hem hem) . . .

# Hibbert and I

## 'My caber-tossing chum'

*Tom Doyle*

Tom Doyle in the *Smash Hits* office, 1988 (courtesy of Tom Doyle).

There he was: clacking away at a typewriter, puffing on a Marlboro Red, quietly chuckling to himself, clearly tickled by whatever he was writing. It was 7 March 1988, the first day of my new job as staff writer at *Smash Hits*. If I wasn't intimidated enough, here I was sharing the same office space as Tom Hibbert.

I can't clearly remember my first conversation with Hibbs. That's probably because, from six o'clock onwards, we were in the pub for the start of a lengthy drinking session. But I vividly recall my first impressions of him: completely unpretentious, totally hilarious – and the poshest person I'd ever met. I'd grown up in a tower block on a grim council estate in Dundee; his father was a celebrated *historian*. We were from entirely different worlds. But Hibbs wasn't snooty in the slightest. From that night onwards, he called me 'my caber-tossing chum'.

Of course – not least because I was only twenty and he was a 'grown-up' thirty-five – I was secretly in awe of him. Aside from his brilliant invention of much of the *Smash Hits* lexicon, he was a masterful interviewer: opening a dialogue with Morrissey with the words, 'What's the matter with you?', or asking Kylie Minogue if her father was descended from a convict (before cheerfully sympathising with her about how the papers were reporting that she was anorexic). Obviously his monthly 'Who the hell . . . ?' skewerings in *Q* were already the stuff of legend.

Hibbs was so busy by this point that he had to give up writing his surreal, rambling responses as Black Type on the *Hits* letters page, and so I was asked by editor Barry McIlheney to take over. It was a tough gig. Hibbs was an impossible act to follow and I could never detail the exploits of Reg 'Reg' Snipton or Uncle Disgusting – never mind continue to lobby for the knighting of Cliff Richard – with quite the same flair or conviction. I felt as if I'd been handed someone else's ventriloquist dummy and was clumsily trying to make it talk without moving my lips.

Other memories flash into my mind when I think of Hibbs. Attending a party at his house and being amazed by how many toys this supposed adult owned. Watching him enthusiastically fronting his occasional band the Love Trousers at the Half Moon in Putney, attacking his guitar and belting out his vocal parts as bassist Mark Ellen grinned away at his side. Hearing him spontaneously and frequently bursting into a loud appreciation of Billy Joel in the office: 'It's myyyyyyy *life*!!!'

The last time I saw him was sometime in 1994, at a do in a bar north of Oxford Street, around the time I'd myself started writing for *Q*. Another *Smash Hits* writer had, a couple of years earlier, let slip that Hibbs had revealed one of his 'secret' interview techniques. He would wait till an interviewee had finished answering a question and then say . . . absolutely nothing. Said rock or pop star would then inevitably feel s/he had to fill the silence. More often than not, they would go on to reveal some deeper truth about themselves beyond the usual promotional flannel.

That night, being in a bit of a 'chatty' state, I decided to compliment Hibbs on this. 'It's amazing you can do that, man,' I burbled. 'Takes a lot of balls to say bugger all, especially if you've got some PR there counting down the minutes . . .'

Hibbs nodded, smiled.

' . . . I've tried it, but I just don't have the bottle. I always end up saying *something*, cause it's just so awkward to sit there and say nothing . . .'

He grinned. Took a deep lug on his fag. Said nothing. I twigged.

'Wait a minute, you're fucking doing it *now*, aren't you?'

He burst out laughing, revealing his famously toothy grin.

In the years that immediately followed, I always kept up with Hibbs's writing, even if it involved me having to buy the *Mail on Sunday* every week to read his never-less-than-utterly-brilliant pop column. One Sunday, instead of reviewing the latest releases, Tom instead informed his readers that all the albums he'd been sent that week were a load of tosh. However, he'd bought a new mop that week, and it had come with a cassette: *Bop While You Mop*, featuring the sudsy sounds of James Brown, Shakatak and Kool & the Gang. Therefore he'd decided to review that instead.

It was great to know that he was now intent on bending the minds of Middle Englanders.

In fact, I've just looked up *Bop While You Mop* on Discogs and it's listed for sale. £1.99 (plus postage and packaging) . . . a snip!

# Smash Hits: 'Bitz' and letters

## Smash Hits, Letters, 19 June 1985

Dear Bryan Ferry,

I have lived in Hampstead for fourteen years and have never heard of (let alone met) anyone called Tarquin or Peregrine (5 June). Neither has anyone else I know. I have therefore come to the conclusion that there are the same number of Tarquins and Peregrines in Hampstead as there are times that someone has sent me a £10 record token so that I can buy your records (i.e. none).

*Tarquina Perigrenne Toadflax, Hampstead*

**Well, where *do* they all live then, brainy slacks? Milton Keynes? North Allerton? Widnes? Eh? Eh? Eh? Got you there, matey, nyah!**

—

Dear **Black Type**,

Help! I think I've been bitten by The Curse of the Damned (7 May)!

You see, the other day I came out of school and this dog started following me home! Maybe it was after my dog-flavoured crisps, but when I got home it just sat outside our house for ages.

Then while I was eating my tea (cheese on toast – yum!) a few cups fell off the draining board, scaring the hell out of our cat Fang.

Later that night I closed my windows before going to bed – but during the night they flew wide open!

I've asked Arthur C. Clarke but he can't help. You're the only person left who can help.

*Dave Vanian's Distinctly Ghoulish Tendencies, Sheffield*

**A DIY Expert writes: Honest, squire, if I've heard it once, I've heard it a thousand times. Wonky windows! Skew-wiff draining boards! Some people never learn! You'd think no one had ever heard of self-levelling rust-proof weather-resistant lead-free multi-sealing poly-adhesive draught-repelling semi-toxic non-absorbent anti-caking simu-grout compound! Works wonders, it does. One dab on a dry, clean surface and, blimey, you won't be bothered by no more stray dogs in a hurry, believe you me!!**

—

I just wanted to say thanks England for giving us 12 points in the Eurovision song contest.

*Sid (Not Vicious), Hardanger, Norway*

**Oh, thank you very much! Rub it in, won't you. If I had my way, there'd be some kind of government enquiry into the complete swizzle that is called the Eurovision Song 'Contest'. After last year's debacle in which the uniquely talented Belle and the Devotions were dis-tracted by a lot of Belgians in beards waving hankies, I did not believe things could get more out of hand! But the sight of our very own flower of song, Vicki, wilting**

beneath the combined weight of Danish midgets and Turks in pith-helmets was too much to bear!! I think the stylish Austrian entry, Garry Mux, summed it up best: 'Boom boom my piano is drowning in sherry trifle' or words to that effect . . .

# Singles reviews

*Smash Hits*, 6 November 1985

## Lloyd Cole & the Commotions: 'The Lost Weekend' (Polydor)

Can this man do no wrong? Well, yes he can, actually – those moody 'n' enigmatic James Dean-orientated expressions he's always attempting just do not work with cheeks so chubby. But apart from that, he's pretty damned impeccable. And this is lovely – chiming guitars sturdily jaunting and winking at an idea based on Iggy Pop's 'The Passenger' with customary jumbly vocal delivery. It all sounds uncharacteristically merry until one starts to pick up the words, which appear to be about contracting pneumonia in Amsterdam, almost dying and then undergoing a religious conversion. I don't think that can be right, can it? I'll just have to listen to it again. (Don't mind if I do . . .)

## Midge Ure: 'That Certain Smile' (Chrysalis)

It's the plush, grandiose pop sound of 'If I Was' once again, only more so – which can mean only four things . . .. 1) 'That Certain Smile' will be a very big hit; 2) You'll be quite fond of it for a couple of days; 3) By the time it's being played on the radio every six minutes you'll be sick to death of it; 4) If he does those stupid theatrical hand wiggles in the video again, you'll scream and scream and hurl the TV set: out of the window and it'll land on top of a police car and you'll be sent to prison for a very long time. Bad luck.

## Topper Headon: 'Leave It To Luck' (Mercury)

If it didn't say right here on the label that the song was written by N.B. Headon, I'd swear that this was a new version of James Brown's 'Papa's Got a Brand New Bag' with different words. Hang on a mo, though, didn't Nicky 'Topper' Headon, former Clash 'sticksman' (for it is he!), once get arrested for stealing a bus stop?! Hmm, it's all a bit fishy if you ask me.

## Single of the Fortnight – The Lucy Show: 'Undone' (A&M)

Guitars nip and chatter while a singer with the sleepy drawl of a British Jack Nicholson gets all sardonic about hanging out on the comer with his stinky friends. Not much of a song tune-wise, but the sound is dashingly gloomy. You can dance to it, you can call it 'art' if you so wish – either way it's *shimmeringly* cool.

## Wham!: 'I'm Your Man' (Epic)

I must say, I do like the cut of George Michael's jib. What usually happens once you've become the world's most famous rising pop star is you get complacent and start making useless records, or you go dotty and stop making records altogether. Not George. George cares about pop far too much to let himself become distracted just yet. He's passionate about pop and he's good at it too: not a great songwriter but a stylish 'craftsman' and a marvellous singer. On 'I'm Your Man' he comes on all breathy and slippery in a racy pumping romp that's a little bit Motown and quite a lot George McCrae. A dignified hit: G. Michael is a proper star. (Not entirely sure what Andrew does on this but, no doubt, he does it very well too.)

## Dexys Midnight Runners: 'This Is What She's Like' (Mercury)

Kevin Rowland's in this pub with this bloke called Bill, who keeps saying, 'Tell me what she's like' to him, right? 'I'm trying. Bill, I'm trying,' Kevin replies – trouble is there's this half-baked Irish showband with a doddery old fiddle player blaring away in the comer so Kevin can hardly hear himself *think*. And anyway, he's getting quite drunk and so keeps losing himself in the middle of sentences and howling along with the showband but not getting the words quite right or the tune for that matter. Bill never does find out what she's like (whoever 'she' might be) and Kevin wakes up next morning with a massive hangover and the awful, dawning realisation that last night he made this simply LUDICROUS pop disc . . .

## Dan Hartman: 'Fletch, Get Outta Town' (MCA)

Dan Hartman doesn't make very good records, does he?

## Phyllis Nelson: 'I Like You' (Carrere)

'I like you', not 'I love you', or even 'I like you an awful lot'. Just 'I like you'. There's little sign of passion in the song either or of anything much else for that matter. Quite clearly, Phyllis Nelson is one of the great hard-bitten cynics of our time.

## Captain Sensible: 'Come On Down' (A&M)

'Win a holiday for two/or a fluffy kangaroo/Genuine vinyl three-piece suite/It will make your life complete . . .' Yes, Sensible is having a sneer at *The Price is Right* and similar gruesome game shows, but he's so jolly and chirpy and inoffensive about it all that Derek Batey, Leslie Crowther and all those other masters of audience humiliation are left without a stain on their characters. In a couple of years, the 'very lovely' Maggie Moone will probably be singing this jaunty cockney trot-along to the contestants on *Name That Tune*.

## The Art of Noise: 'Legs' (Chrysalis)

In an all-too-rare appearance on *Saturday Superstore*'s pop panel, Ms Delia Smith described this record (an achingly hip 'aural tapestry') as 'UNSPEAKABLE' – and who am *I* to argue with the Queen of the Casserole Dish? On second thoughts, I prefer 'UNBEARABLE'.

## Pet Shop Boys: 'West End Girls' (Parlophone)

A tumble through Soho in the seedy wee, wee hours accompanied by the kind of jaundiced horns that are more often found on soundtracks of films about Hollywood actresses hitting the bottle and cracking up with mascara running down their faces (*Valley of the Dolls* springs to mind). Set against this, the electronic bleats and the demi-rap (Grandmaster Flash and the Furious Five's 'The Message' without the baseball bat) create an atmosphere of danceteria sleaze that's almost sinister. Brrr.

## Simonics: 'In This Heat' (Thin Sliced)

The sound of a trickling, ghostly violin – like those played by toothless gypsies in misty graveyards just before the murderer strikes again and the police inspector goes, 'Those same marks on the neck! My God! What kind of creature are we looking for?!' in crackly old horror films – wafts fitfully while the deep, battle-fatigued voice of a male person moans despairingly about a lost straw hat. Absurd?

'Course it is, but its overpowering hypnotic qualities will get you anyway. Ber-rilliant.

## Artists United Against Apartheid: 'Sun City' (Capitol)

## Latin Quarter: 'No Rope as Long as Time' (Arista/Rockin' Horse Records)

Another all-star choir (Bruce, Bono, the saintly Bobs Geldof and Dylan and many more) raises its massed voice in righteous indignation. This time the target is apartheid, Sun City being the South African entertainment resort where international artists – from Queen to Frank Sinatra – perform for flocks of music-loving South Africans (except for black music-loving South Africans, who find it rather difficult to get hold of tickets . . .) 'We ain't gonna play Sun City . . .' chant the assembled ranks, and quite right too. A fundraising event (all royalties to The Africa Fund) to be applauded, but as a protest song in its own right, 'Sun City' seems pretty toothless, any 'message' getting swamped in a riot of jubilant trumpeting and dance rhythm fever. A far, far more potent statement about South Africa is Latin Quarter's 'No Rope as Long as Time' – a quietly despairing tale of an Afrikaner farmer who sleeps with a gun while his country tears itself apart, beautifully sung. No political sloganeering – just humans.

# Hibbert and I

## 'The mystery virus of pop'

*Kipper Williams*

Tom's local pet shop had a fax machine. He used to edge past the hamsters to fax me his scripts for the cartoon strips I drew for *Smash Hits* and later for *Top of The Pops* magazine. We'd occasionally meet up and Tom would hand over his latest creation on a page torn from a reporter's notebook. Looking back, his dialogue still seems incredibly fresh, even funnier and even more bonkers than the first time around.

He took a bit of P.G. Wodehouse and a bit of *The Beano* and jumbled everything together with his own brilliant verbal horseplay. I'd often been a bit snooty (a good Hibbert word) about working from other people's ideas, but when it came to Tom I couldn't wait to get to the drawing board. I felt guilty about having to edit his stuff, but this was only so I could fit his dialogue into the speech bubble space. I thought he was a comic genius.

I'd originally been asked to contribute to *Smash Hits* by editor David Hepworth. I usually drew in the Carnaby Street office, which was where I first met Tom. He was at his desk by the window in the corner doing an unconvincing Sylvester Stallone impersonation – this was at the height of Rambomania. Tom was stripped to his scrawny waist with a bandana round his head, brandishing a set square from the art department, which stood in for Rambo's M60 machine gun.

Hepworth and Mark Ellen originally commissioned me to draw single frame cartoons, and Neil Tennant asked me to draw a full-page strip for the 1985 *Smash Hits Yearbook*, which he was editing. Soon after that, Mark put Tom and me together.

At the time I was also drawing black and white cartoons for the *Daily Telegraph*'s financial pages, so it was a bit of a change to work for the explosion of jokes and colour that was *Smash Hits*. Kylie Minogue, Boy George, Prince and Madonna were all pretty flamboyant – less so the Director General of the CBI. Tom saw the pop stars of the time as being essentially comic-strip characters crying out to be satirised and I was more than happy to join in.

We worked on four different strip titles together over a period of ten years:

## *Bubbles – He's a Chimp!* for *Smash Hits*, 1989

Michael Jackson was a gift to cartoonists, of course – even more so given the news coverage given to his pet chimp, along with his llamas and snakes.

## *Pop Capers – The Masked Avenger of Pop* for *Smash Hits*, 1990–91

Again, this gave Tom the chance to air his grievances about particular pop stars. They were lassooed and put out of action by the Masked Avenger, thus sparing the world from what Tom called their 'warblings'.

## *The Fly – He's Always in the Soup!* for *Smash Hits*, 1990–91

This cartoon had a recurring 'punchline'. No matter what the story involved, the fly always ended up in the soup. So you knew what was coming *(plop!)*, but that somehow made it even funnier. And I love drawing cartoons of flies.

## Ken – The Mystery Virus of Pop for Top of the Pops magazine, 1999

Similarly, Ken possessed strange powers that enabled him to elimi-nate irritating pop stars. It was all deceptively innocent, even a little subversive. The basic premise was, these people are very annoying and silly, so let's find funny and interesting ways of elbowing them off the stage. Tom wasn't much of an eater, but he really tucked in when it came to biting the hand that fed him.

Oh, and sometimes we rounded off a strip with the world ending with a big bang. That'll teach them, eh readers?!

# Part Four

## Q the hell . . . ?

Tom's inimitable interview technique takes him to *Q* magazine
and his infamous series of 'Who the hell . . . ?' features – plus
reminscences from Paul Du Noyer and Chris Heath.

*Best of Q: Who The Hell . . . ?* (Virgin Books, 1994).

'When Mark [Ellen] left Smash Hits to start Q, I became deputy editor and was getting increasingly fed up with having to talk to press officers about Howard Jones every day. Then Mark rang up and said, "Do you want to do some interviews for us?" I said, "Sure."

'We had several long lunches and worked out what it was going to be. It was always going to be irreverent, but I don't think Mark knew how it was going to go. When I was writing, I got very cross with people, so I changed the interview style to be more demonstrative.

'The interview at the front, "Who the hell do they think they are?", was Mark's idea, but he didn't realise how demonstrative it would become, and he got really pissed off at the end because no one would talk to him. I didn't get any trouble from record companies, because I worked from home. Mark got it all. They'd ring up and complain about "this disgraceful article" and he'd have to deal with it.

'At The History of Rock and Smash Hits, I was really fed up with what I was writing about, so I invented sarcasm as a way of dealing with it. That came out in Q.'

Tom Hibbert, 2001

# Hibbert and I

## 'The glorious stupidity of life'

*Paul Du Noyer*

'Twas a dark, stormy night on the frost-embittered moors when first my eyes . . . Except it wasn't, was it, 'readers'? It was probably in a pub, one lunchtime, in the vicinity of London's 'swinging' Carnaby Street. Either way, and it doesn't matter now, I met Tom Hibbert.

Who was this owlish, inscrutable figure? He was already stick-thin, but seemed intent on making himself smaller. The bony shoulders were hunched, the elbows pulled in; his legs weren't merely crossed but somehow entwined around each other, several times. Only the king-sized cigarette, ever present, was allowed to project outside that tightly compressed silhouette.

So this was 'Hibbs', the friend of my friend Mark Ellen. I thought he looked marvellous. Nowadays I can never watch *Withnail & I* without remembering Tom. The elegant dishevelment. The shop-worn clothes, oddly matched, yet completely right. The punk-meets-power-pop haircut. He spoke in a posh-boy drawl I couldn't help liking, despite my chippy class antagonism. He seemed in a state of permanent, private amusement.

Most of all, you were struck by a bright intelligence and, better yet, a deeply inviting sense of fun. He wrote for *Smash Hits*, was fond of 'inverted' commas, and made me laugh. But I worked for the *NME* and there was a gulf between us.

I think back to Carnaby Street in Soho, 1985. Across this tacky, narrow thoroughfare, *Smash Hits* and *NME* faced one another like the rival embassies of two imperial powers. At the *NME* we took ourselves quite seriously. From our third-floor perch we looked down, and not just literally, on *Smash Hits'* second-floor office across the way.

I watched them a little enviously. It troubled me to think they were having more fun than we were.

One day I accepted an invitation to cross Carnaby Street to discuss a new magazine idea, and duly joined Mark Ellen, who was *Smash Hits'* editor at the time, in launching a new rock monthly called *Q*. It was a great success. And one of its key ingredients was a three-page regular called 'Who the hell . . . ?' The idea was that a journalist, nearly always Hibbert, was sent to grill some popular personality that was getting on our nerves. Tom was so good at this that he and 'Who the hell . . . ?' became synonymous.

I think he was at heart a satirist, a great and underrated one. It's said that when you scratch a satirist, you'll find a moralist underneath, and while Tom Hibbert was anything but preachy he did believe in certain standards. Throughout his interviews (in which he deployed a prim silence that panicked his victims into fresh follies of indiscretion), he was ever the sceptical inquisitor. From political braggards to show-biz buffoons, he regarded them as public figures who had let us down. And 'Who the hell . . . ?' was Hibbert's pillory. If it seemed slightly cruel, it was also very hilarious.

'Who the hell . . . ?' ran from *Q*'s first issue, in 1986, until 1997. It was a desperately difficult thing for the editors to put together, especially as the column grew in fame and PR people wised up to its dangers. During my own stint as *Q*'s editor I worried as much about filling each month's 'Who the hell . . . ?' slot as I did about finding a superstar for the front cover.

To add to the pressure, Hibbs was not the most punctual of writers. When printers' deadlines descended, he could leave us sweating
till the very last moment. But his job was tougher than most, being
summoned at short notice to interview anyone from a snooker
player to a seasoned dramatist, while from his subjects and their
minders he faced suspicion and hostility. Yet, when he delivered, as
he always did, all was forgiven and we promptly went to the pub.

He was, in any case, a lovable man. I certainly loved going to
the pub with him. In launching *Q* we'd moved north from Carnaby
Street to the louche old literary district of Fitzrovia. And here he
looked in his element. Away from Soho's new breed of 'meejah'
wonderkids with their ghastly 1980s Filofaxes, he settled instead
in some snug bar unimproved since Patrick Hamilton's day, sus-
tained by a little refreshment from his editor's expense account and
another king-sized fag.

Now he could relax, unfurl his legs a while, and laugh at the wonderful – *and please, sir, can we have some more?* – the glorious stupidity
of life.

# Who the hell does Chuck Berry think he is?

*Q*, May 1988

Chuck Berry is a difficult man.

Towards the end of the recently released Berry documentary film, *Hail! Hail! Rock 'n' Roll*, Keith Richards is seen slumped in a chair, exhausted and exasperated. For the previous two weeks he has been rehearsing with Berry for Berry's sixtieth birthday concert at the Fox Theater, St Louis; he has endured the petulant outbursts of the legend when anyone so much as dares touch the great man's amplifier; he has engaged in heated debate about how the introductory guitar figure in 'Carol' really goes; he has bashed all those old songs – 'Rock and Roll Music', 'Roll Over Beethoven', 'Johnny B. Goode', 'Nadine', 'No Particular Place to Go' – into something approaching tight arrangements, with scant cooperation from the grand old man himself.

And then on the big night what happens? Berry wilfully screws up Richards' labours by changing keys and altering arrangements as he sees fit, by throwing in bursts of unscheduled and singularly rotten guitar playing, and by acting the mischievous and awkward 'showman' the world has come to expect. It's almost as if Keith Richards cares more about Chuck Berry's music than Chuck Berry does and Keith is drained, all patience gone. Chuck, says

Keith, has given him more headaches in a fortnight than Mick Jagger did during the entire Rolling Stones' lifetime. Nonetheless, he adds with a fatigued smile of resignation, he cannot help liking the man . . .

The girl from Faber (publishers of *Chuck Berry: The Autobiography*), on the other hand, cannot but loathe him. At ten in the morning she is sitting in the coffee lounge of the Royal Garden Hotel, Kensington, wearing the haunted look that seems to descend on all those who come into contact with the Berry legend. She may be considerably younger than Keith Richards, and she may possess a full complement of teeth, but still she does a fair impression of Richards' filmed study of sorely tested tolerance. 'I hate Chuck Berry more than anyone else in the world,' she wearily declares. No, I don't think she likes him.

When Chuck Berry arrived in London two days ago to promote his film and his book and to play one concert at the Hammersmith Odeon, his first action, once settled into his Royal Garden suite, was to make a large and clumsy pass at the girl from the publishing house. The hotel chambermaids were merely complaining of pinched bottoms: this was a full-blown *pass*. And when the girl from the publishing house rejected the oily advance of this giant of rock 'n' roll, Chuck retreated into a mighty sulk, locking his doors to all comers. Forty press photographers turned up by invitation to snap the great man and were sent home shot-less when he declined to appear for their cameras.

The chairman of Faber visited Mr Berry's suite with copies of the autobiography for the author to sign – and was sent packing by the great man, who said he did not care to have his sleep disturbed by strangers. The man from *The Times* arrived to conduct a scheduled interview, was kept hanging around for seven hours (while Chuck lingered over a tardy three-egg breakfast, took a post-breakfast nap and did whatever it is that sulking rock 'n' roll legends do) before, finally, he was granted an audience with the great man. The audience lasted all of three minutes – three minutes and Chuck decided he had chattered quite long enough. Everyone, it seems, is paying for the indiscretion of the girl from the publishing house who had the brazen cheek to say *NO* to Mr Chuck Berry, to turn her nose up at the distinct honour of a roll in his love nest.

I arrive at the hotel for the *Q* interview at the appointed time to be told these outrageous tales by the girl from the publishing house. The girl who does not like Mr Berry (because he is 'really disgusting') and who has engaged intermediaries to shuttle betwixt the Berry suite and the press gang camped out in the coffee lounge. The girl who never wants to clap eyes on Mr Berry again. 'I'm afraid you may have to wait around a long time,' I am informed. Chuck hasn't woken up yet (no one would *dare* to wake him) and when he does, in his own good time, he'll be wanting his breakfast and goodness knows how long *that* will take . . . Chuck Berry is a difficult man, but the *good* news is that he seemed to be in a better frame of mind last night when he went off to be charming on Michael Aspel's chat show. (Though the story goes that he only agreed to appear on *Aspel* after a sum not unadjacent to $2,000 in used notes had been delivered to his suite. And when he was asked to perform 'Johnny B. Goode' on the show, he refused saying, 'For second-rate money, you get a second-rate song.' He did a ragged and rather awful 'Memphis' instead.)

Chuck Berry is a difficult man, but perhaps he *is* in a benevolent mood today, for morning has only just turned afternoon and I've been waiting a mere two hours when I am called to the lift to ascend to the legendary presence. Within the inner sanctum of his spacious suite, he sprawls in an easy chair, his legs straight out before him, his head resting on the chair back as he stares in boredom at the ceiling. With his slender moustache, his greased hair and his open beige shirt, he's somehow like a cross between a wizened spiv and an ageing lounge gigolo. Chuck Berry's eyes turn slowly from the ceiling towards me. Was that a nod of greeting I detected? Did a smile of friendship begin to play across his lips? Perhaps not. I sit before Chuck Berry, he leans leisurely forward to pick a Kool cigarette from the packet on the coffee table, and asks, in his sibilant, clearly enunciated voice, 'Did they tell you about the time?'

Did *who* tell me about *what* time?

'Before we begin, you can have maybe three minutes of questions with your tape recorder and then, after, maybe some more questions.'

Three minutes. Is this going to be some revelatory, heart-to-heart confessional with the ultimate living legend of rock 'n' roll? Perhaps not. Chuck Berry is a difficult man . . .

Chuck Berry's book was largely written in 1979 when he was serving his third prison sentence – a short stretch in Lompoc Prison Camp, California, for tax evasion – and one has to hand it to Chuck: this autobiography is most definitely not ghostwritten (well, you'd have to *pay* a ghost, wouldn't you?), as is clear from his quaint and extravagant turn of phrase, particularly when he touches, as he often does, on the subject of his many sexual dalliances ('I embraced her in disbelief that I was about to enter the garden that she had spread before me,' he writes; 'I was ready as a sturdy log twixt two rolling stones,' he writes; 'My determination to get ahead with a bank account helped me manage to withdraw when we did wade nude in the nest,' he writes). It's a strange book: fascinating glimpses of rock 'n' roll's infant years, and pre-Civil Rights prejudice in southern states being crowded out by Chuck's sexy memoirs and personal prejudices. He cares not for those who might try to part him from his money. He cares yet less for journalists. He doesn't like tape-recorded interviews because there's always the chance that he'll be misquoted. He doesn't like *un*-tape recorded interviews because there's always the chance that he'll be misquoted. Until recently he'd only permit *filmed* interviews ('visual-sound consultations') and he'd make sure these weren't tampered with after the fact 'by waving my hand before my face while answering questions to make it too obvious if they cut the scene to insert or omit anything.'

So here I am with my tape recorder and Chuck Berry and three minutes, which is whittled down by his latest journalist-foiling ruse of pausing lengthily after each question, then cupping his hand over his ear and saying, 'Once again?' You repeat the question and your precious time ticks away. Chuck Berry is an intractable customer . . .

'Once again?'

Would you say, Mr Berry, that you, single-handedly, invented rock 'n' roll?

'Single-handedly? Nope. I wouldn't say that I single-handedly invented rock 'n' roll. You see, there's all types of rock 'n' roll. There is *rock*. And there is *roooooooll*. See what I'm saying? And then there's rock 'n' roll, which is rock 'n' roll, hahahaha. It's just a matter of whatever I've accomplished, which is for others to say, I guess.'

How do you feel about those who look up to you in awe and say, That is the man who invented rock 'n' roll?

Pause. Eyes on the ceiling. The cupping of the hand. 'Once again?'

Repeat question.

'Actually, no feeling. I do not feel about such things.'

You have no feelings about the adulation you inspire?

'Once again?'

You have no feelings about the adulation you inspire?

'Nope.'

So you don't really care about your fans?

'My fans? What was that?'

Do you care about your fans?

'Oh, my *fans*. *Sure* I care about my fans. Because fans is money, hahaha. Muh-neeee! And who does *not* care about money? Me, I *like* muh-neeee, haha.'

Throughout the above exchange, if you can call it that, Mr Chuck Berry, alleged instigator of this thing we call rock 'n' roll, keeps one beady eye on his Rolex wristwatch. The precious time is ticking away and time, as we all know, is muh-neeee.

Chuck Berry is a man of few orthodox vices. He smokes his Kool cigarettes at a canter but he swore off the demon drink nearly half a century ago and he has always frowned upon drugs. His regular infidelity to the wife, Themetta (or 'Toddy'), he married in 1948, doesn't count as a sin in the great man's book: 'I keep my home fires burning. To say there must be no other women is a hypocrisy because that's something that is not written upon the heart. Pleasure is plea-suuuure! See what I'm saying?' he tells me with same strange logic. Which leaves only avarice. Chuck Berry likes muh-neeee, this much is clear, and stories of his pursuit of the folding stuff abound. We need not mention his first jail term, for bungled teenage armed robbery, or his third, tax evasion. (The second was for contravening the Mann Act, i.e. girl trouble.)

We need only mention the tales of the man's stage career of the last two and more decades. He wrote some marvellous and imperishable songs in the '50s and early '60s, for sure; nobody had a gift for the wry lyric, the feeling for spry metre like Berry. But he seems to have spent the last twenty-five years desecrating his great songs for paying audiences around the globe. He just would take the money and run. A typical Chuck Berry appearance would go like this: minutes before showtime, the man would arrive, alone, guitar case in hand, and take delivery of concert fee in promoter's office; he'd walk on stage before pick-up backing band he'd never met (band's fee to be paid out of Berry's wodge only if they're up to scratch; no introductions – no 'How d'you do, Mr Berry, and what songs will we be playing tonight?' – no rehearsal), tune up perfunctorily and launch into whatever number popped into his head, hapless pick-up band struggling behind. A bit of crowd-pleasing duck walking, a few old faves with sloppy, idle guitar solos bunged on top, and after forty-five minutes – on the dot – OFF. Even if he were halfway through a song . . . OFF. No encores. Bye bye. Forty-five minutes is what I'm paid for, so forty-five minutes you get, goodnight.

In the film *Hail! Hail! Rock 'n' Roll*, Mr Berry is seen in his garage, a line of his swanky automobiles under polythene wraps. He doesn't want these cars but when he took them for trade-in, they didn't offer him enough muh-neeee. He cannot believe it. He leaves them to rot. And he tells of how he once painted the interior of St Louis' Cosmopolitan Club (where he started out playing in the '50s) and how they paid him $450, which was such a lot of muh-neeee – and he kisses his fingers at the word – that he decided to give up music and be an interior decorator instead (until someone offered him even more muh-neeee – $800 a week – to sing and play his guitar). And he tells of how he sees his guitars not as musical instruments but as 'Tools . . . Tax-deductible, you know . . .' And others tell of how when Keith Richards and the band assembled for the concert featured in *Hail! Hail! Rock 'n' Roll* turned up for rehearsals at Berry's home, Berry Park, they found themselves stuck by the great man with a bill for equipment hire. A bill to appear in Berry's own film. Look after the cents and the dollars'll look after themselves (until the IRS catches up with you . . .).

'Once again?'
   You have often been accused of being an avaricious man.
   'I don't know what that means.'
   Are you a greedy person?
   'Greedy? A greedy person? You mean money? I just take what's my due. You see, sometimes before, I was taken advantage of. I was taken advantage of once. But not twice. That's the smart bit.'

He is referring here, one presumes, to his dealings with Chess Records, to whom he signed in 1955 only to find that his first single 'Maybellene' was credited not only to Berry but also (those were payola days) to the DJ Alan Freed and some guy named Russ Fratto. So Chuck had to split the royalties three ways for a song he had written, and it made him hopping mad. In the book, he fumes at the injustice of it all. But when I mention it today . . .

'I am not bitter because I realise the mistake was mine. The mistake was mine because I knew nothing about business and the accomplishment was theirs. Most commerce is an opportunity to achieve a product that is available and I was available and their accomplishment and my mistake put together is a perfect unity. I'd have done the same thing in their position. It's an incident, not an accident.'

So you didn't object to being ripped off by Chess?

'Once again?'

Repeat.

'Ripped off? Oh, by the way, it wasn't really ripped *off*. There's such a thing as being ripped *off*, of course, but that's under such things as stealing or burglary or something like that. So if I knew the culprit, of course I'd have a grudge and I'd want him to pay the price. But if it's my own fault, if I leave my wallet on the kerb, I have no grudge against the person who picked it up. See what I'm saying?'

It's hard to imagine, somehow, Mr Chuck Berry leaving his wallet on the kerb.

'And that's about all the recording,' he says, consulting the Rolex and pointing a Kool in the rough direction of my tape recorder.

'That machine will have to come off now. That's about all the recording. But you can ask me more questions, I guess.'

And so, feeling impossibly fortunate to get a bonus on my three minutes, I ask him more questions (and find, to my surprise, that once the tape machine is off, and the notebook out, he drops the

'Once again?' tactic – I had begun to wonder if he were, perhaps, a trifle deaf). I ask him how he got on with Keith Richards during the filming of *Hail! Hail! Rock 'n' Roll.*

'Oh, well, you see, me and Keith, Keith Richards, we had our little problems, so to speak. No, let me say that another way. Keith Richards didn't have a problem with me but I certainly had my problems with *him.* Keith has a lot of problems, hahaha. Actually, I don't think that film is so good. They should have done it differently, but what do *they* know? I was in a film, *Go Johnny Go*, and I had a speaking part and that was 1958 – thirty years ago! So what do *they* know?'

I ask him about 'My Ding-a-Ling' – that pitiful example of schoolyard 'humour' which, in 1972, gave Mr Berry his biggest international hit ever – and suggest that it's a shame that he should be remembered for a song so infantile.

'A lot of people liked that song. A lot of people *like* that song. And I *LOVED* that song because that little, weeny song made my wallet so fat and happy, hahaha.'

I ask him what he feels about Mary Whitehouse who, in possibly the one supportable crusade of her career, tried to get 'My Ding-a-Ling' banned.

'Well, Mary Whitehouse . . . I don't really know who the lady is but I heard about her. I think I was shown a picture of her, Mary Whitehouse. Mary White-house – I guess the lady needs a little loving.'

And I ask how long – he's sixty-one now – he intends to keep performing.

'How long? How long, how long, how long, how looooong, hahaha. Who knows? This is not my duty, I feel, you see? Not long, I guess. Not long. I like the money, yes, I like the muh-neee, but more than this, I like myself. I like my-self! *Greatly.*'

And with that the living legend stubs out his latest Kool, rises slowly to his feet and dawdles from the room without a by your leave. This, I take it, is a signal to indicate the end of 'consultation' – and as if in confirmation, the nervous intermediary pokes her head around the door and whispers, 'Um, I think you'd better go now. You've had *twelve* minutes.'

Twelve minutes! And he didn't ask me for a stack of used dollar bills *once*, the cantankerous old bugger.

# Bros: Good morning, America!

## *Q*, November 1989[1]

'Verna,' cries Luke Goss, the drummer. 'Verna! Can I have another triple Hennessy's, please, darl?'

Verna, beleaguered waitress of the St. Paul Hotel, St. Paul, Minnesota – clearly unused to ministering to the needs of upstart pop combos from the United Kingdom and their unruly entourages – obliges and Luke Goss drains the glass. For his supper tonight, Luke Goss, dressed in routine Bros fatigues (be-studded black T-shirt, jeans a-ripped at the knees and held up by a belt with a gargantuan, taste-free buckle featuring the Rolls-Royce motif), is having an ample platter of pasta for starters and as a main course he thinks he'll try the beef. 'Verna? This beef. Has it got bones in it?' 'Er, no, sir,' replies the patient Verna. 'It's . . . it's beef.' 'Oh, right, I'll have the beef. Twice!' 'Er, they're *very large* portions, sir,' explains the stoical Verna. 'Yeh, and I'm *very* hungry, hahaha!'

At the far end of the table, Matt Goss, the singer, is filming the proceedings, this slap-up American feed, with a video camera. His lens alights on Dave, who is munching buttered bread. Dave is Bros's hairdresser, the only man in the world, apparently, who can

---

[1] Technically this wasn't a 'Who the hell . . . ?' piece, but we couldn't resist including it here.

do the Bros cut just so. Dave was flown out from England this afternoon because the boys had run out of hair-gel and felt in need of his particular snip. As Dave eats, Matt makes crude scoffing noises into the vid-cam's built-in microphone. Should be a hoot when viewed.

'Bros is like a very anti-drugs band,' Luke is telling me as he tucks into his bone-less beef. 'You know, man,' he is warning me, 'drugs are very, very dangerous. They scare the shit out of me. Cocaine. Evil. Don't do it. I've seen heroin once in my life. My dad (*Mr Alan Goss was a policeman*) showed us a bag of heroin after a bust. It makes you think . . . Verna! Give us another triple Hennessy's!'

Poor Verna arrives with a large measure of brandy and Luke's second order of beef. He rejects the latter – 'Full up now, Verna' – but drinks the former. Already seemingly well-versed in the ways of proto-excessive rock star behaviour, Luke Goss and his twin brother Matt are just twenty.

Bros, Britain's biggest current mass pop phenomenon, are on their first tour of these United States. The group – Matt 'n' Luke and the stalwart backing musos (bass player Craig Logan, the one no one fancied, is already but a dim memory) – are supporting the blonde and perky teen pet Debbie Gibson (as sponsored by Natural Wonder Cosmetics) on a continental jaunt. But things are not going so well. Bros may be 'huge' in Blighty and points elsewhere (Europe, Australia, Japan) but in America they're unknown – and peeved about it. 'In a couple of years or so,' they tell me defiantly and in unison, 'we'll be selling out Shea Stadium.' Maybe or maybe not. But for the moment they're just a support act to Debbie, strutting their stuff in the confines of Debbie's twee, tot-oriented fairy-tale castle stage set; and Debbie's not selling very many tickets at all.

The St. Paul Civic Center seats 8,000 people. For the Debbie Gibson Natural Wonder Cosmetic experience there are less than 2,000 in the place. Pre-teenage girls in Gibson-styled fedoras with younger sisters in Care Bear rompers clutching the hands of reluctant and apologetic-looking parents who've shelled out big bucks on this regrettable musical event, for the most part. As Bros bound on to the stage at 7.30 p.m. on the dot – Matt nervously shrilling, 'We're from London so we need some help, okay?' and the backing musos striking up a failed call-and-response/product-recognition cry of 'B-R-O-S! B-R-O-S!' – the atmosphere could not be cut with a knife or with any other available kitchen utensil. There is no atmosphere to cut. The Bros 'set' is undeniably 'tight' . . . the first hit, 'I Owe You Nothing', 'Don't Bite the Hand', and 'I Quit' (featuring Matt's quaint philosophical rumination 'Most of my friends were strangers when I met them'), peppered with sturdy and strident electric guitar solos . . . respectable 'rock' music. Bros do the 'biz' but apart from one small girl who flings one small furry toy in the general direction of the pirouetting singer, there is no audience reaction to speak of whatsoever. On stage things begin to go horribly wrong. Matt is muttering sheepish apologies about 'technical problems'. 'This has never happened to us before,' he whimpers. Brother Luke looks distraught. After a fourth song (a version of Stevie Wonder's 'Higher Ground') and a fifteen-minute set, Bros depart the stage. Apparently, I later learn, the 'click track' has gone awry (this means that the drummer finds it impossible to keep in time) and something has gone wonky in the keyboard sample department (this means that it's impossible for Bros to 'deliver' any more of their celebrated numbers).

Matt Goss and Luke Goss are in tears of frustration. 'Me and my bruv, we're *professionals*,' Luke is saying. 'Something like this, it's – this is the honest truth – it's an insult to our art, d'you know what I mean?' The American video director, here to shoot a Bros promo, replete with frugging foxtresses, for the new single, 'Chocolate in a Box', in the twin city of Minneapolis in the morning, courageously feigns enthusiasm; he's never seen Bros before but 'Wow, those guys, they're so *channelled*!' he exclaims. One does not care to enquire just what he means. He seems quite mad . . . Out front, the toddlers couldn't give a damn. Roll on Debbie Gibson and bed . . .

Matt: 'This tour . . . I've been down in the dumps. I've been depressed . . .'

Luke: 'Matt is *this* weak. He's so sensitive . . .'

Matt: 'Everything affects me. Luke looks after me. He protects me. He's physically trained his body now so that comments and problems don't even get into his brain. Not because he's thick. Because he's trained himself to disregard it. But I'm like a dartboard. Sharp things go in, you know . . .'

Luke: 'I cry probably three or four times a week. That's my release. But Matt, the other night he was so tense, I was absolutely terrified. He was on the bed and it took us two hours to try and relax his body. He just couldn't move his body at all and it took me six cups of tea to figure it out. I thought he was going to have a nervous breakdown. I thought this tour was over and that's the truth. He was a nervous wreck and I . . . I have to look after him . . . these people are fucking us up. These people in this industry are fucking us up. It's the whole . . .'

Matt: 'It fucking scares the shit out of me . . .'

Luke: 'It's the whole vibe . . .'

Matt: 'I don't want the press to know how weak I am. Because they'll *get* me.'

Luke: 'It's the whole vibe of this business. It's so lonely, sometimes . . . It's so lonely . . .'

Britain's biggest current mass pop phenomenon are, as we speak, a little the worse for wear, a trifle tired and emotional. We are in the wee wee hours. A post-mortem on the Civic Center fiasco has been conducted at length in the Goss twins' hotel bedrooms. Soundmen have been fired, Goss twins are hopping mad. 'We're so professional,' runs the thinking and the corporate speech. 'We *demand* professionalism from the people behind us. We *pay* them.'

Bros are downcast on this grey Minnesota night. They have let their 'fans' down. (No, I dare not tell them there were no Bros fans in that Civic Center audience.) But the bristling confidence of young men with bristling haircuts is, nonetheless, very much in evidence. Luke leans forward in the hotel foyer sofa and says, 'But we don't want this to be a whinge about this one bad gig and that, know what I mean? It's important that you set the record straight about Bros.' 'Yeh,' says Matt. 'You've flown all this way and you're our release. We want you to set the record straight about Bros.'

This responsibility is somewhat daunting. No matter: let me try. Matt Goss would like you to know that, contrary to popular belief, he *can* actually sing.

Matt: 'I'll fucking . . . I'll go and take on any sod. I'll take on anyone because I know my voice. I can take on anyone, any white singer who wants to give me a go, I'll give him one and . . .' Luke interrupts. 'Yeh, yeh, and they talk about your voice and my drums never even get *mentioned and* . . .' Matt says, 'Yeh, Lukey, but my voice, I'm professional like you are and . . .' And Luke says, 'But listen, 'cos I listen to my drums sometimes and I think, yeh, I'm pretty good.' And Matt says, 'Yeh, *'course* you're good, Lukey, you're the *best* but what I'm trying to say about the singing . . .' And . . . 'Yeh, but hold on, hold on, listen, Matt . . .' Interviewing these south London heart-throbs, evidently brimming with twin sibling rivalry, is possibly one of life's less simple tasks. 'I've never said this before but my drums is so professional, man, know what I mean? Mike Rutherford asked me to play on his album. Mike and the Mechanics asked me to do the album, right? And on the Bros album (*The Time*) I played it all live – bang bang – took me up to twenty-seven hours a track but I did it all live because I'm such a professional!'

So, do not suggest that the golden boys cannot sing or play. It gets their goat and I am here to set the record straight. Worse even than this to the Peckham twins is the insulting intimation that Bros are just one more disposable commodity fabricated by the business-wise – in this case manager Tom Watkins – for teen consumption. Watkins, it is supposed, is solely responsible for the Bros look, the 'style', even the music. I am here to set the record straight . . .

'*Listen*,' says Matt, approaching fury, 'I will tell you *now* that Tom Watkins has fuck *all* to do with my career and . . .' 'Hold on, Matt, bruvs, hold on.' Luke is similarly apoplectic. 'Tom Watkins is not involved with my career. Listen, I'll tell you what happens. We're suggested something and we say yes or no and . . .' The interruption interlude will now go into overdrive . . .

Matt: 'See, people think Tom Watkins saw us when we had long hair and decided to cut it off . . .'

Luke: 'He *did* see us when we had long hair . . .'

Matt: 'Yeh, he *did* see us when we had long hair but we did know what was going down and we actually went into a barber's shop on our own and had our hair cut off for ourselves and . . .'

Luke: 'And we had our hair cut off and we walked into Tom Watkins' office and everybody laughed at us. That's the honest truth.'

Matt: 'Yeh, that's the honest truth because all Bros was was something that needed sticky bits put on it . . .'

Luke: 'It was made a bit more solid . . .'

Matt: 'But we don't need it anymore because we're now a snowball that needs a bit of a shove along now and then and Tom is a brilliant manager but . . .'

Luke: 'Tom is very extrovert and blasé and a brilliant manager but he's done TV and we don't want our manager going on and saying he's a genius and he's a hitmaker. Bollocks! Sometimes he's a bit too big for his boots.'

Matt: 'Hold on, Tom is brilliant. I wouldn't want any other manager . . .'

Luke: 'I tell you, Matt, 50 per cent of his ideas are rubbish. Absolute rubbish . . .'

Matt: 'Yeh, but I wouldn't have any other manager on the planet because . . .'

Luke: 'Because a great band needs a great manager. We're a great band. We need a great manager because you don't put a diamond on a silver setting, right? You put it on an 18-carat gold setting or platinum. Right? Like, you can't make chicken soup out of chicken *shit*. That's very apt.'

Matt: 'But it's like Tom's the greatest manager on the planet but on *The Time* [their second album] he didn't have one lyrical input because he's not a musician . . .'

Luke: 'He can write some good songs, though.'

Matt: 'No, I'm talking about *our* stuff, right?'

And so it continues. The twins in disjointed argument. I am supposed to be their 'release' but I am failing singularly to get a word in edgewise. 'Lukey, let's not talk about this,' says Matt, finally. 'We're on tour; it's the tour.'

Immediately before embarking on this tour, Bros performed at Wembley Stadium to 65,000 of their highly enthusiastic fans. That was the proudest moment of their lives, they will tell you. Everything since has been anti-climax.

Matt: 'Idealistic feelings can be very soothing. You know when I played Wembley Stadium, do you know what it looked like to me? Seventy thousand people in slow motion. There wasn't one bit of hate there.'

Luke: 'No hate there.'

Matt: 'It was 70,000 people all tuned into the same thing. It was almost like playing to a city of love.'

Luke: 'It *was* a city of love. You could feel it. A mini-city of love full of natural energy. It was all love and people were hugging and that's what Bros is about. We've got messages.'

Matt: 'If we do nothing else apart from trying to spread love and trying to spread awareness and honesty, then I'll be a very happy person.'

Luke: 'That sounds, like, really corny but deep down, I am a hippie. I love the idea of love and happiness for everyone. I love that. And we can spread that to our fans. We have an incredible responsibility towards our fans. It may sound corny but we're like God. Take drugs, for example. We're aware of our responsibility so we put a big no entry sign next to our throats. No drugs, drink but drink in moderation, beware of AIDS, beware of diseases. Whatever, we make people aware.'

Matt: 'It's like when I write a song I know that three and a half million fans are definitely going to listen to this song and you just go . . . phew!'

Luke: 'And our fans, for a start, our fans are the best.'

Matt: 'They're our lifeblood. I love them.'

Luke: 'They love us and they're individual. Is your kid on cocaine? Is your kid smoking pot? Is your kid getting pissed out of her brain every night? Or has she got a Bros poster in her room and is she driving you mad, listening to the Bros album every night? Which would you rather have?'

Bros fans – Brosettes – have been perceived, however, as little monsters. There's the Peckham Posse, a gang of particularly obsessive admirers who have been known to turn on rival fans with sharp instruments in piques of jealousy. The Goss boys won't have a word spoken against their public. They take it as criticism of *themselves* and leap to the defensive. 'For God's sake,' says Matt, 'we're Britain's lads. We're Britain's boys and we're not doing a bad job around the world to represent Britain's music.' 'It makes me sick,' agrees the brother. 'We're Britain's lads and people in England should be proud of us but they're all so pessimistic. Why do some people want to hate us so much? Some of the slagging in the press is so incredibly nasty. We've never told a journalist before that it bothers us because we don't want to lower our defences.' 'But it *does* piss us off,' says Matt, softly, almost threateningly. 'It really . . . pisses us off.'

They have been on tour in northern America for just three weeks and already Bros feel that they've got 'the road' in their blood systems. Ah, the road. 'The road,' says Luke. 'Thinking about it, the road is my life.' 'I love the road,' says Matt. 'I love the coach from the bottom of my heart. Because I get to drink, I get to get drunk – not drunk as in pissed but a bit tipsy – and I get to play Nintendo baseball (*exciting video game*). The coach . . .The road is my world. That's the honest truth.'

Later on the boys will show me some of their road movies – home flicks they've shot on the amateur video camera. Skylarks and Spinal Tapism. Here's the saxophone player in a state of some disrepair; he's talking of 'knobbing' and displaying his private parts. Here's the bass player in hog-whimpering state; he is bending over a hotel toilet bowl and, egged on by his young bosses, throwing up his supper. The vulgar clips reel on. Ah, the innocence of youth. 'This is how we unwind,' explains Matt. 'This is our release from the whole vibe of this business.' Luke: ''Cos it's a lonely business.' Matt nods dolefully. 'Lonely.'

Lonely but worth it. They talk a great deal of their pride in their work and their luck. 'We're in such a lucky position to be able to influence people's lives and to give people so much love and pleasure.'

Matt: 'They compare us to Wham!, the Bay City Rollers and the Beatles. And if they want to compare us with three bands that have actually made history, that's fine – but my level of history making will go into a further level. I'm not going to stop writing music and I'm not going to stop performing. People *believe* in us. Our only obstacle is the people who *don't* . . .'

# Who the hell does Tom Jones think he is?

## *Q*, March 1991

The big-boned 'boyo' stands in the centre of the room engaged in an elaborate mime: he crouches as he runs his clenched fists down along his legs; he wiggles his hips 'suggestively'; he purses his lips. He lets rip a blustering laugh born of a million man-sized cigars, wipes his brow: 'Bloody hell, man, hoo hoo!'

Tom Jones, giant-voiced wonder from Pontypridd, has been re-enacting, before my very eyes, the moment enshrined in popular music history, when an adoring and over-excited female member of his audience was first moved to take off her drawers and forcibly fling them at her brute-like idol.

It was 1968 in America, a supper/nightclub called the Copacabana: 'I perspire, you see, and these ladies would hand me table napkins,' says Jones with evident delight. 'But one night . . . I remember it very well.' And in case I missed his lavish impression of de-knickering manoeuvres the first time around, he runs through it one more time with feeling. It is all very exciting. 'Bloody hell! It *was* very exciting!' says Jones, beads of desirable perspiration peeking out on the lightly tanned forehead. 'Bloody hell, man!' Tom Jones has been assaulted by lingerie ever since. If there is one thing Tom Jones is famous for, it is mopping his face with underwear

while trimly trowelled into the tightest of trousers. What a sensational lark it must be to be an internationally renowned machismo-
riddled sexy devil of fifty when you might as easily have ended up a
redundant coal miner with all manner of unsavoury lung disorders.
Bloody, as they say in Pontypridd, hell . . .

Tom Jones, wearing a sensible 'sweater' and a highly polite pair of
spectacles (despite the Bel-Air-styled tan, he looks this day more like
a burly greengrocer than any veteran Sex God of the entertainment
industry), is granting an audience in a friend's home in New Malden,
Surrey. He has just 'de-planed' from Los Angeles, back here to visit
the little wife in Wales, to take part in a documentary film for the
BBC and to complete a new long player for his new record company, Chrysalis. Jet lag doesn't touch this man. As his son/manager
Mark (moustachioed thirty-person in tweeds) brings him a cup of
tea, the Tom Jones pelvis goes into automatic thrust: it's like some
kind of nervous tic, perhaps – Jones stands and his hips go a-wrig-
gling. 'I'm sort of like always full of this nervous energy sort of thing,
you see,' he says by way of explanation. 'Bloody hell!' and the hips
go BOOM!

Jones was twenty-four years old when he discovered that by the
simple trick of moving the lower regions of his magnificent body
about a bit (while perspiring, scrunching up the eyes, dangling the
little finger over the microphone lead and moanin' 'n' groanin'
things like 'It's not unewseworll to be lurved at any tiiiiiime!', 'For
there's a guaaaard and there's a sad old pardaaaaaay!', and even
'So he got some striiiing and he got some woooood!', yup!) he could
drive mature women WILD. He had come from his native Wales
to London, this musclebound boy with the big voice, signed a management deal with Gordon Mills and was performing – as Tommy
Scott and the Senators – in Oxford Street's Beat City club.

'The bloody movements were instinctive!' he says in that deep
and booming Valleys voice. (Watch those nodules, Tom!) 'It came

194

out of the '50s rock 'n' roll, going to the dance halls in Wales and learning to jive and bloody Elvis Presley was, of course, being the one, so you look at Elvis and you think, "Cor! That's bloody good!", and so you try to do it naturally. That's what I did. I was just bloody dancing when I was singing and that's all it was. It was not contrived. But as you go along, you learn that if there's a move that you do and you get a reaction from it, you think, "Bloody hell! That must be a good one. We'll keep that in!"' Tom Jones leaps to his feet to demonstrate a particularly good move that he must keep in: the hips go BOOM! Presto!

'But when I realised the moves were bloody working was in Beat City in '64. What happened was we were one of the resident groups that were there and the Rolling Stones had cracked it and they were playing there one night and I was used to playing to people of my own age but in come these teenyboppers, these bloody kids to see the Rolling Stones. So I'm on stage and I'm doing the thing and I can see these kids looking at me a bit funny . . .' Jones throws his head back and, mouth agape, assumes a look of absolute horror. 'They were looking at me like that, see, because I was very adult for my age. I thought "Bloody hell! These kids are looking at me funny!" So when Mick Jagger came on, I could see the difference in me being masculine and him sort of camping it up and the kids were screaming at him whereas with me they'd just looked at me funny, even though we were doing basically the same kind of material, bloody Chuck Berry stuff, you know. The bloody kids couldn't take me! But I couldn't camp it up. I didn't look that way. I would look like somebody in drag or something. I wasn't pretty enough. I wasn't a boyish-looking person. I wasn't effeminate so I knew that was out. I had to do my masculine thing and hope that it would work.'

The masculine 'thing' has served Jones well these twenty-five years, taking him to Atlantic City and Las Vegas, where his hen night party pieces (for well-heeled hens) made him wealthy indeed, a lusty tuxedoed balladeer going, 'Why why whyyyy Deliiiilah!', 'suggestively' loosening the black bow tie while the hips went BOOM! and the underwear rained down. And yet Tom Jones is not entirely happy with his career lot, he will tell you. He is – yes! – bored with underwear.

'The problem with the underwear,' he says, 'is I don't want it to become a joke. I've had youngsters say to me, "Ooh, ooh, it's tacky, isn't it?" To youngsters it's tacky seeing women do it. Youngsters don't like to see adults do certain things – they don't like to see their parents having sex, you see. And reviews I have, they say, "The place was packed with middle-aged women," which is not true. There's lots of men in there at my shows but they are overlooked and all they ever say is women throw underwear and they never mention my bloody voice. Oh Christ, bloody hell, I don't want underwear to overshadow the talent. The voice is the thing, you see. I don't want to be a caricature of myself. Shit, I just want to get the voice over.'

The voice is a very large voice – 'I don't sing like I'm on bloody tranquilisers. I'm aggressive, you see.' But the voice has not always been well-served by the material; many a Tom Jones' tune ('The Young New Mexican Puppeteer' springs instantly to mind) has been, well, regrettable. Jones would not necessarily agree.

'I'm bloody proud of my records. If you put on "It's Not Unusual" today, it's still a great record. Even "What's New Pussycat?", when I first heard it I thought, "Christ! What the bloody hell do they want me to sing *this* for?" But Burt Bacharach explained, "I want the big voice to sing this bloody crazy song", and you put it on, it's a classic. There's nothing mediocre about the hits that I've had. The problem is I'm just too bloody versatile.'

Indeed. The bloody versatility has enabled him to be everything from token 'raunchy' rock 'n' roller for the over-sixties set to groaning ballad person, from somewhat bland MOR C&W 'artiste' to reborn 'hip' legend with the 1988 Art of Noise-directed 'Kiss'. Jones's musical career has not been a model of stylistic consistency. Mention of this tends to cheese him off.

'It's always been a problem because people don't know where to put you. If you pick up *The History of Rock'n'Roll*, you won't see my name in there but I *should* be in there because I'm a bloody rock 'n' roll singer. I never sold out because I like to do all sorts of songs. It's all about a big voice but it's a double-edged thing because if you are versatile like me, people say, "What are you, then?" Youngsters say, "You sing rock 'n' roll but you're not a rock 'n' roll singer, are you? You sing "Fly Me to the Moon" but you're not Frank Sinatra, are you?" No, I'm bloody Tom Jones! People don't take you seriously, half the time . . .'

One person who failed to take the great man seriously, he recalls, was Janis Joplin, who, in 1969, appeared on his TV show, *This Is Tom Jones*.

'Oh, yes, she thought I was really straight, like an establishment TV figure because being on bloody TV, the rebel side had gone away from it. And we did a duet which was a rock 'n' roll scream up – I don't remember the song – and after it, she said, "Man! You can really sing!" She was so surprised. And so I proved a bloody point there!'

One person who did not fail to take the great man seriously was Charles Manson. Once *This Is Tom Jones* had made the singer an international celebrity, Manson decided, apparently, that the Welsh 'pig' should be 'offed': Jones's name appeared on a hit list alongside Frank Sinatra, Elizabeth Taylor, Richard Burton, Steve McQueen. Manson's wheeze was that one of his female followers should tempt the bellowing idol into a bed situation and therein slit his throat. Oo-eee!

'It all came out at the trial that Manson used to tell all his followers that people like me were all bullshit and I had to be destroyed.

So he wanted to bump me off and that was scary. People like me, we're never safe. It's scary.'

How unusual it must have been for this innocent from Pontypridd to find himself dwelling in madcap Hollywood in the 1970s. Here is a man who was brought up never to swear in front of the ladies, who was trained in primitive pub machismo rituals from an early age. 'There was all these aunties and uncles and all these cousins all going to the same pubs and you've got to be able to drink and they're watching you and your old man is saying, "Are you feeling alright?" and you say, "Yeh!" while the room is spinning, and you've got to try and get home first before you bloody throw up. It's a pride thing . . .' Next thing you know he's a superstar in LA, on a Manson hit list, in Elvis's hotel suite, drugs and girls for the asking etc. Enough, you'd think, to turn a fellow's head. Not this fellow. Oh, no. Tom Jones is proud of his level head.

'I never got into those drugs and mad bloody things like that because of my background and being proud of Wales. The thing is − I'm positive because I've thought about this − if I became a nutcase with drugs and bloody things, if I became a junkie or what have you, I wouldn't be able to go home. I wouldn't be able ever to go home again. And that's always kept me sane. I like being sane. If I didn't, I suppose I would be nuts.'

'Forced' into exile by the hefty tax demands of a Labour government in the 1970s, Jones turned LA residence into a home-from-home.

'They speak English in America so it wasn't like I'd gone to live in France or somewhere which is completely alien, but I had HP Sauce there and a telephone box from Wales, which I put out by the pool. I almost went and bought a bloody Cadillac instead of a Rolls-Royce − that's how pissed off I was with the British government, bollocks. But I thought, No, I'm not a Yankee Doodle Dandy, I'm a Welshman, me.'

Not even Jones's drug-soaked chum Elvis Presley could divert him from the path of sane, Wales-styled living.

'Elvis never took any drugs in front of me, you see. Elvis would go into the bedroom and then he'd come out sort of drunk. I'd say, "Hey, Elvis, let's stick some records on," but he'd be popping in and out of the bloody bedroom and I thought that was a bit funny. And when he went to see Nixon and Nixon made him a narcotics agent, the reason for that was that Elvis wanted a federal licence for a gun – he was obsessed with guns and he wanted to be able to carry a gun anywhere. So he had an audience with Nixon and then I saw him in Vegas and he said to me, "What do you think of this? Nixon has made me a narcotics agent!" And he burst out laughing and all his bodyguards burst out laughing. He seemed to think it was hilarious, man. And I thought, "Well, what's so bloody funny about that?" I didn't understand the joke at all. I was a bit bloody naïve, I suppose . . .'

Tom Jones, naïve, as green as that celebrated grass of home, recalls his first, and only, personal brush with the nuisance that is drugs.

'I was in the Cromwellian one night with a bunch of people and they were handing around like a Vicks Sinex inhaler and I had a cold so I said, "Can I borrow that?" And I sniffed it and I thought, "Jesus! Bloody hell!" It was like if you were on a roller coaster! The bloody thing was full of Amyl Nitrate! Since then I've been in showbusiness parties and they're all in the kitchen around the table with cocaine on there. Carry on, God bless, I say, but it looks ugly to me. It looks horrible to see somebody with a pipe up their nose. Same thing with smoking a joint. Pfffff pfffff . . .' Tom closes his eyes in mock ecstasy, miming the bizarre actions of a pot smoker. '. . . Pfffff pfffff. Uurgh. That's not attractive. I like to go into a pub and have a beer. When I first got into this business I was drinking beer and smoking Woodbines, and Gordon Mills said, "One day you'll be drinking champagne and smoking cigars," and I said, "You must be bloody joking!" But you learn things like that, so I like wine with dinner and I like a cognac afterwards with a cigar and then, if it's early enough, I'll have some champagne. Sometimes I get carried away a bit but that's as far as it goes . . .'

To hear him talk in this innocent manner, to observe the remarkably youthful face (with just a hint of surgery around the nose and gills) as he speaks, you would imagine that Tom Jones is an entirely vice-free entity. Can this be so? What of the ladies, Tom? What of the ladies? Since Jones emerged from a country and western coma that lasted from 1980 to 1986 and re-established himself in the British hit parade with 'The Boy From Nowhere' and 'Kiss', the tabloid press has treated us to a nice parade of 'gymslip'-styled Tomfoolery. TOM JONES FATHERED MY CHILD . . . ROMEO JONES BUYS RING FOR COLLEGE GIRL CINDY . . . TOM JONES: HE TOOK MY VIRGINITY IN POSH HOTEL . . . runs the tittle-tattle, and that's without even mentioning the ancient dalliance with Mary Wilson out of the Supremes. The still-married Welshman seems unruffled by such prying; after all, when you are a singing Lothario whose hips are ever going BOOM!, when you are a macho man from the Valleys who has never disguised his 'sexist' principles ('The man should be the provider and the man should make the decisions. Women are happier that way,' he says), this kind of publicity is hardly likely to do any damage to the reputation, is it?

'Well, no, it's not, is it?' His smile has gone all coy. 'And the reason I haven't gone nuts and taken people to court and all that is because you think, "Now wait a minute, it *is* overblown and it *is* a lot of bloody hearsay but are they saying anything that's *really* bad about me?" If I'm going out with some young lady, that isn't a bad thing to say, is it? They're not saying that I've killed somebody or that I'm molesting children. I'm just a virile chap, so as long as the missus doesn't get pissed off, it's okay. I wouldn't want people to think that I'm jumping on everything in a skirt that moves and my wife is the sweet little innocent Welsh girl that puts up with all this, but it's not that far-fetched what they say about me. I suppose I am Jack the Lad to a point.'

Tom Jones, ladies' man, has his star set down on the Hollywood Walk of Fame. He is colossally proud of that. He is proud, too, of his great big voice – 'The ooold house is still staaanding though the paint is cracked 'n' dryyyyy' – and of his lovely Wales, once more his home. He has, as they say, a sound bottom: he is, it seems, a simple soul. Correct? Towards the end of the interview he gives just one tiny indication that he might, in any way, be 'nuts' when I ask him who (the bloody hell) he thinks he is and he says:

'I'm nobody, really. I'm only a singer. But there's a responsibility there, you see. You can turn love into complete hate. It can be done. When you're on stage sometimes, when everything's going great, you think to yourself, "If I made a wrong bloody move here, if I said something like 'Fuck you all,' I could turn an audience that loves me into hating me." With a few words. If I wanted to. It's there. It's in your mind. Love and hate is very close. Words can do so much, make people that love you suddenly hate you just by something that's come out of your mouth. You could shit yourself, it's so scary!'

To be brutally frank, I am not at all sure what the old boy is going on about here and, alas, I never find out for he must leave now for Wales and he is up on his feet. And what is this I see as he shakes me firmly by the hand? Yes. A distinct twitch in the hip region. Not BOOM!, exactly, but a definite twitch. My undergarments remain secure and shipshape.

# Who the hell does Paul 'Gazza' Gascoigne think he is?

## _Q_, December 1990

'Er, I'm opening a boutique, Brian.' This was the answer that Monty Python's befuddled, inarticulate footballing star would give to any query in an interview situation. 'Er, I'm opening a boutique, Brian,' he'd say in his confusion.

Paul Gascoigne – 'Gazza' to the universe, Britain's biggest footballing star since the 1960s when the nation was told what to eat for breakfast by the TV commercial rallying cry of 'E for B and Georgie Best' – has a fresh variation on the theme. 'Hur,' he begins in his almost impenetrable Geordie accent. 'Hur, I go fishing. I find fishing a very good thing to relax.'

You haven't asked him a question about his relaxation techniques. You haven't asked him anything connected in any way with fish. You haven't asked him where he goes. You've probably asked him something about the 'Gazzamania' publicity machine and whether it's all getting a trifle out of hand, and he says, 'Hur, I find fishing a very good thing to relax.' Brian.

Thus has Gazza sold you another of his child-like dummies . . .

Paul 'Gazza' Gascoigne is not fishing today. (Does he ever, really? How does he find the time, what with all that training, all that footer to play, pizza parlours to open, Best-Dressed Man of the Year ceremonies to attend, tabloid photo opportunities etc., etc. as the 'Gazzamania' machine rolls inexorably onward?) No, today the chubby midfield general in the exciting Holsten-sponsored Tottenham Hotspur shirt, England's cheeky prankster who single-handedly won the World Cup for Blighty (except for the Germans, damn 'em), the star with the greased-back hair and the amusingly poking tongue is in the offices of a record company, RCA, doing promotional chores for . . . oh, God, how inevitable it all is . . . his forthcoming pop waxings. Paul Gascoigne, admired by 'kids' and their mums (drawn to the infant features and babyface grin: at twenty-three, Gascoigne resembles a pram-based tot, a major factor in his appeal and 'profile', surely) all over, has made a single, a rap version of 'Fog on the Tyne' recorded with those veteran Newcastle strumstrels Lindisfarne. And he's made a long player, called – it's good, this – *Let's Have a Party*.

Gazza talks music. What are your primary musical influences, Gazza, if I may call you that?

'Yur. Gazza,' he goes. 'Hur . . .' And he starts to sing. 'I've got a brand-new combine harvester and I'll give you the key . . . Dee deedle dee deedle dee. D'you remember it? It was really good. It was by the Wurzels, weren't it? That's right. And I love Elvis. I like Elvis. "Jailhouse Rock". But I've just really got into "GI Blues". He's got, you know, with "GI Blues", like, he's got . . .' And he starts to sing again. 'You ever you ever get you ever get one you ever get one of them days you ever get one of those days boys . . . I can't remember the words. Dum-di-dum-di-dum. Two two. Er . . .'

Isn't he a little bit on the young side to be an Elvis devotee? Wasn't he an 'Antperson' or a 'Numanoid' or something like that in his 'formative' teenage years?

'Oh, yeah, I like songs,' he replies. 'I like a load of songs. Loads of groups. So that's good. I like Phil Collins. I like Billy Ocean. You know? Hur, it's good for us to make a record, isn't it? It's good, it's different, it's really different, like. But with songs it's, you know, I go training every day and I go back, go fishing. I find fishing a very good thing to relax.'

And to prove his 'point', he picks up an inflatable plastic 'electric' guitar, pretends to reel off a number of irrefutably 'tasty licks' – tongue protruding, Gazza trademark – and then says, 'See that. It's good that, weren't it?' He is pointing to the word 'Elvis' daubed upon the fake guitar in black felt tip pen. 'I wrote that on the guitar meself.'

Paul Gascoigne, dressed in the kind of casual togs that earned him that much-coveted Best-Dressed Man award, is sitting there with his plastic guitar, thumbing through a pile of Paul Gascoigne publicity photos. Beside him sits some kind of minder, a long-haired bloke, sporting a grubby 'Elvis' T-shirt (who, when I ask him who, exactly, he might be, replies, somewhat mysteriously, 'I'm, er, I'm here to look after Gazza,' to which 'Gazza' adds: 'Aye, that's right. Hur. So you can't ask the horrible, bad questions.' I see ... ). Gazza's publicity photographs are all identical – they show the fellow with greased-back hair and playful grin in sensible jacket over what looks suspiciously like the kind of shirt worn by members of Brotherhood of Man circa 1970 – but he studies each one intently, possibly looking for imperfections in the prints, while all but ignoring the interviewer's presence.

How does it feel to be the nation's most feted and famous young rascal, me boy? I enquire.

'Ur. Dum-di-dum,' he replies. 'What's yer name?'

Tom. Tom Hibbert.

'Oh,' he says and proceeds to scrawl 'To Tom. Good Luck. Gazza.' on one of the photos, which he hands over to me as he smiles a beamy grin. I thank him for the unsolicited gift. Where were we? How does it feel to be so very famous, Paul, Gazza?

'I'm, I'm, well,' he shuffles his photo pile, 'I'm ... everyone says that I'm famous. Everyone says that. Nay. I just try and keep being meself, that's all I do. I don't think that I'm famous. I know for a fact that I am famous in a certain way, that people think I am, you know. I know that people think I'm famous because of what I've done in the World Coop, but I don't look at it that way and I don't go round being a big, flash bastard saying, "I'm Paul Gascoigne, me". I will never change. People say, "Yeah, he'll change" and I won't change. I won't change, no way. I will go and relax, I will go fishing because that's a very good thing to relax, and I'm not doing bad for that, am I? I'm doing very well, aren't I?'

Paul Gascoigne is doing very well. Prior to the World Cup finals in Italy, July 1990, Paul Gascoigne – born in a rented room in Pitt Street, Gateshead, Tyne and Wear, on 27 May 1967; kicked his first football at nine months old before he could even walk (or so the tabloid yarn ever goes) – was just a highly talented footballer with a reputation for acting the goat on and off the field. He was called an arrogant, overweight under-achiever; England manager Bobby Robson described him as being 'daft as a brush' (a remark which inspired the 1989 Christmas non-book *Gazza: Daft as a Brush*, a supposedly humorous tome, supposedly written by Gazza himself).

Tell us, Gazza, are you or are you not 'daft as a brush'?

'Yeah, of course I'm daft. I'm really, really daft. But I wouldn't say I'm daft as a brush. Bobby Robson said that. And look at us. I went to the World Coop and done him a favour, see. I did. I'm the same guy now sitting here with yous, I'm the same guy as Bobby Robson called me daft as a brush. I don't think he'll call us daft as a brush again. If he does, I'll play better if he calls me that again. My lads, the lads on the team, they call me Fat Bastard sometimes, but I don't mind. I just play better, me, and be meself like I always am.' . . .

It was England 'skipper' Bryan Robson that all the newspapers were waxing hysterical about before the World Cup tournament began. Captain Courageous. Captain Marvel. That sort of thing. But Robson crocked himself, as per usual, and had to retreat from Sardinia to the doctor's. Cometh the hour, cometh the man. A new hero for brave little England (who managed, somehow, to fluke a win over Cameroon). His name was Paul Gascoigne. Twinkling feet and toddler's attitude.

Cue Gazza's tears. When the boy broke down in floods before the penalty shoot-out in the semi-final against West Germany (he was blubbing because he'd been booked by a crafty referee and thus wouldn't be allowed to play in the final if England got there), the nation wept with him, or so we were told. He had expressed emotion – fine foil for more typical footballing macho 'virtues' – and shown himself to be some kind of 'New Man'. With the droplets streaming down the baby-face, he had bared his heart and a modern folk hero had been born. (Diego Maradona blubbed too, after Argentina lost the final, but Maradona's just a jumped-up Johnny Foreigner dago and a cheating pigeon-chested swine to boot, so his tears didn't count.)

Gazza was the toast of Greavesie and all other 'pundits' on the telly, he was the main topic of dinner party conversation, he was on the front page of the *Sun* and similar journals for days and weeks on end. Except there wasn't much to say about him apart from the fact that he blubbed once, was a bit of a clown (when the England party returned home to national approval and the waiting, adoring crowds aching for a glimpse of the great tubby, Gazza was seen to be sporting fake ladies' bosoms: what a wag, what a sport), and was rather good at football. And so we were treated to half-baked 'sex stories'. 'Why I Gave The Boot To My Gazza . . . World Cup has ruined our love (i.e. he had split up with 'childhood sweetheart' Gail Pringle) . . . Gazza's New Bird (i.e. he had, supposedly, got a new girlfriend, Heidi Shepherd, who was pictured on the front of the *Sun* with rather a lot of her clothes curiously absent). And nonsensical boozy tales: 'Beer Battles Rage As Gazza Makes Merry' (i.e. Gazza once went to a pub and while he was there, somebody else got thrown out) . . .

But flimsy as it all was, 'Gazzamania' still managed to hold the public attention. And just look at the value of contracts and endorsements a man can get through blubbing in public before viewing millions. Crying can get you places, can't it, Paul?

'Hur, it was just something I couldn't stop meself from doing,' he says. 'The fans were brilliant. I was leaving them. And I don't regret it one bit what I did.'

I didn't suppose for a moment that he did regret it.

'No, I cried because the fact is because the fans had been with me throughout all the shit that was wrote saying they were wrecking bars and all that but you've got to realise that the press was going up to fans offering them 50 quid to take photos if they were having a fight or smashing up a bar and all that and that's the English press. They want us to get beaten up and it was the biggest disgrace ever at the World Coop ever, probably we were the only country that done it, we were the only bastard.'

But doesn't he need the press? Haven't they helped to fuel the so-called 'mania', to put him in a position where he'll be a huge millionaire before you can say Jack 'Jazza' Robinson?

'No, no,' he says, putting aside his beloved publicity snaps and looking me, for once, in the eye. His mouth is agape. 'No, the press they're cowardly bastards. There's stupid stories of girls and all that, this girl I never really took out or nothing and the poor lass must have went through hell all because of these horrible, some of them really are cowards, cowardly bastards is all they are. Who needs press? Because of the World Coop, people didn't know me because they read the papers, people seen it on the telly, didn't they? And that's where I really done well is because now this Paul Gascoigne, whatever they call it, Gazza-mania, is because of the World Coop and they watched the World Coop on the telly, didn't they? So I don't need the press because they are all shit bastards, all of them. The fans are brilliant. They know theirselves that it's all shit what's written about us.'

When Georgie Best made his instantly infamous appearance on the *Wogan* show, insupportably drunk, using unpleasant words like 'screw' and being unkind about Paul Gascoigne, there was an outbreak of indignation around the country. How dare the dissipated Irishman be rude about our national hero? And then there was an outbreak of concern. Not about Georgie, poor old fool, but about Gazza. Perhaps, vexed citizens ringing up countless radio phone-in programmes thought, perhaps Gazza might go the Best route: overfeted, famous too suddenly and too soon, squandering his talent. It seems, however, less than likely that Paul Gascoigne will end up as a George Best for the twenty-first century. After all, in George's day footballing stars weren't turned overnight into mini-industries: George didn't have an army of accountants and lawyers, as Gazza does, looking after the star business. What George did was open a club, Brian, and proceed to drink the profits. Gazza is protected from such shenanigans by men in suits. I ask the young man about the George Best syndrome and he gets really quite interested in the 'debate'.

'Yeah, I heard about that and Gazza is going to be like George Best. Yeah, no problem. I would never do that, hopefully, touch wood.' (He raps his knuckles on the wooden table: superstitious breed, footer players.) 'I don't have to be like George Best and go to a newspaper or on *Wogan* and slaughter a young lad like me who's trying to earn a living and who's enjoying hisself just for a bit of cash, because George Best has let hisself down so bad it's unbelievable. He's let hisself down bad, cor, eh mon, well, and I mean the thing is people say, "Cor, that George Best, you see him on *Wogan* and he's a footballer, him", and then us footballers get embarrassed. We think, "Ooh, shit, people think us all footballers is like that drunken fat man and we isn't." Let's think . . .' Gazza pauses to consider the drift of his argument. 'Yur, and you see the fat man's got jealous of me. George Best, the drunken fat man is jealous. He absolutely slaughtered us for a bit of cash and that's a scum bastard.'

At this point we find Gazza's minder in the grimy Elvis T-shirt making untoward throat-clearing noises and looking pointedly at his charge. Sir Gazwell is not here to discuss tears, Georgie Best, his 'psyche' or anything like that. He is here to plug his fabulous pop disc and the minder is reminding him of the fact. And so, in midstream of con-sciousness concerning the relative merits of 'scum bastard' Bestie and 'cheekie chappie' Gascie . . . 'I always been cheeky with me tongue out and relaxed like fishing and that which maybe George Best needs, like' . . . he takes the minder's cue and goes, non-sequitur fashion, 'That's right and the record's going quite well as well.'

Oh, alright, then, tell us about your dreary record.

'I didn't want it to be released if it sounded shit. If it were sound-ing like shit, me record, people might think, This sounds like shit and that wouldn't be much good, like. But people say, Yeah, it'll do well, so I released it and I done an eighty-minute mix with twenty great singers on, fantastic, and I've got Gilbert O'Sullivan on and it's called *Let's Have a Party* and . . .'

Gilbert O'Sullivan? Gracious! And who are the other nineteen 'greats', pray?

'Yur, wait a minute, and it's called *Gazza and Friends* and Danny Baker's on it and me sister's on it and her friend and some of the lads but they're only singing like not a song but just at the end (Gazza proceeds to sing once more): All you need is love ba ba ba ba ba and whatever it is and it's the first album with Elvis on.'

Pardon? Could you clarify this peculiar statement, Gazz? His 'minder' does it for him by saying, 'Er, ah, you see, it's the Elvis medley that was out some years ago and it's been re-edited and it's the first time it's available on CD.' 'Hur, that's reet,' says Paul Gascoigne, footballer, twenty-three.

I ask Gascoigne, pop hopeful, what he thought of his Tottenham teammate (and new England 'skipper') Gary Lineker's choice (Dire Straits, Simply Red etc.) when, recently, Lineker was purred at by Sue Lawley on *Desert Island Discs*.

'*Desert Island Discs*? What's that?' he responds. I try to explain the concept of the celebrated radio programme.

'Oh, I see. I didn't see it. What, do you want me to go on there?'

Er, no, it's not really in my power to select Ms Lawley's guests.

'Oh, I'm sorry, yeah, yeah, that programme's on telly, isn't it?'

'It's a radio programme, on Radio 4,' hisses the 'minder', losing patience with his charge.

'Oh, it's a radio programme?' says Gazza. 'Oh, I just put a compact disc on all the time. It's sort of snobby, radio, isn't it? If you want me on your *Desert Island Discs*, it's got to be a lot of tracks off Elvis.'

No Dire Straits? All footballers adore Dire Straits.

'Who's that? No, hang on, hold on. On the bus to the Hungary game in the World Coop, I give 'em, I put on Elvis and the lads really sang along to it so I'm not doing too bad, am I?'

Ignoring the fact that England didn't play Hungary in the World Coop, the history of footballers making pop records is a sad and grim one, indeed, from Kevin Keegan's 'It Ain't Easy' (major flop) and 'Head Over Heels in Love' (on which the be-permed supremo was backed by the super Smokie and got into the top forty in 1979), to the relatively recent chart-storming efforts of Glenn (Hoddle) and Chris (Waddle), it's a catalogue of aural indignity. Gascoigne seems unaware of footballing solo singer history.

'Hur, Kevin Keegan made a record? I'm trying to think . . .'

'Minder' butts in. 'The trouble with Keegan was he was trying to sing.'

Gazza: 'Oh, I see, yeah, he was trying to sing. I can't sing. I can rap, uh hur. Now I just enjoy it. I go training and I go fishing to relax. It's a very good thing.'

And with that, he rises from his seat and says, 'Cheers, mate. I didn't think there were any more questions because I got to go . . .'

Go? Go fishing? Brian?

'I got to go to Luton.'

And so to Luton, beaming like the child who scoffed all the Mars bars, he goes . . .

# Who the hell does Gary Numan think he is?

## Q, May 1991

Thank Christ for this 'Siberian snap' and all this snow, is all I can say. Thank Christ that 'it's cold outside' (as G. Numan sang on his jolly big hit, 'Are "Friends" Electric?' years and years ago).

At an airfield somewhere north of London sits a Second World War aeroplane, a Harvard, painted in vaguely Japanese colours to resemble a kamikaze affair; its owner and pilot stands disconsolately beside it, gazing out at the thick white blanket of snow on the runway. There'll be no flying today, chaps. And Gary Numan *did* so much want to take me up, up, up for a spin and a few hair-raising exhibitions of snazzy aerobatics.

He's given joy rides in the Harvard to over 170 poor souls in his time, he says, and only twenty-seven of them have actually thrown up. If you are taken queasy in Gary Numan's Harvard, you have to clean up the resulting 'accident' yourself. So thank Christ for all this snow. Looping the loop with a barmy old rock star like Gary Numan – he who has been dubbed 'The Biggles of Pop' by many a newspaper – at the joy-stick is not, quite frankly, my idea of relaxation and ultimate fulfilment. Delta, Tango, Echo, Foxtrot . . .

Fifty years ago, this airfield rang to the sound of gallant young men with extravagant moustaches saying 'Scramble!' and 'Ginger's

212

been burned to a crisp'. Today the place is a private affair where a (rich) young man without a moustache but with preposterously dyed black hair (i.e. Gary Numan) can indulge his private passion for aeronautics, pretend he is Douglas Bader and Wing Commander Guy Gibson (out of *The Dam Busters*) all at the same time. We won the Battle of Britain and we got Gary Numan. And here he sits upon a battered sofa in the airfield's ex-operational hut, surrounded by photographs of daring and dead young men in Spitfires and other craft, talking aeroplanes.

When Gary Numan, toothy and fleshy of face, talks aeroplanes, your mind goes a bit numb. Like a madcap trainspotter or a fanatical stamp collector or a bloke with a thing about cars or barn owls, he just doesn't know when to let it lie. For a good half hour before this interview proper commences, he bores the pants off me with talk of vintage military aircraft and his Harvard Formation Team and Cessnas, Pipers and De Havilland Beavers.

Gary Numan has a new LP out. It's called *Outland* and it sounds like the others. It is with much reluctance that Numan's concentration is turned from aeroplanes to popular music. When did you first decide to be a pop star, Gary?

'I never did, really,' he says. 'When I was eleven or twelve we had a careers talk at school and I wanted to be a pilot, actually. I wanted to be glamorous and rich and have lots of girls around. Totally unrealistic, I suppose. Aeroplanes were always the thing with me. But I always fancied Mike Nesmith, I suppose . . .'

Gary Webb – for this was his name at birth, 1958 – was a punk rocker in 1977, singing in a hopeless group called the Lasers. The Lasers became Tubeway Army and released their first LP, *Tubeway Army*, in 1978. It didn't sell very many copies. It was no good.

'I didn't like the music very much. I didn't like punk rock very much. I've never liked any fashions very much, actually, but I didn't really have anything alternative to offer anyone.' But then Numan made his Grand Discovery: quite by chance he stumbled upon electronic music. 'It was just pure good luck,' he confesses. 'There used to be this studio in Cambridge called Spaceward and it was really cheap, so I went there a couple of times and one of the times I went there the session that had been there before had left behind a Minimoog that they'd rented, and so I just had a quick go. I couldn't play keyboards or anything. It was one of those really bizarre things where I pressed it and it had a really good sound on it. So I just thought that you pressed a synthesizer and that's what they sounded like. It sounded great. It could have gone *ik* and sounded really crap and I'd have gone, "Fuck, them synthesizers are a complete pile of shit, I won't get involved with them." But it sounded great, like a hundred guitars all going at once, such a powerful instrument . . .'

And so armed with the Grand Discovery, Numan proceeded to create an electronic LP called *Replicas*, which was to include the jolly big hit, 'Are "Friends" Electric?' There he was on *Top of the Pops* with his juvenile techno-fantasies all dressed in black right down to his painted fingernails like some futuristic goon from a failed nightmare. 'The emblem of a bleak, de-personalised future in which machines and monotony had replaced people and passion,' as somebody put it. Or, ahem, the 'voice of alienation'. Etcetera. Numan takes great exception to this latter sobriquet.

'Me? The voice of alienation?' he says, scowling as he always used to before a microphone on the telly. 'That's utter bollocks. I've never been the voice of anything, 'cept me. I've got no idea what people think or what they're interested in. I don't sing about the problems of the world because you have to live with them to understand them and I *don't* live with the problems of the world, really. The only thing I really know anything about is aeroplanes. I just sing about stuff that is applicable to me and then I get slagged off because all my songs say I and Me. Most of my songs are like diaries, things that happened to me – but I have to make them more interesting than they really were. I did a song for the RSPCA once. That was my token nod to doing something worthy.'

But what about the 'image'? He may have *looked* like a *Thunderbird* puppet, vacant and useless, but he was obviously trying to portray something chilling for a bleak, android-dominated future (or something along those lines), was he not?

'I wasn't trying to be nothing,' he snaps. 'I only had that image for about a year. Since then I've had all kinds of stuff (*yes, there was a sort of vague gangster phase and then he turned into Mad Max and bleached his hair, much of which promptly fell out*), but the black stuff is the one that's remembered. It's like David Bowie's always going to be Ziggy Stardust for the rest of his life. It must irritate the fuck out of him. What happened with my image is there was a bloke I saw wandering round all dressed in black and he looked really good so I bought black clothes and it was really good and the thing about not smiling was I was terrified and so nervous I was shitting a brick but the fans seemed to like it so I thought, "Oh, I'll do a bit more of that." I'm not a natural performer. I'm shy by nature.'

Success came suddenly for Gary Numan. Was this something of a surprise for the failed punk rocker?

'Well, you're a bit arrogant when you're young, aren't you? I always thought it would happen, which is very arrogant considering it wasn't very good stuff I was doing at that time. "Are 'Friends' Electric?" and all that stuff was pretty naff. It was shit. The production was shit, the sound was shit, it really was squiddly. I didn't even tune to concert pitch then. But the thing that was a surprise was how fast it happened. It was a matter of weeks from never doing an interview and never doing television to being number one with half the people telling me I was the biggest pile of shit since turds were invented.'

Ah, yes. Gary Numan, pasty-faced robotic-type, was never to be popular with the music press. Someone called him a 'fat white grub'.

'Yeah, Paula Yates, that was. Fat white grub. That was rich, coming from her.' Someone suggested that Numan's parents, Beryl and Tony Webb, should have been sterilised in order to prevent this pop mishap. 'I will never forgive that, criticising my parents for giving birth to me. There's no excuse for that whatsoever, and all this thing about, "You're in the public eye, you must take it," is utter rubbish. They say, "Don't take it personally."'

Oh, *really*?

The abuse of yesteryear still rankles, it is clear.

'I never understood why the press hated me so much. I've never encouraged people to become drug addicts. I've never been drunk. So it's not as if I'm an example for the bad side of life, corrupting the young impressionable people who buy my records. So why am I such an enormous turd? It must be jealousy. If I can earn six or seven million pounds doing something that's such utter crap, then who's the idiot? I've had a really good life and if I can carry on writing such shit and generating such large amounts of money, then I will. I used to drive past *NME* in my Ferrari, thinking, "Oh, yeah, slag me some more, I'm *really* upset!"'

Numan was a big pop star with silly synthesizer symphonies like 'Cars' and 'I Die, You Die' – ever a dab hand at singing gibberish for the masses. It was inevitable that the tabloid press should attempt to entertain us all with tales of the surly singer's sexual exploits.

'Yeah, that was all quite good, wasn't it?' he says with an unseemly smirk. 'I did an interview once with the *Daily Mail* and this woman came over and she wanted to do, she said, an article about my daredevil exploits in aeroplanes, display flying and all that, because it's quite dangerous. "Oh great," I thought, "I'm going to be a hero." And it ended up with the headline "Confessions Of A Sex Warrior". I said nothing about sex at all. She said, "Are you gay?" I said, "No." She said, "Have you ever *wanted* to be gay?" I said, "Well, not really, as a rule." And she said, "Well, couldn't you *say* you wanted to be gay?" I said, "What's that got to do with aeroplanes?" She said, "Do you like lesbians?" And she ended up with a two-page article about sex . . .

'And there was another one. Who was that girl? What was her name? Linda Fox. She sold a story that said I stood at the end of the bed and sang "Land of Hope and Glory"! Hahaha!' Numan laughs – a rare sight to the general public. 'That story was *true*, actually. I was on tour in America for the first time and I was feeling very patriotic and very homesick, so I sang "Land of Hope and Glory" wearing nothing but socks. So at least she told the truth. I'm the biggest perv on earth. I really am.'

At the height of his fame, this grand perv was also subject to a number of death threats, bizarre and over-excited 'Numanoids' vowing to do the hero in.

'They were worrying at first, the death threats, but nutters are nutters and I didn't get all paranoid and fucked up like everybody thought. I like shooting and clay pigeons, so one paper tried to make out that I was a paranoid nutcase with guns everywhere, but that isn't the case at all. I mean, if some nutter came at me trying to kill me, I'd shoot him. But that's self-defence, isn't it? I'm not paranoid, but there's a lot of jealousy involved. The death threats, most of them I think were like boyfriends of girls who'd bought my records and had posters of me on the wall and it goes on from there. I've got two guns, but there's nothing unusual about that at all.'

In 1981, after two years at the top, our gun-toting perv, our aeronautical Sex Warrior, decided to take a break from the pressures of celebrity and fly around the world. His first attempt went all awry when he crash-landed in India and was arrested on suspicion of smuggling and spying.

Apparently, the Indian officials didn't even *recognise* the international superstar! It's an outrage! Numan does not have fond memories of India. The mere mention of the sub-continent turns him foamy. He narrows the already small eyes and bares the teeth as he snarls, 'India is the pighole of the world. No *wonder* they want to come here. Terrible place. The arsehole of the world. You actually see turds on the street. I've seen people sitting in the street, crapping in the street in front of everyone, seen lepers begging, seen people living in mud huts, seen women renting out their children to beggars, never seen so much fucking corruption in my life. Terrible, dirty, stinking, crap-filled country of shit. I met that Mother Teresa when I was there. She couldn't give a monkey's. I just shook her hand. Indonesia's a shithole, too . . .'

At this point Numan launches into a lengthy account of his flying-around-the-globe adventures. These are of a too technical and tedious nature to detain us here – graphs, fuel, wire, oxygen, twin engines running at 'full chat', staring into the eyes of the Big D – death, Piper, Alpha, Tango, Zulu, Zzzzz. I attempt to bring the fellow back to terra firma – not an easy task once he's got his head around an aeroplane-styled topic. Very interesting, Gary. Very, very interesting. But could we talk about music?

'Oh. You know, I've lost my interest in music. I haven't read any music-type things for years. I don't watch music programmes at all. I don't listen to music. I just keep well out of it. I have very little to do with the business at all. The flying thing is my life and passion.'

Evidently.

So Gary Numan flew all around the world – 'It seemed like a jolly idea. What fun. But it was the most frightening thing of my life' – and when he returned, well, he was yesterday's phenomenon, a musician forgotten by all except the staunch Numanoids. A career in tatters. He blames it all on Radio 1 who, he says, have refused to play his records since 1983. Sounds like some madcap conspiracy theory, doesn't it?

'It *is* a conspiracy,' he insists. 'I don't know why they blanked me, but they did and they've been doing it for the last eight years. Something happened. They'll deny it until they are blue in the face, but something happened. I'm supposed to say nice things in case they might change their minds one day but Radio 1 blanking me like that has damaged my career terribly. It's amazing. It's very sad. They've done it to Five Star, they've done it to Nik Kershaw, and they've done it to me and I'm lucky because I'm the only one that's just about hanging on by my fingertips because I can still go out and tour.

'In 1983 they stopped playing my stuff and I still haven't been able to find out why. It's amazing. They said my stuff wasn't suitable, but how can you have a record in the top twenty and not get one play? Something weird's going on there, you know. Maybe I did something rude with the daughter of someone important at Radio 1. Maybe I pissed them off because I'm a perv and said bad things about Band Aid because I thought some of the money should have gone to England to cure cancer or something because I'm patriotic. Maybe they don't like general aviation. I don't know. We used to keep surveys of it and then make up big letters absolutely *proving* that there was a bias against me. But I was pissing in the wind.'

The dastardly Corporation have tried to destroy this innocent man, it seems. It really is not fair.

'I don't care about not being so famous as I was,' he says. 'I never wanted to be a hero, anyway. I never understood my fans, fighting with Duran Duran fans and all that. I always thought that people that deserved to be heroes were people that had done something brave or really, really clever. Like Douglas Bader (*the leg-free flying ace so magnificently portrayed by Kenneth More in* Reach for the Sky). Though it doesn't *have* to be in aeroplanes for you to be a hero. Lifeboat men, people like that. They're the most people in the world of being heroes. I remember people saying, "Oh, it's really *brave*," when I put out a ballad for the first time. Fucking hell, what's brave about that?

Oh, yeah, rock on, that's *very* manly, isn't it? But if somebody dives into a fire and rescues somebody from an aeroplane, you don't even hear about them and that just seems wrong. People who save little kiddies are heroes to me. Not pop stars.'

Gary Numan never wanted to be a hero. But he *did* want to be terribly, fantastically rich. Didn't he?

'Oh, yeah. It's all ego, the business, isn't it? Ego and money. I've made money. A few million quid. I'm not ashamed of that. I *like* money. I'm not a true blue Tory, as everyone says, but I'd rather drive a Ferrari than a Mini. I see nothing wrong with the capitalist way of things and if somebody is good at something that benefits mankind, I think they should be paid for it. I like having a lot of money and if lots of people want to come and see me singing my songs and I've got something they want, they should *pay* for it. So give me your money!

'I'm enriching people's lives and they value that enrichment to the tune of five quid or ten quid, so why should I give 90 per cent of it to somebody else who ain't got a skill, who hasn't got off their arse and *done* something like me? I'm a great capitalist pig. So what? I don't want to be remembered. I really don't give a *fuck* about being remembered. Just want money. Yeah, I'm a pig.'

The pig, the perv, the Sex Warrior called 'Biggles' shuffles away from the decrepit sofa to join his mum Beryl, his dad Tony, his girlfriend Tracey as they stare out at the snowed-under runway. 'It would have been great to go up today,' says the son, sadly, as he gnaws upon a bacon sandwich from the airfield's canteen. 'Oh, it'll melt soon,' says Gary's mum, consolingly. Her son shakes his head. 'It would have been good to go up today. It would've been good.'

Call me a coward, but thank Christ we didn't, is all I can say . . .

# Who the hell does Ringo Starr think he is?

## Q, June 1992

Ringo, why do you wear two rings on each hand?

'Because I can't fit them through my nose.'

Beethoven figures in one of your songs. What do you think of Beethoven?

'He's great. Especially his poetry.'

How did you find America?

'We went to Greenland and made a left turn.'

But that was nearly thirty years ago, innocent times when the small one – Ringo, how tall are you? 'Two feet, nine inches' – with the extended nose sat with the other three before the press of the world and cracked his mop-top jokes, playing the clown and acting the goat, The Lovable One, the one you could take home to meet yer mum and yer dad. In The Great Throne Room at Buckingham Palace, 26 October 1965, the Queen asked the 'Fabs' how long they had been together and, quick as a flash, came Starkey's reply. 'Forty years!' The wag.

It is now much later, April 1992, but that 'natural' Scouse 'wit' of olden times remains intact: The Lovable One clambers aboard a podium at London's Dorchester Hotel and drily announces: 'My name is Ringo Starr.' The assembled members of the press

221

laugh loudly at the pithy sally; a female reporter from Belgium, in the excitement of the moment, squeaks, 'Yah!' It is quite like old times . . .

We are gathered here today to hear exciting news. Ringo is about to release a new LP and it is called *Time Takes Time*. Furthermore, his new amusingly named All-Starr Band – featuring Dave Edmunds and Joe Walsh and Todd Rundgren and diminutive trampoline champion Nils Lofgren – is touring Europe in the summer. Cameras clack and the PR woman sternly warns us to limit our questions to 'the present and the future' (i.e. nothing about *them* – the Beatles – and nothing about alcoholism, if you please). And so the probing begins as a girl from Sweden asks the occasional drummer why he is starting his tour in Sweden: 'Why not?' Uproarious laughter. And a girl from Italy asks him why he is finishing his tour in Italy: 'Crazy question. It may be a surprise to you, lady, but I am a musician.' Hoots. And a girl from somewhere equally foreign asks him if he is 'reaching out to the new generation' – 'You had zis Thomas Ze Tank Engine, no?' – and he says he's just playing his kit now because he is a musician and he likes to feel the 'love' flowing from an audience because it's in his blood. Somewhere along the way we learn that Ringo has absolutely no intention whatsoever of playing with George Harrison at tonight's Albert Hall concert in aid of the Natural Law Party because what Ringo's doing now is promoting his album which is really jolly good and everything so everybody should buy it . . .

Two hours later, upstairs in a hotel suite, Ringo Starr is staring at me through his darkened spectacles. The expression on his somewhat wizened face is somewhat sour. 'This record deserves to be a number one,' he is saying. 'It's a fine album.' The ready quips are not dropping from the lips of The Lovable One this afternoon. His impressive nose is twitching in irritation. I have made a dreadful mistake. I have dared to ask him about . . . them.

He had entered the room in seemingly stony mood. He had thrust himself down upon a sofa and had glowered. 'Is this yer first time?' he had muttered. Er, come again, Mr Starkey? 'Is this yer first time?' My first time what? My first time in a posh suite at the Dorchester hotel or what? 'Just joking,' he had muttered bemusingly. My opening question had been designed to be one of the most psychologically challenging – nay, disturbing – ever to be posed within the context of a rock interview. It was this: Have you, Mr Starr, or have you not, felt a twinge of pity ever for Pete Best (The Good-Looking One who was booted out in favour of Ringo, of whom John Lennon was once heard to remark, 'When I feel my head start to swell, I look at Ringo and know perfectly well we're not supermen')? There was a pause containing the faintest twist of menace. 'Crazy question,' The Nice One murmured, adding a withering stare for good measure.

'Did. I. Ever. Feel. Sorry. For. Pete. Best?' Yes, that was the enquiry. 'No. Why should I? I was a better player than him. That's how I got the job. It wasn't on no personality. It was that I was a better drummer and I got the phone call. I never felt sorry for him. A lot of people have made careers out of knowing, er . . . the Beatles.'

He has said it. He has uttered that word, that thing that we are not supposed to mention because Ringo has 'moved on' and is living for today and for tomorrow and not for, in the word of his old mucker in the rhythm section, yesterday. He has said 'Beatles'. So can we talk about the Beatles, then? Ringo shrugs his shoulders. 'Sure,' he grunts. So tell me about your image. You were The Goofy One. Was this an imposed personality or was it the real Starkey or what?

'That's not how I am. That was how we were in the movie, in *Help!* and *A Hard Day's Night*. That was what people felt we were like.'

But didn't you mind always being given the goony songs to sing, 'Octopus's Garden' and 'Yellow Submarine' and that awful one about 'the greatest fool who ever made the big time'?

'They were writing a lot heavier songs than I was and the ones they wrote for me were never that heavy, either. That's what made the combination that we were. All completely different but together we were a mighty force.'

Presumably this 'difference' in personalities was what made the break-up of the Beatles particularly acrimonious and acid. Discuss.

'That's stupid. We'd changed. We didn't have the time to put in all that energy. We were all married then. Most of us were married. I had children. John had a kid. George got married. So it was a natural end to it. We finished. That's it.'

At the morning's press conference, Ringo had been banging on about how you can't beat the feeling of playing live, of how he's 'addicted' to it, the love teeming from the audience, the 'buzz', the 'vibe' etcetera. But if we examine the history (and leave out the Ringo Starr and his All-Star Band jaunt of '89), we see that since '66, he has played on stage hardly at all. This is not a criticism, I was just wondering whether . . .

'Look, playing live is how I started,' he snaps. 'That's where my blood is. We played live for four years as the Beatles, but in the end it was impossible because the reaction we used to get was so loud that I was turning into a bad musician because I could only keep the off-beat, so we were deteriorating. How often do you want to play stadiums? We as the Beatles lost the contact. I want to feel the love from the audience and you don't get that in a stadium. Bruce Springsteen loses the love and the audience contact and Guns N' Roses and the Stones and Paul McCartney, they all lose the love and the contact. They just forget that it's a great privilege to play to an audience, so on my tour I'm playing Liverpool and I'm playing Hammersmith and . . .'

And so he goes on for several weeks about all the intimate sheds he's going to bash his drums and sing that one about 'You're six-teen and you're beautiful and you're mii-iine,' or whatever it is, in.

So stadiums are useless. I had always imagined, in my simplicity, that the Beatles at Shea Stadium was just one of the most thrilling moments in all of popular music history. Am I entirely incorrect?

Ringo tuts and he crosses his arms, a huff-orientated posture.

'Shea Stadium was *brilliant*,' he goes. 'We were breaking new ground. Of course it was brilliant. But if you see the video on Shea Stadium, you see how crazy we all were, anyway. John wasn't playing it note-for-note. John went mad. It was a thrill.'

Did Ringo go mad all those years ago, what with all those American girls saying he should be President and swooning at his shaking fringe?

'It wasn't only American girls, you know,' he points out, helpfully. 'It was English girls and Swedish girls. So, yeah. I went absolutely mad round about 1964. My head was just so swollen. I thought I was a God, a living God. And the other three looked at me and said. Excuse me, *I* am the God. We all went through a period of going mad.'

Presumably drugs made a major contribution to the mental mayhem.

'The drugs came later. Well, there was always some element of alcohol and amphetamine and then several other substances came into play and then the Beatles was over.'

And in '68, you all went to India to 'groove' with Mr Maharishi Mahesh Yogi. That was mad . . .

'Well, I was in hospital with my ex-wife [Maureen] delivering Jason, my second son, and I got back and there was two messages on the answerphone, a message from John and a message from George, and they were saying, we've been to see this Maharishi guy. So I said, what's that all about? So they told me how great it all was and I met Maharishi and I fell in love with Transcendental Meditation and I got to India and I took two suitcases, one full of clothes and one full of baked beans because I don't eat curry, and

225

it was high for a while and then I thought, "That's the end of it for me, thank you very much" . . .'

By this time, the drummer of the Perky Personality had embarked upon his unlikely career as a screen actor, playing a gardener who has love on billiard tables in the hippie sex romp *Candy* (which featured Marlon Brando as a guru personage not a billion miles removed from Mr Maharishi), and then a foil for Peter Sellers in the simply awful *The Magic Christian* (and then being actually quite good as a Teddy Boy drummer in *That'll Be the Day*). Ringo doesn't think that talking about his Thespian pursuits is very interesting at all because he's moved on and music's the thing, like . . .

'We just decided we wanted to be an actor. I'm not interested in that acting anymore . . .'

In the mid-'70s, Starr made (along with some really dud LPs) a couple of splendid pop singles: 'Photograph' and 'It Don't Come Easy'. The man who, in 1963, said, 'Whenever I hear another drummer I know I'm no good' (and who sits here today peering at me with a certain chill and insisting 'I am the best rock drummer on earth and it's not just me saying that, many fine musicians say that' when I have never even questioned his capabilities) comes over refreshingly modest for once when I say I liked those tunes.

'Well, I just decided to make some singles because the Beatles always took so long to make albums and so I started to write but I could never finish a song. I was great for two verses and a chorus but I could never finish a song so I'd have to ask George to finish it and we'd just have rows because George would always put in the "God verse" and I don't sing about God, so after a few smashes it all went downhill because, er, well, yer know . . .'

I do know. It all went downhill because Ringo was hitting the sauce with alarming abandon.

'It was my addictive personality. Suddenly you're starting to drink at nine in the morning and I was procrastinating me balls off and I was just trapped as an alcoholic, a drunk.'

He was too drunk even to pay any great attention to the shooting of John Lennon, he says.

'I wasn't well when he got murdered and I wasn't well after it. I was in such great pain that I hardly noticed . . .'

The voice of Thomas The Tank Engine and The Fat Controller was killing itself with booze. But then – hey presto! – Ringo booked into De-Tox Mansions, USA, and everything was all right again.

'One day I had a second, maybe half a second, of clarity and I was in so much pain and I knew that Barbara [Bach, second wife who he met on the set of the dismal *Caveman* film in '81] had mentioned a sort of re-hab situation. She had a problem, too. She found this place in Arizona. I haven't had a drink or a drug since and that was October '88 and I've given up smoking cigarettes, too.'

Ringo was cured of his urges by the power of love.

'It was love. It's love. And the proof of the difference in my lifestyle is that I've put a band together, I've made this album and . . .'

Ringo takes this opportunity to tell me what a great musician he is and how his new LP is really jolly good and everything until I interrupt to suggest that however good his new LP is, it can hardly hope to top *Abbey Road*, can it? He looks at me as if I am deranged:

'What, as an album? My album can't beat the *Abbey Road* album as an album?'

That is, in a nutshell, what I was driving at.

'Well, the so-called B-side of *Abbey Road* is one of my favourite sides, the one with "Bathroom Window" and "Polythene Pam", but just by chance I was re-listening to *Sgt. Pepper* the other day and that's a fine album too and it's a bloody marvellous album, it's a bloody fine album and *The White Album* was great because we were like a band after *Pepper* and all the craziness and *Rubber Soul* was great and the first album which took twelve hours to put down was an achievement . . . So I don't know what you're talking about. That was thirty years ago, man. I'm still making records and you can hear that I'm a great musician on the new record, *Time Takes Time*, if you can ever be bothered to mention it. This is an actual bloody *legend* in front of you. I'm not expecting you to comb the bloody legend's hair but you could mention the new LP and these other fine musicians I'm still playing with.'

Ringo Starr is close to rage and I don't know quite why. I decide to placate him by talking about his All-Starr Band. This ploy is not a success. What is it like working with Todd Rundgren, I enquire? Todd Rundgren's a bit mad, isn't he?

Ringo lunges forward in the sofa, almost doing himself a mischief.

'What? *What?* Have you met him? Why would you say shit like that? You don't even know the man. How dare you say shit like that about a friend?'

I meant 'mad' as in 'genius'. It is a compliment.

'You're talking shit. That's like saying Frank Zappa's mad. Frank Zappa's probably the nicest man I ever met in this business. I've been in the game too long for this shit! I've done my bit. I've made a record, I've made the thing and I hope it's a number one because I've done my bit, I'm promoting the thing . . . or I am trying to promote the thing . . .'

What manner of umbrage is this? Ringo Starr seems to feel – and strongly – that my failure to spend this interview discussing his new LP and the brilliance of Tom Petty and Jeff 'Skunk' Baxter and Harry 'Schmilsson' Nilsson and everybody else who played on it – is impudence of the first order. But wouldn't such an interview be a trifle limiting and boring and . . .? I am unable to make this suggestion because The Clown, The Lovable One, seen here in his updated role of Pop's Mister Crosspatch, continues to rant away . . .

'If you bothered to listen to the single "Weight of the World" you'd hear this line in it which goes . . . er, er . . . well, it says that you can't live in the past and that sums it up. Because you're living in the *past*. As far as this interview has been going on, it's *shit* because it's been the Beatles interview and you haven't even mentioned *Time Takes Time* or 'Weight of the World'. But that's okay.

You've got the time. That's what you asked. I've answered your questions. And . . .' Ringo rises from the sofa, two feet nine inches of unbridled anger . . . 'That is *it!*' And it is. He flounces from the room, a cry of 'Thanks a lot!' that oozes with sarcasm, his cheery farewell. What this man needs, in my estimation, is a stiff drink, or a cig, or both . . .

That night, on stage at the Albert Hall, George Harrison played 'Taxman' and a lot of other aged songs and then announced 'a blast from all our pasts' and on bounded Ringo. How could this be? Had not the man assured us earlier in the day that he would most definitely not be gracing this political rally thing with his presence? Well, there he was, anyway, and he played drums on 'While My Guitar Gently Weeps' and 'Roll Over Beethoven', no doubt feeling all the love wafting up from the auditorium. Then, at the conclusion of this horrid old rock 'n' roll novelty, up strode some representatives of the peculiar Natural Law Party to talk embarrassingly about this 'night of magic' that the crowd had been privileged to witness. And as the spiritual oration continued, a lone cry of protest rang out from the back of the stage, a bellow of annoyance, a sharp 'Shut up!' The culprit of this ill-mannered intrusion was identified only as a man with drumsticks and a great big nose . . .

# Who the hell does Roger Waters think he is?

## *Q*, November 1992

'So how's Syd these days?'

If one happened to bump up against an existing member of the legendary rock combo Pink Floyd in some 'social situation' (cocktails at Brands Hatch, probably), that's the only thing one would be inclined to say. 'How's Syd?' one would go and the existing member of Pink Floyd – whether Dave Gilmour or Nick Mason or the other one – would, no doubt, blink briefly, pop a cheese 'n' pineapple-savoury-on-a-toothpick into his mouth, bray "What? Cor! Frightfully good, these canapés!" and wander off to hobnob with Nigel Mansell or somebody really interesting.

'Syd' is, of course, Syd Barrett, original member of Pink Floyd, beautiful boy who wrote extraordinary things like 'Apples and Oranges' and 'Astronomy Domine' and flipped his cork and disappeared. But there is another original member, no longer in the legendary rock experience that was 'Floyd', who appears to be a degree off beam: Roger Waters. He's the one who invented giant inflatable pigs, the one who tortured schoolyards of children by making them sing his catchprase ('We dahn nee nur edercays-hun, we dahn nee nur fort corntrawel') all out of tune, the one who once recorded a 'song' called 'Several Species of Small Furry

Animals Gathered Together in a Cave Grooving with a Pict', the
one whose doomy sound 'anthems' about 'alienation' and how
awful everything is have worried listeners all over the world for
several years.

In the guest lounge of a genteel hotel in the picturesque town of
Stockbridge, Hampshire – where Waters has a home because the
fishing is excellent down here apparently – the lofty rock icon sits
gazing at the cover of an ancient *Country Life*, a pint glass of local ale
before him. He's got jeans on. He's got long hair. And he's wearing exactly the same T-shirt (well, it's a different shade – pink not
black – but of identical cut) that he was sporting on the cover of
Pink Floyd's 1969 LP, *Ummagumma*. One has to ask. 'How's Syd?'
'I don't know. I haven't seen him for ten years . . . more than ten
years, probably. I don't know what went wrong with Syd because
I'm not an expert in whatever it is, what they call schizophrenia. I
don't know a lot about it. Syd was extraordinarily charming and
attractive and alive and talented but . . . whatever happened to
him, happened to him.'

Roger Waters is thought, by many, to be the gloomiest man in
rock. *The Wall* was gloomy and his solo LPs, *The Pros and Cons of
Hitchhiking* (1984) and *Radio K.A.O.S.* (1987), were gloomy, and his
latest work, *Amused to Death*, is frightfully gloomy. Waters' voice
drones along to warn us that: a) there's a squaggly Jeff Beck guitar solo coming up any minute; b) everything is horrible, especially
television, war, the entire universe and Andrew Lloyd Webber. In
recording *Amused To Death*, Waters has utilised a snazzy new sci-
entific recording concept that's called 'Q Sound' (nothing to do, I
hasten to add, with this magazine, which should immediately sue)
and with this natty new technique, if the listener sticks his/her head
in the correct place betwixt the speakers, all sorts of amazing things
happen!

Isn't technology fab?

I tried this at home. It didn't work that well because I have a deaf-ness problem, but standing and forking my neck at an uncomfortable angle, I could clearly detect (I think) the sound of a peacock rattling pencils inside an old electric kettle (or something). Marvellous! More discernible still was the gloomy groan of someone who was saying how ghastly everything is . . . Roger Waters folds his arms and defies his beer as I compose a second question. Which is:

'Are you or are you not the gloomiest man in rock?'

'You can't expect me to take a question like that seriously,' he says, in his posh, soft voice. 'I refuse to answer that question on the grounds that it is stupid.'

Immediately I warm to the man. He has such a chip on his shoulder it's a wonder his arm doesn't drop off.

'I've been reading the nonsense that's been written about *Amused to Death*. Adam Sweeting [music journalist who said, in the *Guardian*, that the LP wasn't much cop], well, he's a complete prat. Always was, always will be.'

I protest. Adam Sweeting is not a prat; he's entitled to his opinion and a very nice man to boot, I say.

Waters will have none of this.

'Sweeting is not a nice man. I don't know him but I know him. He says I write twaddle. He's wrong! He's one taco short of a Mexi-can meal. Sweeting is not the only arsehole: there's other cunts like Andy Gill and Charles Shaar Murray.'

'Andy Gill and Charles Shaar Murray, they write for *Q*.'

'Do they? Who gives a fuck who they write for when they can't fucking write?'

This man is argumentative. This man is, er, several bass guitar notes short of a decent tune.

'It is extraordinary that Andy Gill and Adam Sweeting and Charles Shaar Murray didn't notice *The Wall*. They are supposed to be music journalists; how could they not have noticed this extraordinary well-constructed, deep and meaningful and moving and important piece of work? What the fuck's the matter with these arseholes? And now, with *Amused to Death*, they've missed another one, Adam Sweeting and Andy Gill and the other fucker and all the rest, they should be in hospital. I am confident that I am really clever and that I am really good at what I do so I'm not going to have prats like Sweeting and Andy Gill and Shaar bloody Murray telling me that I'm no good because they're wrong. *Amused to Death* is fucking, fucking good. Isn't it?'

He fixes me with a steely eye and I say that *Amused to Death* is probably magnificent but I can't really tell because, due to my 'technical problems', I cannot appreciate the superb and magnificent benefits of 'Q Sound'.

He accepts this weedy excuse. He says: 'Well, anyway, I am one of the best five writers to come out of English music since the War.'

Let us turn the clock back. Let us go a-whizzing away to the 1960s when the world was young and Pink Floyd were wearing preposterous neckerchiefs and singing about Arnold Layne, a character given to stealing women's underwear, on drugs in clubs like UFO. What grand times those must have been.

'No, they weren't,' says Mister Gloomy. 'I don't want to go back to those times at all. There wasn't anything "grand" about it. We were laughable. We were useless. We couldn't play at all so we had to do something stupid and "experimental".'

This is too much. Pink Floyd's first LP, *Piper at the Gates of Dawn*, is an absolute monument of, er, a record that's quite good.

'Well, that was Syd. Syd was a genius. But I wouldn't want to go back to playing "Interstellar Overdrive" for hours and hours.'

Waters doesn't seem to like being in pop groups very much at all. In 1973, his group recorded *Dark Side of the Moon* and billions of people bought it (even though it was useless) and, naturally, this commercial success cheesed off Roger enormously.

233

'We'd cracked it. We'd won the pools. What are you supposed to do after that? *Dark Side of the Moon* was the last willing collaboration: after that, everything with the band was like drawing a tooth; ten years of hanging on to the married name and not having the courage to get divorced, to let go; ten years of bloody hell. It was all just terrible. Awful. Terrible.'

Yes, Waters, the Mister Glum who refuses even to sniff at his brimming beaker of beer, is the gloomiest man in rock. He's enough to depress a gadfly. Perhaps I should jolly up the proceedings by telling you, soaraway-twingo-bingo-Sun-style . . . Twenty Things (Trimmed Down to a Handy, Fun-Packed Eight) You Didn't Know about Roger Waters, probably:

1. He doesn't much care for Radio 1!
   'Radio 1 won't play my fucking single ["What God Wants"] because they know it's no good. They know it's not as good as Erasure or Janet fucking Jackson. They know that the British public shouldn't be listening to it. It makes my blood boil! If you're not seventeen with a baseball hat on back to front, they don't want to know.'
2. He's crackers!
   'It is very important, in our current predicament, that we try to give each other the change to confront our feelings about things. There's some branches of the medical profession that now agree with me, saying that it's vital to hang on to what you felt when you were sixteen or seventeen or four, retaining a grasp on that stuff we had when we were children, when we saw the picture of the world in bright colours and strong sensations before it was turned into a grey, uncaring mush by Adam Sweeting and Andrew Lloyd Webber.'
3. He doesn't (unlike other people) much care for war!
   'What irritates Adam Sweeting and Charles Shaar Murray and Andy Gill and all you journalists is that I gloomily and boringly

234

enough find that my concern with war as big business doesn't diminish as the years go by. I feel just as gloomy about it at the age of forty-nine as I did when I was seventeen. I'm sure that my hatred of war was spurred on by the death of my father [killed as a pilot in the Second World War]. I find myself compelled to feel for everyone's father or son who is killed in a war – and for what?'

4. He's crackers!

'It's important for people to grasp sensations, like the kind I get when I am fishing. Some of us are gatherers and some of us are hunters. I'm a hunter. I need the mud of river oozing between my toes. It's like Proust.'

5. He doesn't much care for Sinéad O'Connor!

(Ms O'Connor appeared at Waters' 1990 performance of *The Wall* in Berlin, in aid of Leonard Cheshire's Memorial Fund for Disaster Relief.) 'It was very, very hard work organising that *Wall* concert but everyone was fabulous to work with – Bryan Adams, Van Morrison, Cyndi Lauper, bloody brilliant. All brilliant. Except for Sinéad O'Connor. Oh, God! I have never ever met anybody who is so self-involved and unprofessional and big-headed and unpleasant. She is so far up her own bum it's scary. With *The Wall*, she was so worried that there weren't any other [adopts Irish 'brogue'] "young people on the show". I and everybody else were old farts in her opinion so she was worried that she was doing something that wasn't "street" enough. And because it wasn't "street" enough, she came up with this brilliant idea: she said that I should employ Ice-T or one of those people to re-work one of my songs as a rap number! I am not joking! And neither was she fucking joking! That's the sad thing – she was serious! And then a couple of months after the show, when the record was out, she did an interview on American television, millions of viewers, and she rubbished the whole thing, said *The Wall* concert was a load of wank. I don't give a fuck what she thought about it but she should have kept her fucking mouth shut because it could only hurt the charity, the memorial fund and everything that Leonard [Cheshire] had done. She doesn't understand anything. She's just a silly little girl. You can't just lie in the corner and shave your bloody head and stick it up your arse and occasionally pull it out to go (*'brogue'*) "Oh, I tink this is wrong and dat is wrong" and burst into tears.'

6. He doesn't much care for 'stadium rock'!
'Rock 'n' roll in stadiums is genuinely awful. These concerts are just like Tupperware parties – held in honour of the Great God Tupper – with 50,000 people, only they don't buy Tupperware, they buy hot dogs and T-shirts and occasionally look up to watch those disgusting video screens that are all out of sync and make you feel sick and torture you. It's funny how people try to work their way around the greed of it all. Like U2, whose rationale is (*feigned Irish accent*), "Ooh, we have to play in stadiums 'cos all our fans want to come and see us". Well, fine; give your fans a really shitty show in a stadium – but for fuck's sake don't charge them twenty-five quid for it!'

7. He's a wag!
'Michael Jackson performs in stadiums, too – but he's not doing it for himself, he's doing it to save all the little children in the world.'

8. He's crackers! But not *that* crackers because he doesn't much care for Andrew Lloyd Webber!
(There's a lyric on *Amused to Death* which runs thus: *'Lloyd Webber's awful stuff/Runs for years and years/An earthquake hits the theatre/But the operetta lingers/Then the piano lid comes down/And breaks his fucking fingers.'*)
'Andrew Lloyd Webber sickens me. He's in your face all the time and what he does is nonsense. It has no value. It is shallow, derivative rubbish, all of it, and it makes me very gloomy. Actually, I've never been to one of his shows but having put

that slightly savage joke on the record, I thought I'd better listen to some Andrew Lloyd Webber and I was staying in a rented house in America this summer and the people who owned the house had a whole bunch of his rubbish so I thought I'd listen to *Phantom of the Opera* and I put the record on and I was slightly apprehensive. I thought, Christ, I hope this isn't good – or even mediocre. I was not disappointed. *Phantom of the Opera* is absolutely fucking horrible from start to finish.'

Yes, the music of 'Sir' Andrew Lloyd Webber is rather horrible – but has not Waters, in condemning *Phantom of the Opera* as 'fucking fifteenth rate from beginning to end', as he does, missed something? Has he not noticed something uncanny about *Phantom of the Opera*, the title song, something about the opening notes that go 'DAAAA-da-da-da-da-da'?

'Yes, "Echoes"!' he booms. ('Echoes' was an LP-side-long, and rather-good-actually, track on Pink Floyd's *Meddle*.) '"Echoes". Yeah, the beginning of that bloody *Phantom* song is from "Echoes". (*He sings*) DAAAA-da-da-da-da-da. I couldn't believe it when I heard it. It's the same time signature – it's 12/8 – and it's the same structure and it's the same notes and it's the same everything.

'Bastard. It probably is actionable. It really is! But I think that life's too long to bother with suing Andrew fucking Lloyd Webber. I think that might make me really gloomy.'

Waters has spent many years of late in a suing situation. This is because what he does not much care for most of all is the new so-called Pink Floyd. In 1983, after the *Final Cut* LP, Waters flounced from the band. Four years later, the others, Gilmour, Mason and Wright, assembled, called themselves Pink Floyd, played lots of Waters' songs on stages before huge and enthusiastic audiences, and made pots of money. Meanwhile, Waters toured to promote *Radio K.A.O.S.* but he wasn't called Pink Floyd so nobody gave a hoot. This made Roger gloomy. Lengthy litigation ensued. The animosity lingers.

'When those people went out calling themselves Pink Floyd, it made me very, very gloomy. And it made them very happy. Well, I don't know if it did make them happy. I don't think they are happy, actually. You should ask them. Ask them: "Are you happy? You sold out. You sold out everything. Did it make you happy?" I mean, how can they find it within themselves to go on stage and do my songs – songs from *The Wall*? I wrote *The Wall* as an attack on stadium rock – and there's "Pink Floyd" making money out of it by playing it in stadiums! Oh well, that's for them to live with.

'They have to bear the cross of that betrayal. They have to live with the denial of what the work was about. But when all that nonsense started, it made me fucking gloomy. I stood by a river and stared at myself in the water.

'Pathetic, I said. They despoiled my creations and there was nothing I could do about it. My one pathetic victory was that they had to put testicles on the pig [i.e. the blow-up pig he designed for the cover of the *Animals* LP, the pig that broke loose from its moorings at Battersea Power Station and ran amok through the Home Counties' skies]. If the pig had been exactly the same as the pig that I designed, I could have stopped them using it. Fuck them. Gilmour and Mason now own the name "Pink Floyd". They keep it in a box.'

Waters chuckles a chuckle born of loathing and self-pity. If only I had a shiny sixpence, I might press it into the old man's palm. Earlier in this conversation, Waters 'pointed out' that he was one of the five best writers of music since the War. So who could possibly rank above him, I wonder? With furrowed brow he ponders the question.

'John Lennon,' he says. 'I'm trying to think,' he says. 'Er, I can't think of anybody else. You see, I don't much like listening to records. I'm a bit isolationist and insular. I'd rather be fishing. The list of great writers is very, very short but I am definitely in it. Er, who else is there that's better than me? I really don't know. Freddie Mercury, maybe . . .'

Roger Waters stares into his untouched pint pot. Then he picks it up, apparently toying with the idea of putting it to his lips. He smiles to himself and then he grins at me. He does not take a drink. Careful, as they say, with that axe, Eugene . . .

# Who the hell do Status Quo think they are?

## *Q*, January 1993

> *'She wears denim wherever she goes/Says she's gonna get some records by the Status Quo . . .'*
>
> 'The Concept', Teenage Fanclub, 1991

Easing a hand, cagily, carefully, into a pocket of the over-tight blue jeans, Francis Rossi extracts a blue plastic comb. He totters towards the dressing-room mirror, pauses (comic timing), pats the head, drops the comb, delivers the punchline, 'Not fucking worth it, is it?' Get it? No? Well, you see, Francis Rossi (despite sporting the ponytail that time and fashion forgot) has scarcely any hair on top but this doesn't matter, because if you're in Status Quo, you're supposed to be all creaky and grizzled; you're supposed to be of the balding tendency. If you're in Status Quo, you're still playing your heads-down-no-nonsense-mindless-boogie-con-legs-splayed-in-trim-fit-denim even though you're over forty and, consequently, old enough to know better. This is the quip. This is why all Britain holds the Quo in such affection.

This is why when Rossi sits down upon a chair in his dressing room, he does it slowly and gingerly like a codger while (humorous bonus) making a farty sound with his lips (flatulent codger).

And then, in case you'd forgotten that even though the Quo are ancient they're still 'lads' and, er, 'diamond geezers' all at the same time, comes an inevitable and negligible Knob Joke, at which everybody in the room – the management people and the equipment people and the sundries – endeavours to cackle as loudly as possible.

Crikey, 20,000 years at the top, I say, attempting to open an interview amid dressing-room japery. Er, 20,000 years at the top: this must make you feel all sort of, um, 20,000 years at the top-ish. Rick Parfitt – the other 'proper' Quo – looks at me all furrowed brow and gravity.

'I think,' he corrects me, 'I think you mean twenty-six years, don't you? Not 20,000.'

*'Get down deeper and down/Down down deeper and down/Down down deeper and down/Get down deeper and down.'*
'Down Down', Status Quo, 1974

At the ice rink, Ryde, Isle of Wight, hard-core Status Quo fanciers – teenaged softies with wavy hair and wonky spectacles and distressed denim jackets festooned with sew-on patches that say *Extreme* and *Bon Jovi: Slippery When Wet* and *Status Quo* – are gathered by the foot of the stage. Behind these throng other examples of the Quo Public. It takes all sorts. There are women in white high-heels sipping yellowish cocktails out of plastic beakers, there are thick-necked bruisers with failed moustaches and shell-suits eyeing said women up; there are kiddy-winks of the Nintendo generation hand-in-hand with grandmothers togged up in sequin-fronted jerseys for the beanfeast; there are couples of middle years in their Sunday Asda-shopping-expedition best. There are sorts who look like gangsters and sorts who look like wets. The appeal of Status Quo knows no barriers. Status Quo, they're the ones who strummed for Prince Charles in their waistcoats and for charity and they're 'down-to-earth' and 'just-like-us'.

And they don't even take drugs anymore, bless 'em . . .

Rick Parfitt is attempting to conjure up a memory but he's not doing very well, so he turns to Rossi for assistance.

'You remember, '78 or '79. The guy was called Brian and we were in LA and we got into coke. There was a party in the hills and he offered us a line. It was Brian whatsisname, remember?'

Rossi: 'Robertson?'

Parfitt: 'No. Brian. Him with the glasses, you know?'

Rossi: 'Brian?'

Parfitt: 'No. Brian. Brian, you know, the one . . .'

Rossi: 'Oh, *that* Brian. Yeah. Ur, I don't know what you're talking about.'

In simple conversation they do make an acceptable double act. And Roy Hudd complains that music hall is dead.

Parfitt: 'Yeah, anyway, so Brian got some toot out and so we thought we'll have a go at this and we had a line each and then we went outside and sat in a car and said to each other, "Is anything happening to you yet?" "No, nothing's happening." So we thought, "Well, we're not bothered with drugs then, that's great!" But then six months later . . .'

Six months later, the drug was sampled again and, alas, this time it seemed to do the trick. Hooked. While Rossi murmurs assent to a tale of woe, Parfitt, like reformed 'fiends' are wont to do, embarks upon a lengthy thesis called Drugs Aren't A Very Good Idea, On The Whole. 'Blah blah,' he goes. '. . . vicious circle . . . blah blah . . . horrible spiral . . . blah blah . . . vicious, er, spiral . . .' He was on the stuff for ten years.

'I needed a toot just to get into the shower' – and, oh dear – 'Ten years is a lot of dough and it's a lot of brain cells and it's a lot of shit been talked. I spent four hours one night just trying to teach Francis how to shake hands with people properly. Remember?'

Rossi: 'Yeah . . . I'm going to tell Tom about the pen.'

Parfitt: 'No. No, don't tell him that . . . Er, Francis gave up on the coke before I did, though, didn't you?'

Rossi: 'Yeah . . . but I got a good party trick out of the coke. Because my septum's gone and my nose doesn't work properly anymore, I can put a cotton bud up one nostril and it goes up and I pull it out the other side.'

If only I had a Q-tip about my person, I could ask Rossi to demonstrate this remarkable nasal feat.

Status Quo in the early '80s were, says Parfitt, 'smashed on gear and booze. But the band just got bigger because, in all truth, we never did coke on stage.'

Francis Rossi, with the gesture of a contrite schoolchild about to confess to mischief behind the bike sheds, puts his hand in the air and says, 'Ur, I did. I did coke on stage.'

Parfitt seems disappointed. 'What? You never told me! I knew you went out on booze – but not coked up. Did you?'

'Oh, yeah,' says Rossi. 'I did. I just thought, "Fuck this. It's rock 'n' roll." Rock 'n' roll sounds marvellous when you're pissed and coked up. You think you're fucking wonderful. And nobody dares tell you that you're crap.'

I am longing to tell Status Quo that they're crap because they haven't made a decent record since 'Whatever You Want', but I can't get a word in edgeways.

Rossi: 'I'm going to tell Tom about the pen. I am. Ha ha. I was staying at Rick's house and we'd been in the studio and doing a lot of coke and he came down one morning and he looked like death and he said, "Oh man, my fucking nose, for fuck's sake, my nose hurts." And then – dunk! – out his nose comes the centre piece of the pen we'd been snorting through. It had been up his nose all night. Ha ha ha!'

This unseemly anecdote has sunk Parfitt into a dark frame. 'It wasn't the centre piece of the pen,' he grumbles. 'It was the bit on the end where the actual ball-point is.'

243

*'When I look up to the sky I see your eyes a funny kind of yellow.'* 'Pictures of Matchstick Men', Status Quo, 1968.

In March 1968, Esther and Abi Ofarim were number one in the British Hit Parade with the bewildering 'Cinderella Rockafella' and Status Quo were at number seven with 'Pictures of Match-stick Men', a grand example of English pop psychedelia. 'Pictures of Matchstick Men' – the best thing the group ever did (if you don't count 'We ain't Got Nothin' Yet', recorded when they were still called the Spectres) – never features in a Status Quo live set. Just like Spinal Tap, who never like to be reminded of their 'flower power' period, Status Quo are ashamed of their flitty beginnings.

'We were a plastic-haired bunch of pop stars,' says Rossi, stressing 'pop-stars' as if it were an alternative term for 'neo-Nazi-pederast-calamity-misfits' or something worse. 'We'd been on the telly so we were . . . pop stars.' 'We didn't know what we were, really,' says Parfitt. 'We didn't really know how to dress, so we dressed like everybody else did, with bell bottoms, flares that were about 14 feet across, and frilly shirts and the business. We must have looked like a couple of poofs.'

Rossi wrote that first hit sitting on his lavatory.

'I was on the bog because I couldn't get away from the wife at the time. I'd only just got married and I moved in with the mother-in-law and the wife – ex-wife now – in this prefab in East Dulwich and the best place to get away from them was in the bog. But it was tricky because those prefabs had narrow bogs. You had to sit like that. (There's a mincing-buttock-mime here to the accompaniment of appreciative laughter from Parfitt.) So I went to the bog and I sat like that and I started writing this song and then the mother-in-law and the wife went out so I went into the lounge and started on the lyrics and then they came back so I went back in the bog. It was my favourite room in the house. So

I wrote all the lyrics in there and it was easy because it was just dream-sequency . . . anything that comes into your fucking head that sounds stupid.

'I just wrote this thing that sounded slightly "pissed-adelic": I didn't know what they were going on about when they were talking about "psychedelic", all those hippies and people back then. The closest I knew that "psychedelic" meant was when you went to gigs at colleges they'd put up coloured gels *(blobby 'light shows')* that moved around and made you sick all over the fucking place. And Marsha Hunt would always be there. So, anyway, I'm just in the bog going, *When I look up to the sky* – fine – *I see your eyes a funny kind of yellow* – that's fine. That'll do.'

One must give them this: Status Quo have a refreshingly honest approach to the art of lyric-writing. There will be no Bernie Taupin-styled coffee-table books of so-called 'poetry' from these geezers, no Lou Reed-type 'analyses' in the posh Sundays.

Rossi: 'When we got big and famous, there were all these critics saying Status Quo's lyrics are meaningless, but I agreed because as far as I know our lyrics mean nothing. *"Down down deeper and down"*. What's that mean? Fuck knows. But then you hit Australia and they say, "Phwoarrr, down down, eh? I know what you mean, mate!" because they think it's all about sex. Same with "Roll Over Lay Down": everybody thinks that's totally sex – "Woooargh, you crafty devil, you!" – but it's not sex at all, it's just the opposite because it comes from my ex-wife. I'd come home and if she had the hump, she'd be sleeping on my side of the bed so I'd have to wake her up to get in so I'd say, "Roll over."'

This discursion upon The Imagery of the Quo Lyric proves so fascinating that I find myself asking Rick Parfitt how he came to 'pen' 'Mystery Song' – the one that goes: *'The boys know what you're giving/You give the boys such a lot of fun/dum-di-dum-di-dum-something/You really got me going, baby/Baby can you give me a price?'*

'I've no idea,' he replies. 'All I remember about that was I was doing some sort of drugs at the time. I don't remember what sort of drugs they were.'

Rossi: 'Hang on, I'd given you some speed that morning, remember?'

Parfitt: 'Oh, that's right, yeah. We were in the studio and I was feeling a bit rough because I'd been out the night before so you said to me, "Come to the toilet with me," and we went into the bog and I'd never done speed before but you gave me some speed.'

Rossi: 'Sulphate.'

Parfitt: 'Sulphate, yeah, and I thought, "This is great!"'

Rossi: 'We left you at midnight sat on a stool and we came back the next morning and you were still on the stool with the guitar, writing your fucking song. And the reason it's called "Mystery Song" is you couldn't remember what you'd called it in the fucking first place.'

Parfitt: 'Yeah. Right. But what happened was you spiked me, Francis, mate, and the speed was great so I put these chords together and done these lyrics about this girl I was supposed to have known who Francis knows who she is but I don't.'

Rossi: 'What the fuck are you talking about?'

Parfitt: 'Basically, the song is about a prostitute. I don't know who she was – but you don't when you're on drugs, do you?'

They are not very ideologically sound, the Quo, are they, readers? Their attitude to women (particularly ex-wives) is hardly New Man, they use words like 'poof' and 'wop' with no blink of realisation that it might give offence (though 'wop' is all right because Francis Rossi comes from an Italian ice-cream family).

They did their very first protest song only recently: 'In the Army Now'. How did it go? *'Smiling faces as you wait to land/But once you get there no-one gives a damn/You're in the army now, oh-wow-oh . . .'* Brilliantly observed polemic or not, there is little point in being in Status Quo if you're of the protest persuasion: Quo and rebellion, just like oil and water and blood and bleach, simply do not mix.

Rossi: 'You're right. I'm forty-three years old so I'd be pretending if I said I'm twenty years old and I'm an angry young man, wouldn't I?'

Parfitt: 'Yeah, that's right, because the other night there was this woman in the audience and she was amazing and she had a warm glow about her and she was really old, like seventy or eighty, and I find it much easier to smile at people like that than I do at regular Quo fans. I find it a pleasure and a privilege smiling at an old lady like that.' Even a Jimmy Tarbuck-type, or one of Tarby's golfing-Sunshine-Variety-bus-chums, might wince at this onslaught of 'sincerity'. Rossi, at least, has the common decency to place his head in his hands and mutter, "Christ."'

In the late '60s, they'd go on stage in their Carnaby Street kaftan togs – the 'poof' clobber – only to find that the dolly birds would 'scream a darn sight louder for Amen Corner or the Love Affair or Marmalade than they did for us'. So they discovered gym shoes and denim and long hair and a dumb method of nodding the head and a kind of boogie music that Rick Parfitt eloquently describes thus: 'Durm-durm-durm-durm-durm. It's a sort of shuffle rhythm. There's something horny about it. You can stand there all night going durm-durm-durm-durm-durm, can't you?' 'Yeah,' agrees Rossi, 'that's how we became boring.' Durm-durm-durm-durm-durm and they never looked back.

They pioneered the hard rock/HM denim look. (In 1975 there was even a Quo brand of denim clobber available in the shops. Rossi: 'There was Quo jeans and Quo jackets and it was all in C&A and Woolworths and places like that. It was stuff no one would buy – wash it once and it went green. There's only one guy who ever bought it – a guy who's actually changed his name to Status Quo. He's got "Status Quo" tattooed on his neck and he's changed his name by deed poll. Status Quo. That's his name. He is Mr Quo and his friends call him Status . . .') They murdered John Fogerty's 'Rockin' All Over the World' and popularised the lame boogie (durm-durm) and they became a National Institution. They are like Marmite and they are like the ravens at the Tower of London. Like the Queen Mum and Cliff. They are just there and not an ounce of harm in them . . . yes, they are rubbish, aren't they, Status Quo?

'I've always liked Jim Reeves,' says Rick Parfitt (apropos, seemingly, of nothing). 'What I mean is we've never been the world's most fashionable band and our image has gone boring over the years with the jeans and stuff like that, but I think that's gone in our favour. That's why we are what you said – the Queen Mum.'

'When we did Live Aid,' says Francis Rossi (apropos, seemingly, of less), 'we were the only band on that bill not to have product out. Everybody else on that show had product to promote. And I thought, "Hang on, I thought we were doing this for charity!" And that's Quo, right?'

Outside in the cold of the skating rink auditorium, the people shuffle to music rasping from the p.a. (Survivor's 'Eye of the Tiger', mostly) as they wait for the evening's main feature. Any moment now there'll be these blokes up on the stage hopping about in plimsolls for an hour or so, shaking their manes to their pub-rock stuff. One of them (Rossi) will shout 'Shit!' very loudly into the microphone and the people will cheer the naughty slice of wit. Durm-durm-durm-durm-durm. Status Quo: the band that became a parody of itself.

'Yeah, it's right what you said about Quo,' Francis Rossi is telling me minutes before showtime. 'We're the Queen Mum. That's fine. I like the Queen Mum, me, so what if people say we're boring and only do three chords? There's no point in getting hung up about it.'

Rossi and Parfitt nod their wise old heads in unison.

'But sometimes,' says Rossi, 'sometimes, like when "Marguerita Time" came out, I was really desperate for that song to prove a point, although I don't know what the point I wanted to prove was . . . but I was listening to Capital Radio and they had that comedian on, that Richard Digance, and he played "Marguerita Time"

248

and he said, "Great to hear from them again, same old bleeding three chords." But there's two or three minors there in that song. If you're going to be totally honest, "Marguerita" is actually a six-chord track.'

Rossi is becoming quite heated here. Gone is the tiresome tomfoolery of farty lips as he defends the National Heritage that is Quo. 'Like, I always used to get laughed at when I was young because I was brought up with Italians and every wop in the world sings opera. I grew up with that. I'm not ashamed of it. And take "Nessun dorma", the basis of the choral section of that has three chords, "La donna è mobile", the basic section of it that everybody knows also has three chords. Verdi and Beethoven – quite a lot of that stuff is just three chords. So . . . so . . .'

'Um, yeah,' says Rick Parfitt, leaping to his colleague's crumbling defence. 'And . . . "Whatever You Want" has *five* chords.'

# Who the hell does John Lydon think he is?

## *Q*, June 1994

The interview, *Q* vs Lydon, should have taken place several months ago, but when I turned up on his Fulham doorstep and rang his bell, he failed to invite me into his lovely home. 'Go away!' the unmistakable voice came whining from the entryphone. 'I'm fucked up. Go away!' I went away.

Fortunately, all this time later, the singer now has 'fresh product' to promote – his punk rocker memoirs, *Rotten: No Irish, No Blacks, No Dogs* — and so, in a First Class carriage of an Intercity train bound for Manchester (where he is to sign copies of the book for his adoring public), he is holding court. Ever the arch exhibitionist, he is showing off again. The trademark toxic glare is very much in evidence, the baggy, ballooning suit can only be described as comical, the voice swoops wildly, his every word an upper-case italic, as he moans about how extremely *BORED* he is just sitting there on platform 15 and why can't the train just GO! (Well, possibly because this is the three o'clock train and it's not quite ten to . . .) 'Doesn't the driver know *I'M* aboard?' he wheezes, swivelling those piercing eyes like a man possessed. 'Could he not feel the waft of arrogance as I walked down the platform? I'm HERE now, driver. We can GO.' A high-pitched snigger (another Rotten trademark:

'Heh, heh, heh, cough, splutter, heh,' it goes) serves as the full stop to the comedic interlude.

Yes, Lydon, the boy who was Rotten, is arrogant alright. In *Rotten: No Irish. . .* the co-author (he had more than a little help from his friends) admits as much with glee. No one is safe from his scathing insults – Malcolm McLaren and Glen Matlock and the Clash and Cliff and Elton ('a fat buffoon') and the teacher who expelled him from school (Johnny later pissed on Mr Prentiss's grave) and poor old Bill Grundy, scorned and savaged all – except for himself. He invented punk rock all by himself, and his withering sarcasm and his ability to annoy are marks of genius. And the Johnny Rotten persona was a brilliant creation of Lydon's making; believe it or no, 'Johnny Rotten' was based on Laurence Olivier in *Richard III*. Pardon? 'Having seen it aeons ago,' he writes, 'I took influences from Olivier's performance. I had never seen a pop singer present himself quite that way. It wasn't the norm. You're supposed to be a nice pretty boy, sing lovely songs and coo at the girlies. Richard III would have none of that. He got the girls in other ways.' But he says, 'Oh, you shouldn't believe everything you read, dear boy!' How Johnny loves to contradict himself. 'Arrogance is something I have aspired to and something that didn't come naturally. It's been perfected. It's a skill that I had to learn. I did a crash course through the Pistols.'

Lydon claims he's given up beer – 'I've had a spot of the Botticellis' – but when the PR woman from the publishing company goes to the buffet, it is beer Lydon calls for. This is a relief: John without beer and belching just wouldn't be John, somehow.

It's nearly twenty years now since this swaggering figure shocked the world by throwing up in airports, by throwing 'filth' at our 'pop kids', by throwing abuse at our own dear Queen. In the book, he appears to claim, 'What do I appear to claim in the book? I haven't read it yet, heh heh heh . . .' In the book, he appears to claim that

251

'God Save the Queen' was some kind of act of revolution, that he single-handedly paved the way for the monarchy's present travails and parlous condition.

'Yeah, it's just bog-standard conversation now, isn't it, being rude about the royals? But that's the way life is. Somebody does it first, gets their head chopped off for it, and then it's alright. The only thing I feel sorry about is that Fergie did it ever so much better than me, heh heh heh, which is a real pisser. It makes me really like her, her whole attitude from start to finish was wonderful: milk it for all it's worth and then leave the sinking ship. I don't mind Fergie wanting to keep the curtains in her new luxurious manor. Why not? Much better than going out and buying a new set of Laura Ashley prints, isn't it?'

It's nearly twenty years since the boy brought a chapter of musical history to a close at San Francisco's Winterland, crouching on the stage and grumbling, 'Ever get the feeling you've been cheated?', the Sex Pistols' famous last words. What a terrible racket the group made that night; one has always imagined that the words were directed at the audience, but no. As Lydon tells it, he was asking himself the question – because the Sex Pistols had been a 'disaster' from start to finish.

'Ever get the feeling you've been cheated? Yeah, I was talking about myself and the band and everybody really all-round. It's not a bad observation to have made. It's just fact, you know. It was just the whole sorry sourness of it all. The Sex Pistols just became a publicity fiasco rather than something with actual content and purpose. All that was thrown by the wayside and we ended up as some sorry rock 'n' roll sad, sad thing that I didn't want to be a part of.'

In the beginning it was three blokes who couldn't play (well, Glen Matlock could, a bit) and one bloke who couldn't sing, in a rehearsal room, loathing one another. 'I still can't sing,' Lydon says with evident pride. 'My voice is an instrument of torture and that's good enough for me. I'm an expressionist.' A Situationist? 'Ooh, no, no, certainly not that. No poncey Left Bank politics from Paris for me.' Steve Jones and Paul Cook, the wideboys, wanted the band to be like the Faces. Johnny Rotten, the arty one, very much did not. Glen Matlock dug the Beatles; Johnny didn't. Why did he persevere with this seemingly hopeless project?

'Because what else was there to do? It never occurred to me to be in a band and to make music. They tried to get me to sing "Maggie May"! It was impossible. It should never have worked. Every day it just seemed to get worse – pitfalls, booby traps and mines. You must understand that when I joined the Sex Pistols, I had no prospects whatsoever and this was my last chance to do something and I tried to use it to the best of my ability, without being a cliché. I gave myself some weird disciplines and rigid morality codes to try to work things out in. I made it work.'

Yes, in the end it did work, didn't it? They swore on the telly and then they made some of the most exciting records ever and then they broke up.

'We could have been the weediest band ever. But it couldn't have worked without Steve being as structurally limited as he was. I found it absolutely thrilling to be next to him on a stage, the power that would come out of that poxy little amp with usually three strings, because that's all he could remember to hit at one point . . . But Glen's tunes I never came to terms with very well – too many memories and Beatles influences in there that I found completely unrefreshing. They would always remind me of my mum and dad's record collection, everything Glen ever did. He'd turn out some crappy old Beatles thing on a Dansette. Not very nice.

'I think what I learned in the Pistols was that I never wanted to write a love song in my entire life: it was a daily battle in rehearsal rooms because that's what they insisted I should be doing. They always wanted me to write love songs. Always. Seriously, Malcolm wanted some kind of, like, naughty version of the Bay City Rollers and that's what Glen wanted with his Soho poof's ideas. I had no training, no nothing, so I had no fears. My subject matters would be not based on anything previous at all. That's the best way to be. Ignorance leaves you without fear. It is a wonderful tool.'

John Lydon downs a can of beer, opens another, belches a satisfyingly loud belch, much to the consternation of fellow First Class 'customers'.

The Sex Pistols' encounter with Bill Grundy on the telly, the episode that prompted some daft bugger to kick his TV set in and worked the tabloid newspapers up into a froth of gleeful indignation, was shown again on Channel 4 the other night. And looking back on it, one is hard-pressed to recall what the fuss was all about. It was so tame. And that Johnny Rotten fellow appeared to be so timid.

'Yeah, but I'm sure that Kenneth Tynan [first person to use the F-word on the box] would look timid now, too. That's the point, small steps. But, yes, it is staggering to look back on all that and to see how pale it all was. When you look back on that, you really feel embarrassed. People should really feel sorry for me. A lot of what the Sex Pistols did was so tame, but you have to look at it in terms of history. There's no point in shocking people these days, there's no gain in it. It's trivial. I've got other emotions to tamper with.'

Are Nirvana 'shocking'? Are they the Sex Pistols of the 1990s? I ask the punk philosopher, knowing full well with what scorn the enquiry will be greeted.

'Huh!' he goes and rolls his eyes. 'Huh! Well, that's Rory Gallagher, isn't it? That's the Rory Gallagher fan club. You take one look at those shirts and that's it. Those shirts just put me off. I'm sorry. Nirvana should lay off the Black Sabbath albums. Although I can see the good in everything – except for Guns N' Roses, for some peculiar reason. Actually, I was going to work with him, Kurt [Cobain], at some point last year. Kurt and me were going to meet but he would only meet me if I would take him to the zoo, him and his kid. It was just bizarre. I wasn't walking around a bloody zoo with him and his brat!'

In the autobiography, Lydon makes the astonishing revelation that Paul McCartney once expressed a desire to work with the spikey-topped star, too.

'Yeah, but I think he only wanted to do that to amuse his kids. Jesus! Things like that are just daft. They are embarrassing to remember. And I handled that all very badly because I just shied away without confronting it, locked myself in a room rather than cope with it, because it just made me feel so middle-aged all of a sudden. It was so hurtful. It was the industry getting back at me in the worst way possible. Oh, John, Paul would lurve to make a record with you. Oh my God! What have I done wrong? Has it come to this? You can't do that kind of thing. You just turn into Johnny Showbiz. You might as well call yourself Matt Monro or Des O'Connor and pack up your troubles. That's when you're looking for the pension and you end up doing these dreadful charities, singing along with all the old farts, a big jam session at the end with 100,000 people thinking it's splendid. It's not. It's horrible. It's misery. Live Aid would have been spectacular and great if only three people had turned up . . .'

John rants on, spilling bile on charity concerts and 'Free Nelson Mandela', for several centuries. Charity concerts really get John's goat. But then so does almost everything. Glen Matlock (fed with a spunk sandwich at one point in the book)?

'No, I don't hate Glen,' he corrects. 'It's just his lifestyle to me is deeply silly. He was frightened of "God Save the Queen" because his mummy wouldn't like it and he thought the song was about fascism, which it certainly was not. It's funny that the only person in the country who came to that conclusion was Glen Matlock – and he was the bass player. But there again, before I formed Public Image, I don't think anybody ever listened to bass players.'

The Clash?

'Joe Strummer's never been over-endowed with wisdom, has he? I never liked that band. I always thought they were far too serious and far too childish. It was sloganeering. Pick up a copy of Karl Marx, underline a few sentences and call that "attitude". It's just daft.'

The Sex Pistols after John had quit the band?

'That "Frigging in the Rigging", everything that went on after I left, was just awful. They shouldn't have carried on that way. It ruined it, completely shattered it. We should have ended with a full stop in San Francisco but they kept on and on at it and it's been to their detriment ever since. Going to Brazil to see bloody Ronnie Biggs – I found all that embarrassing and childish and stupid. I'm very bitter about that element of it. I don't applaud liars and cheats and thieves. There was nothing clever about that. People that hurt people to steal other people's money: where's the fun in that? Disgraceful.'

Malcolm McLaren, the self-styled Svengali of Pop (or something)?

'Malcolm was scared of me. I wasn't the stupid little gobshite that he originally perceived me to be, so he did his best to wreck the American tour. Him and Vivienne [Westwood] are manipulators; they like to manipulate the gullible. I took them on at their own game so they tried to write me out and pretend I'd never existed after I'd written some of those songs that put them on the map. That was annoying and very hurtful.'

Nancy Spungen, Sid Vicious's idiotic American girlfriend (deceased)?

'No, I think Nancy could have been a decent person. It's impossible for me to imagine, but I could go on for years about Nancy. It would make a stunning play. Or *Nancy: The Musical.* Imagine that. Opening scene on some toilet, a massive shooting party going on. No, Nancy was dreadful. I don't feel bad about speaking ill of the dead, not at all. I mean, I'm hardly nice to the living, am I, now I come to think of it?'

Sid himself? Does Lydon feel any guilt about Sid's death? Does he feel he could have done more to keep his oft-preposterous friend away from all those frightful drugs?

'Yes, well, that is, unfortunately, getting into hindsight, which is a thing I don't like. I don't know what I could have done to save Sidney. What could I do – hide his Lou Reed albums? I suppose that would have been a good start, because he did believe all that drugs and rock 'n' roll nonsense to be something marvellous. He just did not see the humour in Lou Reed at all. He missed that completely. And then he had Nancy telling him that he was the real star of the Sex Pistols and Malcolm was doing that too and he believed it. And through the years, Sid has been mythologised to the point where he's seen as some kind of superhero when, I'm sorry, but the reality is very different. He was just stupid, bent on a slow suicide, which should not be seen as something graceful or skilful or smart. It's just sad and stupid.'

The beers are slipping down a treat. Lydon talks of his glittering career as a Hollywood actor (ten years ago he appeared in the not-very-good *Order Of Death* alongside Harvey Keitel). 'Harvey's really famous now, isn't he? I like to think I helped him along the way, heh heh heh. I still get offered parts in films but the offers are so appalling, you just don't want to know. I don't like doing films. The endless takes, you just get *BORED*. Good actors have to be incredibly dull people because if you've got any kind of personality at all, it's just not going to work. But I heard I got a bit in *In The Name of the Father*. Apparently, I'm on a poster in the prison. It makes the film, dear boy. I should get an Oscar for that.'

He talks of Chrissie Hynde, who Lydon once agreed to marry (immigration reasons) in exchange for two quid, then chickened out and sent Sid Vicious along as groom substitute (but, of course, Sid was too blotto to make it to the altar). 'Why didn't I marry Chrissie? Need you ask? Listen to any of her albums. No, to my mind you don't make commitments like that lightly because it would have been a lifelong commitment. I could definitely feel that there was a clinging going on with Chrissie which I didn't want none of, thank you. I have a fear of being mothered, I suppose. Women just want to mother me and smother me in marriage.'

Does Nora (Mrs Lydon) mother and smother you?

'No. Not at all, not at all. She won't let me get away with anything.'

Are you frightened of your wife?

'Yes, very much so.'

Is she the only person in the world you are frightened of?

'I think so. Oh, yes. Well, apart from my father, actually, because I can't fool him, not at all, not about anything.'

What did your father make of the Sex Pistols' 'outrage', the airport puking and like unsavoury antics?

'(*Adopts Irish accent*) Oh, Jaysus, John, you're a fockin' disgrace! He thought we were throwing our lives away, which I must admit I felt we were doing many a time. It did all seem rather useless. Life is so disappointing and mediocre. That's why I want more of it, heh heh heh . . .'

Finally, he slumps back in the First Class seat, yawns, belches and, for no evident reason, turns his attention to the subject of baldness. 'Howard Devoto [one-time singer with the Buzzcocks and Magazine] just gave up, didn't he? He went bald. It's very difficult when you're bald. People tend not to take you seriously. It's the end of your life. Coming back and promoting this book and dealing with this Sex Pistols stuff all again, I'm amazed just how many people from that period are now bald. It amazes me. I always had very, very thin hair but Clairol and all the hair bleaches I've used over the decades have done wonders for me . . .'

The queue at Waterstones book shop in Manchester that patiently awaits the appearance of the punk rock star of yesteryear, here to scribble his exciting signature for the public delight, contains many a bald or balding person. There are men in shell suits with their Manchester United-shirted sons. There are what can only be described as grizzled hippies in overcoats of distressed condition.

There is a matron of middle years who bears an extraordinary resemblance to Elizabeth Taylor (bloated version). There is not a spiky-top or safety pin to be seen. And a strange dearth of leather. Where are you, punkers of yore? And when John sits at the book-stacked table to carry out his promotional chores, he is politeness itself, pressing the flesh, chatting to Peter 'Hooky' Hook out of New Order and saying 'Thanks for coming' to all and sundry in non-sarcastic tones. There's no gobbing, no larks with vomit, not even a lusty belch, this evening. Ever get the feeling you've been cheated? It is, as the saying goes, like punk never happened.

# Hibbert and I

## 'Did you know the Pale Fountains once refused to walk on a frozen canal?'

*Chris Heath*

I've a folder in an old filing cabinet, Tom's name on it, that I hadn't opened in a quarter of a century. There are dozens of articles I'd ripped out of newspapers and magazines, saved for the saving of it all. Today I'm randomly browsing through the errant genius of it all: an *Observer* Pendennis column, this one seemingly about watching England play cricket at the Oval until Tom explains apologetically – well, actually not all *that* apologetically – how by mistake he has turned up at the *Kerrang!* Awards instead; an article from the *Mail on Sunday*'s *Night & Day* magazine where Tom actually plays tennis with three veteran tennis stars (with photos: for added preposterousness, he's sporting a T-shirt showing Mexico's 1994 football team); a TV review column which begins – I've hit an improbable sporting seam – 'Among my many achievements in life is having once played croquet with one Huey Lewis, the singer out of that most irritating of American rock combos Huey Lewis and the News, and beaten him hollow. Mr Lewis sulked rather a lot after this sound thrashing . . .'; an article from *Details* magazine about gin, in which Tom reports offending the corporate spokesperson, who tells him, 'four bottles of Gordon's gin are consumed every second of the day and night' with the riposte 'Well, that's Elizabeth Taylor for you'; a page from what looks like *The Sunday Times* magazine about skinhead culture, concluding with the single-sentence paragraph 'Are you screwing my bird?'; a music column from long-forgotten *Top* magazine detailing Tom's ten favourite records of 1988. The first nine of these – a good Tom snapshot; for all his muttered asides that no one else was fit to darn Alex Chilton's socks, and the suchlike, he had open-eared broad taste – are by Dinosaur Jr, Velvet Elvis, the Bangles, Game Theory, Julian Cope, Salt-N-Pepa, Brian Wilson, Pia Zadora and Kim Wilde. The tenth is Gigantic Death Orgy's *Gospel Favourites and Eskimo Sick*. 'On this, their ninth LP,' he explains, 'the "Giges", as they are known to their countless fans, go all "introspective" . . .' and on and on he continues, describing a 'quite, quite beautiful' record whose only minor, entirely unmentioned shortcoming might have been its failure to exist.

Among all this writing, I also find a handwritten and drawn photocopied invitation to 'a garden so-called "party"' one July Saturday, at his and Allyce's house. It offers a list of 'Important things to remember', the first four of which are illustrated in an artist's-own drawing.

A.  Bring some grog (see Fig. 1).
B.  Bring a brolly (see Fig. 1) as it's certain to rain.
C.  Bring some galoshes (see Fig. 2) or something as it's bound to be a total washout.
D.  Bring a good book (see Fig. 3) in case you get bored.

When I first started to work occasional days in the *Smash Hits* office (day rate, if memory serves me, £27.50), I was assigned to help Tom writing 'Bitz', the miscellanea of news and other short stories at the front of the magazine. I was twenty-one. Tom was thirty-two, or so I can calculate now – at the time, and maybe always, he seemed kind

of ageless. I think I realised pretty quickly that he assumed I would turn out to be one more bright-eyed idiot who didn't quite 'get it'. I worried that he was right.

It was a good day, then, the first time he seemed to think of me somewhat less so. The least glamorous part of writing 'Bitz' was the interstitial brief news stories, announcing a new record or video in some slightly diverting way. The sentence which met with Tom's approval appeared on page 4 of the 14 February 1985 edition of *Smash Hits* among a column of equally helpful items about Shaka-tak, the Jonzun Crew and Zak Starkey. Appended to news of this particular group's imminent album and single, it stated: 'Astonishing Fact! The Pale Fountains once refused to walk on a frozen canal!!' (I knew this because Paul Rider, who presumably came by the office that day, had shared some version of this non-information from a recent *Melody Maker* photo shoot he'd done.)

Tom liked that. I guess I could make a torturous case as to *why* it may have chimed. How there was something glorious about the pure doubled-down banality of it – a not-interesting possible event hadn't happened. How it dramatised *Smash Hits'* endless Sisyphean joy and despair in finding ways to have a humdrum world be more interesting and entreatingly shaped than such a world easily allows, while refusing ever to fake it. But really it was no more than something that was just about half-amusing for a moment or two. Filled three lines. Did what it should.

If you weren't too much of a fool to realise it, you soon knew that the list of things you were never going to do as well as Tom was a long one. Being funny was only the most obvious; there were plenty more. So it felt like a great compliment whenever he treated you as worthy of coasting for an instant in his slipstream. Quietly, he was a fine teacher, and I would learn a great deal from him. Along the way, this first 'Bitz' moment became a kind of code, or touchstone, or password, between us. Much later, when our careers and lives had veered along separate paths, I might run into Tom somewhere, after not having seen him for many months, and he would sidle up to me, give me that owlish deadpan look.

'Did you know, old chap,' he'd say, 'that the Pale Fountains once refused to walk on a frozen canal?'

In the early months of the pandemic, I found myself reading the book *Niche: A Memoir In Pastiche*, by Scottish musician and artist Nick Currie, who works under the name Momus. It's a highwire-act autobiography in which Currie tells his own story by serially adopting the voices of great and distinctive prose stylists: Dylan Thomas, Franz Kafka, William Burroughs, Yukio Mishima, George Orwell, Albert Camus, James Thurber, and on and on and on. (As Currie writes in the introduction: 'So here they are, my heroes, brought back to life. They're discussing me. What narcissistic arrogance!')

It seemed perfectly fitting to me that on page 178, following Muriel Spark, Tom Hibbert takes over for a while. In those weird and disassociated times, and caught by surprise as I was, it was moving to find Tom there. Even if Currie's ventriloquism does, at times, veer towards a more generic mid-'80s *Smash Hits*-speak than inhabiting Tom's precise voice, he's well worthy of the honour and the context. Though, self-reflexively, it strikes me that the Tom who speaks in Currie's book would have doubtless considered the whole business a very rum do indeed.

Later, in that same issue of *Smash Hits* as the Pale Fountains news story, Tom interviewed Mick Jagger. It was a Q&A, and the first question was quite probably not the one Jagger was expecting.

*Hello. You're the very first person in the pop world to have been interviewed by me since Morrissey.*

'Morrissey? Who's that?' Jagger replied.

*The singer in the Smiths. A pasty-faced fellow, often quite ill. He's not quite as famous as you, of course . . .*

And, having gently thrown Jagger off balance and set the tone on his own terms, Tom was off. I think, as his career evolved, it sometimes got lost what a smart and canny interviewer he was. I always had mixed feelings about his *Q* magazine star turn 'Who the hell . . . ?' because, even though when it worked best it was magnificent, it risked making a kind of mannered stunt out of what Tom did naturally. He was a great, curious inquisitor who proceeded without fear or favour. Yes, he had a particular appreciation for those with a sense of their own ridiculousness, coupled with an ever-ready willingness, when faced with a less self-aware interviewee, to do the necessary heavy lifting for them. He sliced through pretension and pomposity and – maybe to him the greatest sin of all – being dull, with calm, superficially polite brutality. But – and this is the part I worry sometimes gets lost along the way – I don't believe that he did so as a snarky trick, or because he relished cutting people down to size, but because he had a true interest in what he was always hoping might lay beyond that.

I think 'Who the hell . . . ?' was supposed to be able to embrace all of this, but often I think you could feel the awkward tension from what its format relentlessly demanded, as though the moments where he wasn't taking someone down a peg or two were off-brand or off-message. His gift was greater than that. He may have eagerly played up to the most visible and obvious part of his persona, the grumpy contrarian and curmudgeon, but like the best curmudgeons, in truth he came at everything less with negativity than with a sense of disappointment that the world and its inhabitants so often fell short of their wondrous potential, and with a latent sense of excitement and expectation that this time they might not. He was a tremendous, and tremendously precise, enthusiast for when people got it right, capable of immense rejoicing at those moments when the world did not disappoint. What I think he really wanted, you might say, was to take the world up a peg or two.

There was one final item on that list of 'important things to remember' in Tom's July garden-so-called 'party' invitation. Like much else that he wrote, I guess it stands, then and now, as good enough advice. Says just what it says, and maybe a little bit more:

'Don't forget where you live, as you'll probably want to go home at some point.'

# Part Five

## Madcap grandees

Tom's personal pantheon of heroes was a narrow but select group of damaged cult figures (not including 'Fab Macca Whacky Thumbs Aloft'). In these three great pieces, Tom is at his least sarcastic and most reverential, plus Bob Stanley remembers his journalistic hero.

Tom with 'Fab Macca' doll, 1984 (photo by Paul Rider).

*'The real old farts – Neil Young, David Crosby – are great, people like Alex Chilton and Arthur Lee. I'm talking brain damage, basically. Meeting Roky Erikson at his mother's house was really sad. I took him out for a meal, took him to a charity shop. There was no communication. He'd point at cuddly bears and ask, "What is that?" But I enjoy that weird situation more than a straightforward sit-down interview, because you can write about it and put colour into it. Or meeting Arthur Lee, who was as mad as a meat axe. I met him in a hotel on Ladbroke Grove, watching that bloke with the sideboards who does the racing, John McCririck, and he spent the whole interview saying, "What is that guy on?" I loved that. Roger McGuinn invented my life, basically, because I think the Byrds were the best group ever, but when I met him he was a completely boring arsehole.'*

Tom Hibbert, 2001

# Arthur Lee: Right church, wrong pew

## Q, July 1992

*'I feel real phoney when my name is Bill.'* This may not mean very much to the younger generation, but for those who struggled through adolescence in the late 1960s, the line (from 'The Red Telephone' on *Forever Changes* by Love) was . . . well, just sort of great.

You could live your life to a line like that. And then, from that same LP of 1967, there was *'Oh, the snot has caked against my pants/ It has turned into crystal'* and *'We're all normal and we want our freedom'* (cruelly parodied by the Bonzo Dog Band on *The Doughnut In Granny's Greenhouse*: *'We are normal and we dig Bert Weedon'*). *Forever Changes* was an album of such intensity of strength and beauty, with weirdness as a topping, that, for once, the word 'classic' means something, and it was clear to all perceptive teens that Love's singer/composer Arthur Lee was a giant among poets. It was also clear that, like all giants among poets, Arthur Lee was scarcely normal at all . . .

The passing of the years has turned Arthur Lee into a bloke of Rock Legend. He ranks right up there with Brian Wilson and Syd Barrett, on the podium just above Roky Erickson and Sky Saxon, as one of pop's Madcap Grandees. Like Brian, like Syd, Arthur Lee (who at one point preferred to be known as Arthurly and at another as plain old Arthur Two Ex-Lax) started out by creating music of genius and then went, not to put too fine a point on it, mad.

Conversations between old hippie types invariably turn to Arthur Lee sooner or later, and they always run like this: 'I wonder what happened to poor old Arthur?' 'He's probably in the bin. Remember the wig? Ha ha!' 'Ha ha! I was playing *Da Capo* last night. Poor old Arthur . . .' But not anymore. Arthur has returned. He has not released a record since *Arthur Lee*, solo album, in 1981; he hasn't released anything of substance for some twenty years. But now he has a new band called Love and a new LP to remind one that a) his voice, which can turn on a sixpence from silky Nat King Cole to gruff punk rocker, is a wonderful thing; b) he always could write a lovely song (or a crazy one, too); c) he is still engagingly eccentric.

Arthur was flying in to London for a promotional trip and two shows, so rumour had it. But Arthur wasn't at his hotel at the appointed time. This wasn't altogether surprising: his reputation for never being quite where he is supposed to be (the recording studio or the concert hall) had gone before him. Two hours later, his young American manager came into the hotel foyer with Arthur's suitcase and said that there had been this 'hassle' at Immigration (Arthur had forgotten to bring his work papers) but that Arthur was here now. Except he wasn't. 'Oh,' explained the manager, 'yeah, see, Arthur's here, we just drove up now, but Arthur's gone to find a tobacco shop.' A tobacco shop? His first time in London in God knows how many years and the first thing Arthur does is go to find a tobacco shop. A tobacco shop? Did the manager not know the story about Arthur and the LA concert debacle of 1981? Well, so it's said, there was Arthur on stage with this band in this club playing old Love songs, which were being recorded for a live album when, halfway through the set and in the middle of a tune, Arthur decided he was feeling peckish, so he put down his guitar, climbed down from the stage, walked through the audience, out the door, across the street and into a supermarket. Nobody saw him again for months . . .

There are lots of stories like the concert-flounce yarn about Arthur Lee and his peculiarities; most of these, the Love Master has never felt inclined either to confirm or deny: so often in abeyance, he has granted few interviews in his career and those he has given have been nigh incomprehensible (read on for the latest example). From tales of eccentricity, the Legend of Arthur Lee has been fashioned . . .

It started in Los Angeles in 1965, a band called Grass Roots playing in a tiny club called Bido Lito's, Kenny Forssi, Johnny Echols, ex-Byrds roadie Bryan Maclean, Don Conka and this handsomely funny-looking bloke from Memphis called Arthur, who was about nineteen (his actual date of birth has never been confirmed). Arthur was rather strange: he used to walk around all the time with only one shoe on and wearing these triangular spectacles with one blue lens and the other red (and psychedelia hadn't been invented yet). There was another group called Grass Roots so Arthur Lee's band changed their name to Love and, signed to Elektra Records (the label's first rock band), released their first LP, *Love*. On the cover, Arthur Lee had a lighted cigarette stuck in his ear; on the record, he sang about hard drugs, which was most *outré* at the time.

Arthur Lee wanted to make pots of money and he demanded that the record company erect a giant billboard featuring the celebrated Love logo (a design, incidentally, that Lee was once fond of claiming as his own creation, though it was the work of another) on Sunset Strip. But then he made the mistake of introducing Elektra boss Jac Holzman to a group called the Doors and Holzman signed them. It was the Doors, not Love, who got the Strip billboard. It was the Doors, not Love, who sold lots of records and became teen idols. All of which made Arthur hopping mad . . .

According to Jerry Hopkins, Love's first manager, Arthur Lee was the very first person in Los Angeles to 'walk around on acid twenty-four hours a day'. Perhaps this accounts for Arthur's unusual relationship with his hair. (Arthur hair stories include: he once bought a wig that he hoped would turn him into Brian Jones – 'I look in the mirror and I see a Rolling Stone,' he said; then he tried to iron his thatch into a spectacular new style, but the procedure went awry and it caught fire – as seen in Michael Jackson Pepsi-Cola commercials; the moment he saw Jimi Hendrix, according to Holzman, 'he went right out and bought a fright wig'; once, in a fit of pique, he shaved his head bare; later, he took to wearing an Afro wig but it didn't fit properly.)

Perhaps this also accounts for Arthur's unusual relationship with his band. At one point the members of Love were ensconced together in a *Munsters*-styled horror mansion in LA and they didn't get on at all well. 'They got big heads,' complained Arthur. 'Snoopy can't hold a beat,' complained Arthur about Alban 'Snoopy' Pfisterer (drummer who had replaced Conka for the second LP, *Da Capo*, and found the frenzy of Arthur's '7 & 7 Is' rather hard to manage). After *Forever Changes*, Arthur sacked the lot of them. In '69, he hired a new Love, sterling musos, for the excellent *Four Sail* and for the deranged *Out Here* (barking double album featuring, on 'Doggone', a song about Arthur's pet dog who'd left home and a stupendously awful and lengthy drum solo). They all walked out on him as they didn't understand his peculiar ways. He hired another Love for 1970's barmily engaging *False Start* (which had Jimi Hendrix on the opening track). They all walked out on him, too. 'I called the album *False Start* because I made a false start with Love but now I'm gonna show the real music inside of me,' said Arthur. Brave words. Nothing much happened for the following two decades. There was a staggeringly loud and disturbed-sounding solo album, *Vindicator*, in '72, a brand new soul-brother-type Love who made the dull *Reel to Real* LP the following year. The rest was silence. And stories . . .

In 1970, Arthur Lee and Love, the *Four Sail* line-up, staggered into Reading University to play a show. They were headlining over

Mighty Baby. It was not a good night. For an hour or more, while his band tried hard to play marvellous Lee songs like 'August' and 'A House is not a Motel' and 'She Comes in Colours' behind him, Arthur just stood there slumped over his guitar with his tongue hanging out, swaying slightly, not singing, not playing, just staring and staring at nothing. He had no hair that night. He was a Legend.

And the Legend has returned. Not just back from obscurity but, much to my surprise, from the tobacco shop. I enter Arthur Lee's cramped and modest hotel room and there he is, hair intact and impressively unkempt, sprawled upon the bed looking up at the tiny TV that's playing Channel 4 Racing. John McCririck, the daft bloke with the deerstalker and the side-whiskers who waves his arms about and shouts about betting odds, is on the screen. Arthur is enthralled. 'Man,' he says as he gazes at the telly. 'That guy is really weird!' He flicks the ash from a cigarette into an ashtray that is filled with loose change, twists his body so that he's lying on his back, smiles up at me and, in his husky Southern slur that suggests otherworld-liness in itself, says, 'Helllloooo, man. How do yo do?' Then he laughs. 'Hahahahaha.'

*It has been years since the world heard of Arthur Lee. Why has it been so long?*
'Because I got involved in a lot of difficulties. My stepfather was dying of cancer and I went home to take care of him and I just said, "To hell with the music for a while," and when I said that, they were all busy cashing in on my dough, uh, whatever that would mean. I had to look at myself to be a sort of normal normal, man. I stayed away from myself because I was having a good time but it was a drag. I threw my stuff out in the street because I got tired of the fame thing. I wanted to be an everyday Joe. I wanted to see how that everyday life was and now that I've seen that that stinks, I want to make Love better than it ever was. You can't put Love on a scale. Love is

273

the omnipotent supreme. I like good music, man. *(Sings)* 'Chestnuts roasting on an open fire . . .' I like good music. Hahaha! Know what I mean?'

*There's been a rumour that you've been away so long because you spent some time in an institution.*
'Oh, man, you know, the sparrow sings, the sparrow dies. I learned a long time ago there's more than one way to skin a cat if you're in the cat-skinning business, you know. And there's more than one cat to skin. So let's get skinning! The reason I'm here now is because of God Almighty and I really appreciate that because He loved me first and that's why I love God. So I wanted to sing for God first and then myself and then the people. It's a chore, man. You have to sit up and sing your song! But I want to sing my song. I hear a lot of things that sound like my things on the radio from a long time ago. The Fuzztones call me up and they played "7&7 Is" on the Fuzztones' album. Alice Cooper did it and somebody called Bob did it, I don't know his name, whatever. So a lot of people do what I do because there's nobody who can sing like me. Copy that!'

*You were influential from the start, weren't you? The Leaves stole your version of 'Hey Joe' and had a hit with it.*
'Yes, they did! It's weird! Not only that, they asked for the words and Johnny Echols gave them the wrong ones on purpose and the song became a number one in LA. That's the truth, man.'

*And you invented the Doors.*
'I helped the Doors a lot, man. I got the Doors on Elektra Records. The Doors . . . I made the Doors. Loving your neighbour as yourself and praying for those who trespass against you, that's a difficult task, man. It is. I've learned not only to forget but to forgive and the forgiving thing is really something. There's all these people

who have done things to me, said slandering things about me, talking about me, the worst things. I just want to do my horns and strings and things like that as well as my punk shit.'

*Do you feel bitter that Love were never as famous as they deserved to be?*
'Bitter? There's a book called *Roots* by Alex Haley, you know, one should know who one is. My mother's white, my father's brown, black, whatever, you know . . . my mother looks white, anyway. My father was a cornet player, my mother played piano. My mother's ninety years old now. In February, she's ninety years old. I just feel good about what I'm doing. I'm glad to be here to live because this is not a permanent place, it's just a few minutes, your life, man. You change, the next thing you're looking in the mirror and there's somebody else in there. Me, fortunately, I've been able to hang on to the same old *(sings)* baby face . . . hahaha . . . It's cool! I've got all my organs and parts working in here. I'm having a ball. I really enjoy London. Thank you. Jimi Hendrix was here one time in London when I was here.'

*You were a friend of Jimi Hendrix.*
'Yeah. Well, he came to my house once and he told me, he said, You know, I have enough money to buy five houses like these, why am I living in a motel? I didn't say anything. I was a vegetarian at the time. I was a vegetarian for five years. I felt everybody should be a vegetarian, hahaha. I felt, Whatever I am, everybody should be that. I know the way, this is the way . . . well, you know, that's a bunch of baloney, man. I wasn't here to see the first wind blow and I won't be here to see the last.'

*What was Hendrix like?*
'I don't know how the birds are fed everyday if the humans don't feed them. What was Jimi like? We got along together, we sort of had the same behaviour patterns except for the flip-flop thing.'

*The flip-flop thing?*
'Flip-flop? Er, peaches in both back pockets. Gingerbread man. You know what I'm saying? But I don't like to criticise any behaviour pattern of any person, you know, you're going to die of a fever or a cold anyway . . .'

*How would you describe your current 'behaviour pattern'?*
'I try to express my feelings through my music. But that's quite contrary to my everyday lifestyle. I'm mostly a loner. I don't want much. I don't like birthday parties too much, anyway. To die with unfinished songs, man, that would be a drag.'

*Is it true that you used to only wear one shoe?*
'Yeah. I walked about with only one shoe for about a year and a half. I was young, man. Anything it took to be recognised. I had triangle glasses. I still have those glasses. And one shoe on whether it was raining or not. Except if I had to go to a restaurant. If I had to go to a restaurant, I wore one moccasin. Sometimes they would deny me entrance.'

*It's been said that in the early days of Love you were on LSD twenty-four hours a day.*
'Who are you talking about? You're talking about LSD, right? I don't know what you're talking about, man. I've seen quite a few things in my day, I have to admit. But I haven't seen any coloured balls falling for quite a considerable amount of years. And if I do, it's just raindrops falling through a window.'

*Love's first LP contained an early example of an anti-drugs song, 'Signed DC'.*
'I didn't write a song about that. I wrote a song about the District of Columbia. "Signed DC". If you want to stop taking drugs, stop taking drugs, try shoe-shining – that's a good interest – shoot marbles or be an alcoholic or a Born Again Christian. You've got your

choice. It's up to you. It's not up to me. If you're a Born Again Christian, keep it to yourself. I've never been strung out on drugs. I've never been strung out on any particular thing. Alcohol. Alcohol helped me a lot. I could sit there and think about what I wanted to do but I was too lazy to get up and do it. It started with a beer. *(Sings)* And then it happened . . . you took me by surprise . . . sweeter than wine . . . hahaha . . . *(gazing up from a supine position at John McCririck on the telly)*. Man, that guy is weird!'

*The original Love fell apart after* Forever Changes. *What went wrong?*
'Love? I started that name, man. I thought of that name, Love. It was my idea. The whole Love thing, man, it's not a household word yet, it's not like the Deadheads or Madonna, but I hope it will be because I want to make Love a nice four-letter word. I started that name, Love. Bill Graham, that's my friend but he passed away, but I used to play the Fillmore West, Fillmore East and I played the Colosseum in Denmark and I played a bunch of places. I went on tour with Eric Clapton. Boy, what a drag that was! I had a cold look at life then, huh? Shaved my head and everything. I was in the right church in the wrong pew. But the more I think about *Forever Changes* and the things I've done in the past, I like my music more than anybody's music I've ever heard . . . That didn't sound too corny, or anything?'

*Going back to the original Love . . . You were once quoted as saying that all the other members got too big-headed, so they had to go.*
'Well, the thing about it was, they got big-headed. But it wasn't just those guys, it was myself, as well. I got that swollen head thing. I was wearing a guy's jacket and here's Love, man, it's the Beatles. Shit! I couldn't care less about all that stuff.'

*Do you find it bemusing to be one of rock's great 'legends'?*
'I am Arthur Lee, whatever that means. I never knew about the Legend thing. I don't hardly ever read articles about myself because

I know what I say. I say the same thing over and over, just about. All it is is I got a black and white band together and I named them Love and then it became more important and the more I went back into my childhood and fooled around and got in trouble and carried on with foolishness, the more Love meant to me. God is Love. And the name means I have to act accordingly. I intend to do the best I can to carry on for as long as I can because my music, it don't mean a thing if it ain't got that swing! And I'm not gonna die, man. I'm just going to try to figure out this woman thing and where I'm going . . . hahaha . . . You know what I'm saying? *(Sings)* "Ooh-ooh-ee, baby, baby". Hahaha . . . I love Smokey Robinson . . .'

# Roky Erickson: His own private realm

## *Mojo*, June 1995

On the fringes of Austin, Texas – down past the jumbo shopping zones and the fast-food outlets designed to resemble gigantic sombreros and the like – there's a down-at-heel porno store. 'Wayne Bobbit: Uncut – The Video', it advertises in letters peeling from a makeshift sign. Cut through behind this dignified emporium and you'll see a battered shack with hardly a window to its name; and from this dilapidated pile you'll hear coming all manner of strange music and voices, a cacophonous melange of sound. You have arrived. You have reached the residence of Roger 'Roky' Erickson, one-time leader of Austin's psychedelic music pioneers the 13th Floor Elevators and long-time 'cult legend', a hero to those who like their idols 'dysfunctional' and bizarre *in extremis*.

We slip inside this house, Roky's friend King Koffee (drummer of the Butthole Surfers) and I, through the unlocked screen door, and it really is a different and strange 'ambience', a set-up from some low-budget, out-of-focus horror flick, that I spy. All over the living room space there are TVs – old TVs, several of the monochrome persuasion – all turned on, all tuned to a different channel. News, cartoons, sports with cars in, a woman in a leotard working out, flicker away and babble in competition. In competition with the several radios – again tuned to different stations – that are fed through ancient valve amplifiers to create a 'music', an impressive and horrifyingly loud mixture of country, hard rock and traffic reports that hasn't even been invented yet.

Wires trail all over the shop, vying for space with the magazines strewn carelessly about the darkened room. In one corner, an ancient word processor is switched on, its screen all green and shaky and covered in layers of dust. On the walls, advertisements ripped from journals – ads for anything from running shoes to ice cream – are pinned up in random, willy-nilly fashion. Multimedia indeed, with no apparent purpose. Oliver Stone, you should be living at this hour. And in an adjoining room – well, you could hardly grace it with the word 'room', as the shack has the consistency of a pre-fab from hell – lies Roky on his mattress, with no shoes on, watching another elderly telly, seemingly oblivious to the white noise around him.

He gets up from the bed and greets me with a warmth that is touching indeed, all back pats and believable smiles and (possibly) small talk. Although over this preposterous racket I can't hear a word he is saying, and he surely can't hear mine. (His latest single, on King Koffee's own Trance Syndicate label, is called 'We Are Never Talking' – how very apt in these surroundings.) Roky's top front teeth are worn down to fangs of minimalism and his hair is matted and his trousers hardly fit at all, but you can still see the outline of a beautiful boy, which is what he was. Back then. Before, due to unforeseen circumstances, he decided he was a stranger to Texas and the world, an alien from Mars and insisted upon having that fact notarised . . .

Let me take you back then. To Texas in the mid-'60s. California or London was where it was all 'happening', we've been told, but with a peppering of our trusty friend hindsight it is simple to see why the 13th Floor Elevators are often credited with having 'discovered' psychedelic music. They were barmy from the start.

'The most noticeable thing about the Elevators was their rationalisation of their environment and way of life,' wrote Larry Sepulvado in *Mother Magazine* in 1968. 'Though there has always been a religious connotation linked with drugs throughout history, the religious ramifications that the Elevators attributed to them was unprecedented in rock music.' No, I don't know what he was rambling on about either, but notice that 'was', a past tense in 1968 – the Elevators already almost a thing of history. What a sorry state things had come to. Their first LP, *Psychedelic Sounds* (1966), was an item of no little genius. Mind-altering Music for Texans, a novel concept. But Tommy Hall, another prime Elevator, was greatly given to saying things like 'Man has the power to identify with anything. If you want to turn yourself into a Coke bottle you can, and it's much easier on psychedelics', and other nonsenses.

And Roky? He was tongue-tied from the start, preferred to play the part of 'child God with the voice of an angel', as one writer put it in *Not Fade Away* magazine, back in 1975. But when he DID talk, well . . . There's an old and odd and rather brilliant Elevators song called 'Fire Engine' (on *Psychedelic Sounds*, subsequently covered by Television). Roky talked about that once, a million years ago. The song had a line in it which went, *'Let me take you to the empty place'*. Roky: 'We would actually say, "Let me take you to de empty place", and it would sound like a spade saying "the empty place" like Uncle Remus, and he says, "Let me take you to DMT place", which is DMT, which is dimethyltryptamine, which gives you a trip for fifteen minutes of beautiful hallucinations. What you do is smoke it and you hold it in as long as you can and you can feel it going into your skin. It just penetrates and all of a sudden everything is spinning like fire engine wheels. So we said, "Let me take you to DMT place" and it was like a fire engine ride without the calamity of a fire, as if all the negativity could be taken away from the fire itself.'

The sleevenotes of *Psychedelic Sounds*, meanwhile, had this to say: 'Recently, it has become possible for man to chemically alter his mental state and thus alter his point of view . . . He can then restructure his thinking and change his language so that his thoughts bear more relation to his life and his problems, thus approaching them more sanely. It is this quest for pure sanity that forms the basis of the songs on this album.'

Sanity? Oh, yes. Policemen in Texas were most impressed by the Elevators' professed admiration of narcotics. This was even before *Easy Rider*, remember, where the nasty rednecks stove in Jack's head and shoot Peter and Dennis from off their bicycles just because rednecks object to hair and drugs. So this group were constantly brushing up against the forces who confiscated equipment and tore amps to pieces looking for mind-altering evidence and would run the band out of the most conservative towns.

Sanity? Roky, King and I leave the Erickson homestead (Roky turns off not one electrical appliance) and, pausing only for King to feed Roky's cat who's called Black (well, actually, it isn't – Roky gave it some multisyllable name which King never got the hang of, and as it is King who comes round each day to feed it outside the Erickson portals, he thought it might be simpler to christen the thing 'Black'), we go past the porno mart and step into King's extremely unswish transportation device. Roky wants to go shopping. 'What were you watching on TV, Roky?' I ask. 'What was I watching? When? Just now? *Top Cat.* You know, that guy is WEIRD! He lives in a TRASHCAN! Can you believe that?'

'Do you remember Tom?' asks King Koffee of Roky as King negotiates his vehicle up the short dirt track before Wayne Bobbit Land. 'He met you in London, England, in 1980.' Roky: 'London, England? I went there. It's like Japan. It's the same as London in England. Did I go there? Are you hungry, King? Yeah?'

In King Koffee's old dumper truck, we drive out to a shack that is a Tex-Mex restaurant, Roky smoking cigarettes in the front and asking King to explain the intricacies of car ashtray technology to him.
'How do I do this, King?'
'You just flick the ash in, Roky.'
'Wow! Hey, like this?'
'You got it, Roky.'
Pause.
'How do I do this, King?'
'I told you, Roky. You just flick the ash in.'
'Hey! Like this?'
'That's right, Roky.'
King Koffee is a patient, dear man.
At the restaurant:
'This place is great. How did you find this place, King?'
'I was just driving by and there it was, Roky.'
'Really? Is that so? Is that so? . . . This place is great . . . How did you find this place, King?'
'Someone told me about it, Roky.'
'Is that so? This place is great. Blood, Sweat & Tears. D'y'all remember them, that band? I hated that band.'
I hated that band, too, goes me.
Roky looks at me with a beaming grin. 'Really? You hated them. That must mean your middle name is Alan. Is his middle name Alan, King?'
'Why don't you ask him, Roky?'
'Hub, huh, HUR! This place is GREAT!'
Etcetera.
As we leave the shack establishment, Roky takes his time at the door, bidding farewell to the proprietors who don't know him from Adam and who evidently consider him a trifle crazed. 'I'll be careful now!' says Roky. 'Thank you, thank you!' He waves. 'Seein' you! I'll be careful, now!'

'Roky's always saying that,' King whispers in my ear. 'I'll be careful. Most people say, Take care, now. But Roky . . . I don't know. I think it's to do with the electric shock treatment. He was taught to say that in the hospitals . . .'

The 13th Floor Elevators' second LP, *Easter Everywhere*, was released in 1967. By this time the group members were dipping into LSD with some abandon. Roky was writing extraordinary songs such as 'Slip Inside This House' – which featured the singalong refrain: 'If your limbs begin dissolving in the water that you tread/All surroundings are evolving in the stream that clears your head' – and live shows were centred around the killing of music as we then knew it: endless feedback, rhythmic incontinence, mad acid racket. God bless 'em.

In 1968, guitarist Stacy Sutherland was killed in a domestic dispute. In 1968, Roky was busted for a couple of pot-filled cigarettes, an imprisonable offence. He didn't want to go to chokey, so he convinced the authorities that he was insane and was sent to Austin State Hospital. He escaped, but failing to go on the run, deciding to resume his musical career, he was apprehended at a gig and sent to the Hospital for the Criminally Insane in Rusk, Texas. He was there for three years, fed all sorts of 'improving' drugs, given the electroshock treatment. (After his eventual release, he claimed he was still receiving electroshock 'therapy' from Rusk through the power lines.)

Roky was never quite right again. This is scarcely surprising. And yet give him a guitar and a mission to make music and he could be splendid just like before. 'Two-headed dog, two-headed dog, I've been working in the Kremlin with a two-headed dog.' That was his comeback single of 1975: 'Red Temple Prayer (Two-Headed Dog)' by Roky Erickson and Bleib Alien ('Bleib' being an anagram of 'Bible', as you can clearly see), produced by Doug Sahm (once of Sir Douglas Quintet and an enormous Texan hat).

In 1980, Roky's renaissance continued when Stu Cook of Creedence Clearwater Revival produced an LP known to fans as 'hieroglyph' because it had no proper title, just a spooky squiggle, by Roky Erickson and the Aliens. This contained such majestic madcap songs as 'Creature with the Atom Brain', 'I Walked with a Zombie' (both inspired by Roky's favourite shaky old black and white horror flicks and featuring the excellent arrangements and guitar playing of Duane 'Bird' Aslaksen, aka 'Dwalien') and 'Stand for the Fire Demon'.

By luck or happenstance, this waxing got the man a contract with CBS in England. He was brought, attended by a pair of humourless bodyguards, to publicise the LP in the summer of that year. I met him, my hero, in a CBS conference room. His hair was long, his beard was black, he was confused and so was I: I was the first person in the history of the world to interview Roky outside America ever. Impressed? No? I was. The interview, if one can call it that, went, edited, something like this . . .

Me: 'What is your song "Mine Mine Mind" about?'

Roky: 'Oh, it's just about Demonism and stuff like that, y'know.'

Me: 'What about "The Interpreter"? What's that about?'

Roky: 'What about it?'

Me: 'Is it about spies?'

Roky: 'Huh? . . . Spies?'

Me: 'Spies in Moscow . . .'

Roky: 'No, it's not about spies.'

Me: 'There's a line in it about Moscow . . .'

Roky: 'There's nobody in Moscow.'

Me: 'Never?'

Roky: 'No.'

Me: 'Why not?'

Roky: 'I don't know anybody in Moscow I like.'

Me: 'Oh. You once wrote a song called "President Ford is a Square Queer" . . .'

Roky: 'No, I think you did.'

Me: 'I did?'

Roky: 'Yeah.'

Me: 'Did I?'

Roky: 'Yeah.'

Me: 'Oh. Well, you once wrote a song about Bo Diddley . . .'

Roky: 'A song about Billy?'

Me: 'Bo Diddley.'

Roky: 'You wrote a song about Bo Diddley?'

Me: 'No, you did.'

Roky: 'Huh?'

Me: 'Do you like Bo Diddley?'

Roky: 'Yeah, sometimes I do. He was eaten up by the piranhas. He was in the Amazon or a river or something, y'know.'

Me: 'Doug Sahm was a witness when you had it notarised that you came from Mars . . .'

Roky: 'No, he said he came from Mars.'

Me: 'So you don't come from Mars?'

Roky: 'I come from somewhere. Or I don't . . . I don't really know. I'm not into that kind of a horror, I mean that meat kind of a horror. I'm more into being a kicking kind of a horror. Kick some-body's head off or something like that, y'know?'

Me: 'Let's talk about the 13th Floor Elevators . . .'

Roky: 'I don't like the Elevators.'

Me: 'Not at all?'

Roky: 'I think people today are a bunch of worms. I think a bunch of chicken shit . . . bastards at least.'

Me: 'Why?'

Roky: 'I don't know. I think they're all scared of something. I don't know what it is. They're scared of feet, I guess . . .'

Fifteen years later and Roky doesn't do interviews anymore. He long ago lost his CBS contract and lives on welfare and has been back on the inside. In 1990, he was charged with mail theft and appeared in federal court (he believed he was there to help the judge through a spiritual crisis). He was sent to the federal mental institution in Springfield, Missouri, then to the Hays County Correctional Institute, south of Austin, then to Austin State Hospital. He was diagnosed as suffering from organic brain damage with possible underlying schizophrenia. But still he makes marvellous music – his latest LP, *All That May Do My Rhyme*, released on Trance Syndicate, is lovely in parts – and still he smiles and greets one as a long-lost friend and thinks your middle name is Alan.

The Tex-Mex feast over, Roky says, 'What d'you want to do? I'm having a good time. Are you? Let's go for a ride. I'd like to do some shopping. That'd be great? I saw *Poltergeist III*. That was kinda scary.'

And so we go shopping, to one of Austin's Goodwill (chain of charity) stores, where misfits browse among decaying furniture and bits and bobs and racks of terribly faded Hawaiian-style shirts. But before we can go shopping we must swing by Evelyn's house – Evelyn is Roky's mum – because Roky has no money and must needs borrow. Evelyn is almost as 'eccentric' as her son, if such a thing were possible. She has cats everywhere and clapped-out musical instruments everywhere but money nowhere, and so all she can do for Roky is write him a cheque for $5. I make small talk with Evelyn – about cats, mostly – while Roky turns on the colour TV to watch beach volleyball, which amuses him greatly. 'These guys are weird. Hur hur. That guy's got no feet.'

At the Goodwill store . . .

Roky wanders around the expansive shop seemingly entranced by the elderly goods on store. He points to an 'occasional' table and asks me, 'What is that? Is that some kinda futon?' No, I think it's a table, Roky. 'That's weird! That must cost a million dollars!' No, it's priced at $30, Roky. In the electrical section, Roky comes over all like the proverbial child in the proverbial sweet shop. He picks up a telephone. 'What is this?' It's a telephone, oh Rokperson. 'That is weird. How do they do that? That must cost a million dollars.' Price, eleven. Then he finds a device with knobs on that calls itself a 'microphone mixer'. 'What is this? How do they make this? This must cost a million dollars!' Price, seven. 'Will you buy this for me, King?' 'Are you sure you want it, Roky?' 'What is it? I want this. Must cost a million dollars.' I'll buy it for you, Roky, I 'generously' afford. And I buy it for him. He is delighted . . .

It's sad. And it's sad to have to write about a musical hero this way. But it's not that sad, because Roky Erickson can still make haunting and marvellous music when he can be bothered, when friends like King Koffee egg him on to non-indolence. And look at him now, back in his blaring shack, sticking leads into his new acquisition, the 'microphone mixer', turning the knobs and making the cacophony of his abode yet stranger and more cacophonous still. He knows what he's doing. I *think* he knows what he's doing.

'Gremlins have always taken care of me all my life,' said Roky in 1978. 'Mainly there would always be one behind the door of my bedroom and I would tell my mother there was a gremlin, demon, grandfather child behind the door and she would ask him to leave . . .'

In 1995, Roky, in the politest way, is asking me and King to leave. We leave. Outside the screen door, Roky takes me firmly by the hand. His eyes are smiling. 'I'll be careful,' he says, then laughs. 'I'll be careful . . .'

# Vivian Stanshall: Madly missed

*Mail on Sunday*, 12 March 1995

'A cup of char, old bean?' It was with these kind words, delivered in the trademark plummy 'n' fruity voice, that Vivian Stanshall, eccentric and gifted leader of the '60s comedy-pop troupe the Bonzo Dog Doo-Dah Band, welcomed me into his delightful home (a cluttered bedsit in north London) some five or so years ago.

The ginger and bewhiskered old gentleman, dressed in a garish dressing gown and red shoes, boiled a kettle and proceeded to tell me about the first time he went into a mental home.

Where would the 'wonderful' world of pop music be without the odd eccentric, the batty crank, to make it all worthwhile? Stanshall, the man who once put raw meat into Ringo Starr's drum kit (while the Beatles were recording *Revolver*) in an attempt to 'foil the Fabs' sound', who sang, memorably, about 'My pink half of the drainpipe' and 'We are all normal and we dig Bert Weedon', died in a fire at his abode last week and it's all very sad.

Yes, pop music needs a healthy supply of eccentricity to keep it exciting and upon its toes – but there is a woeful dearth of madcaps on the present-day 'scene'.

These we have loved:

- Syd Barrett. Creative force behind the (early) Pink Floyd. Notable achievement: using margarine as hair gel.

- Roky Erickson. Guitarist/singer of 'legendary' psychedelic Texan band, the 13th Floor Elevators. Notable achievement: imagining that he was, in fact, an alien from Mars – and visiting a lawyer to have this 'fact' officially notarised. (Incidentally, Roky has a new LP upon the Trance Syndicate label called *All That May Do My Rhyme* – crazy ride, crazy record, crazy guy! – which is madly lovely.)
- Arthur Lee. Leader of '60s legends Love. Notable achievement(s): shaving off all his hair for no evident reason, walking off stage during concerts to go to the supermarket.
- Sky Saxon. Singer with cult acid-rock pop stars from California, the Seeds. Notable achievement(s): wandering the streets of Los Angeles in kaftans, enquiring of dogs, 'Pardon me, sir, could you tell me the time?'; choosing to live in a dustbin just like his hero, Top Cat; etcetera.
- Keith Moon. Drummer of the Who. Notable achievement: you know, Rolls-Royces in swimming pools, that sort of modest caper.
- Prince. Small fellow with the word 'Slave' currently emblazoned on his cheek. Notable achievement: shouting to the audience at his recent London gigs, 'What's my name, what's my name?' and getting absolutely no reply because he has, of course, changed his name to an entirely unpronounceable squiggle.

Definitely non-eccentric are Duran Duran, unless you count Simon Le Bon's boating antics aboard the good ship *Drum* some years ago (the yacht kept falling over, you may recall) or the fact John Taylor has married Amanda de Cadenet – that dreadful 'wild child' who used to conduct celebrity non-interviews on *The Word* – for reasons best known to himself. There again, maybe the fading New Romantic beauties are a trifle potty after all. If their new LP, *Thank You* (Parlophone), is anything to go by, they may well have mislaid a modicum of marbles. Like Annie Lennox's feeble effort that I mentioned last week, this is a collection of cover versions of songs that worked perfectly well for their original owners but are complete duds in this second-hand setting. Lou Reed's 'Perfect Day', Elvis Costello's 'Watching the Detectives', Iggy Pop's 'Success' – it is something approaching blasphemy when Duran Duran (who once changed their name to Duranduran, which is quite eccentric, I suppose – or maybe just idiotic) tackle works of this quality.

The last words Vivian Stanshall said to me as I left his bedsit all those years ago were, 'Bugger it, I say, old bean. Bugger it!' I couldn't have put it better myself.

# Hibbert and I

# 'The appalling Graham Nash'

*Bob Stanley*

Unlike most of the contemporaries who tried to keep up with Green Gartside's critical theory or wrote lavish praise for Elvis Costello's increasingly gruesome puns, Tom Hibbert had wildly individual taste and wasn't afraid to share it. He loved to enthuse about '60s B-sides, had no time for rock iconography and made the whole business of music writing generally seem like fun.

*Smash Hits* was the vehicle for much of his most memorable work. He described Salt-N-Pepa's DJ Spinderella as 'rather handsome'. David Bowie was rechristened Dame David Bowie (at a time when Bowie said that his declaration that he was bisexual was 'the biggest mistake I ever made', this was nicely pointed). Other gags came at the expense of less substantial acts: Scottish wholemeal-soul duo Hue and Cry were written about as if Hue was the singer and the other bloke was called Cry. And there was a surreal, long-running joke about Madonna's supposed pet cougar.

But what made Hibbert my writing hero was a book called *Rare Records* that he published in 1982. He was all over obscure records that wouldn't become fashionable until years later – a whacked-out, breakbeat-laden album by *Department S* actor Peter Wyngarde; Bowie-inspiring one-man-band the Legendary Stardust Cowboy;

the Monks' 'disturbing' *Black Monk Time*. It was also full of great photos, most of which I have never seen anywhere else: a glorious shot of Liverpool's football pools supergroup the Vernons Girls; ex-Shadows Jet Harris and Tony Meehan standing on giant snare drums (or are they biscuit tins?); a two-page spread of 'Canadian buffoon' Hughie Green as well as one of the Electric Prunes; and the Swinging Blue Jeans scowling unhappily in a greengrocer's.

The prose in *Rare Records* was equally unorthodox. What we had here was a writer who collected records while finding much of the rock world quite ridiculous. I hadn't come across anyone bold enough to baldly dismiss – without explanation – 'the appalling Graham Nash', or to refer to something as unobvious as the Yardbirds' flop 'Happenings Ten Years Time Ago' as 'possibly the greatest 45 ever released'. Here was someone who clearly loved pop music but also loved to mock it, who revelled in Billie Davis' 'beautifully controlled, shivery voice' as much as the Del-Vetts' snotty garage punk masterpiece 'Last Time Around'. He nailed Adam Faith's mangled vowel sounds. He talked about his crush on Annette Funicello (despite her 'hopeless lack of talent'). And like my other early inspiration Nik Cohn – who wrote that the Silhouettes' 'Get a Job' alone was of more worth than the Doors' entire back catalogue – he found Jim Morrison's god-like status preposterous.

Tom Hibbert was my people.

In September 1986 I started a town planning degree at the Polytechnic of Central London (just as Suede's Brett Anderson would, a year or two later, pop pickers). As I was moving from Peterborough to the capital, I did what I thought an entirely normal thing to do and sent Tom a copy of my fanzine, plus a letter saying how much I liked his work – and, er, would he like to go for a pint? He wrote back and said 'Yes', which again I thought an entirely normal thing to do. I know now that it really wasn't normal at all to accept such an offer from a 21-year-old fan.

*Rare Records: Wax Trash & Vinyl Treasures* (Proteus, 1992).

We went to a pub on Fulham Broadway, where Tom told me he'd seen Tim Hardin playing in the mid-'70s. That must have been amazing, I bibbled. No, said Tom, it was not. Hardin had played all his best-loved songs – 'Reason to Believe', 'Misty Roses',

'If I Were a Carpenter' – by smashing the keys with his fists and singing them like Tom Waits with a rotten case of piles. Hardin had writer's block, it transpired, and his way of dealing with it was to annihilate the great songs he'd written just a few years earlier.

Naturally, we talked about *Smash Hits*. He was hilariously rude about a couple of my favourite writers from years gone by. The thing he seemed proudest of was sneaking in 'facts' about McDonald's, such as their playing a sped-up human heartbeat subliminally through the speakers to get people in and out faster. There was another story about an elephant called Ronald McDonald. Presumably he'd obtained all this info from the McLibel folk and it is quite astonishing that EMAP failed to spot these inflammatory yarns popping up next to posters of Madonna's cougar and Morten Harket's sculpted hair.

I told him how much I loved *Rare Records* and he looked rather sad. It turned out the publishers had captioned all the photos without running them past him. He'd memorised some of the worst and spat one out – 'a member of the Riot Squad!' I had no idea about such sloppiness in the wonderful world of publishing.

Apparently Tom had also accepted a commission from the same publisher to write a Billy Joel biography. They rejected his manuscript when they noticed that the first eight chapters were taken up by Joel's scrabbling days in soulful '60s garage band the Hassles, with only the last two dedicated to his huge commercial successes in the '70s and '80s. Lines such as 'he soon soared to the heights of mediocrity' weren't exactly what they were looking for.

While Tom spent the evening directing me towards a trove of garage punk and '60s teen pop 45s I'd never heard of, I didn't have much to put his way. But I suggested he might quite like a new Creation Records act called Primal Scream, who, at this point, were led by Roger McGuinn-mad guitarist Jim Beattie as much as by outrageously fringed singer Bobby Gillespie. A few months later he got back to me, after hearing Primal Scream's first album, *Sonic Flower Groove*, to tell me that he thought they were piss-weak – I'm sure in time, when they became genuinely famous, he would have found their none-more-rock 'n' roll stance to be as side-splittingly amusing as the Doors and Vanilla Fudge were before them.

We met up a couple more times and Tom introduced me to his lovely American wife Allyce (American, how glamorous! I thought), and I remember watching episodes of *Cheers* in their flat. At some point we had talked about forgotten 1963 hit 'Hey Paula' by Paul & Paula; I owned a copy of their first album that Tom was welcome to. We arranged to meet at his flat the following week, but when I got there, Paul & Paula's debut under my arm, there was no one at home. As I was living in a hall of residence, Tom had no way of contacting me, but it turned out he'd been invited to interview Margaret Thatcher at the last minute. I was rather pissed off. Thatcher! Wouldn't he have rather spent an evening listening to Paul & Paula's 'First Quarrel'? Maybe, but then he did have a job to do.

*Q* wasn't my world – David Gilmour and Robert Cray appealed to me rather less than a-ha and Annette Funicello – so I didn't follow Tom's writing past *Smash Hits*. We drifted apart. A few months after that Thatcher night, I landed my first review in *Smash Hits* – Paul McCartney's *All the Best* (8 out of 10) – and had begun working towards my dream job. To my horror, the editor told me the magazine was making a concerted (if drawn-out) attempt to move away from Tom Hibbert's singular vision by dropping the inverted commas and iconoclastic nicknames. I jumped ship quickly and headed for the 'inkies', first *NME* and then *Melody Maker*. It's safe to say Tom's *Smash Hits* house style followed me, as well as the knowledge that most pop music is mediocre to dreadful – the best thing you can do is to write something that's more entertaining.

# Part Six

## The Male on Sunday

Fed up with pop stars, Tom diversifies into columns for the
*Mail on Sunday*'s *Night & Day* magazine and the *Observer*.

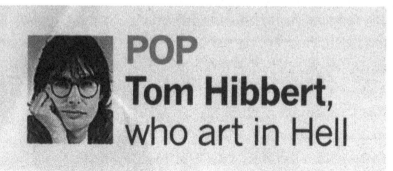

*Mail on Sunday*, 28 August 1994.

*'I made the leap from* Q *to the* Observer *in 1996 because Jocelyn Targett – who was a big fan of the "Who the hell . . . ?" pieces – rang me up and offered me a column. I swore, when I went there, that I'd never interview a pop star again. Emap Metro were paying no money and I fancied writing for a national newspaper. They'd just cancelled "Who the hell . . . ?" and Lynn Barber had stolen the idea. By the end, they were getting me to interview third-rate actors from television that no one cared about. Robson and Jerome. What could you say about them apart from, "two crap actors who make dreadful records"? I've been told that* Q *had changed by then, but I wasn't a big* Q *reader. I just read my pieces to see whether they had cut my jokes out.*

*'That's what's boring about rock now. I sound like such an old fart, but it is everywhere. When your father knows more about Echobelly than you do because he's read about it in* The Times, *you know something's up.'*

Tom Hibbert, 2001

# Drinking: With gin, the legs are the first to go

*Details*, November 1990

I'm sitting in an English country garden, swigging a Dog's Nose (two fingers of gin mixed with dark beer). It tastes disgusting, but it does the trick: legless before the ice cubes begin to rattle. As Lord Byron, most distinguished of gin imbibers, once said, 'Gin is the source of all my inspiration.' Of course, he died young. Though an Englishman, I do not drink gin often. Neither, it seems, does anybody else these days. Gin – the *chicest* of all drinks, once patronised by royalty, as British as the Union Jack (two-thirds gin; one-third crème Yvette) – has fallen from favour. Which is only fitting, since that's how it began – a drink despised and frowned upon.

A distilled, pure-grain spirit flavoured with juniper berries, herbs and spices, gin was originally produced in Holland in the mid-sixteenth century. But it was the English, with their great propensity for inebriation, who acquired a taste for it. Almost immediately, gin palaces, gaudily decorated public houses, started shooting up around town. By 1743 over a million gallons of gin were being sold in London a year. It was sold in factories, workhouses, barbershops, brothels and even prisons (in the King's Bench Prison, 120 gallons were sold each week). In gin cellars, men, women and children sat on straw, propped up against the walls until the effects of the spirit wore off and they could hit the bottle once again.

Gin passed into coarse slang. *Gin bottle:* a dirty, abandoned, debased woman; *gin lane:* the human throat; *gin trap:* the mouth. Mothers fed their babies the cheap liquor to still the infants' bawling. Mothers-to-be attempted do-it-yourself abortions by swigging a draft and clambering, reeling, into a hot bath.

Such vulgar behaviour was not taken lightly. In 1736, by Act of Parliament, gin prices were hiked beyond the means of the common herd. And, wouldn't you know it?, as soon as gin was made expensive it became respectable, a drink for the terminally fabulous and the would-be intelligentsia. (Sociologists will note similarities with the history of cocaine.)

Gin went on to become the high-octane rocket fuel of the cocktail age, that heady time of hedonistic paaaaartying between the wars when everyone said amazingly witty things, dressed in shiny dinner outfits and danced the Tango (two measures gin, one measure sweet vermouth, one measure dry vermouth, two dashes curaçao, juice of quarter orange).

Americans, realising what a fine and cultivated lot the Brits were, got in on the gin jag, too. It was 1925. In Paris, Ernest Hemingway strolled with his chums F. Scott Fitzgerald and Scott's loopy wife, Zelda, into the celebrated Harry's New York Bar. Zelda ordered some newfangled cocktail called a White Lady (two measures gin, one measure lemon juice, one measure Cointreau, teaspoon of egg white). 'It's sweet and delicious!' piped the barking Zelda. 'Then I'll have a White Lady, too,' cooed Scott. 'For you are sweet and delicious.' Ernest, somewhat repelled, ordered his usual: 'A martini for me. Distinctly dry.' Later on, he killed himself.

Frank Sinatra is still alive. During his Rat Pack days, it was Tanqueray gin all the way. Bob Hope likes a drop of Tanqueray. Joan Crawford was a Gordon's man, it is said. Mary Jo Kopechne too. So what happened? All these heroes of literature and comedy and cinema and underwater swimming loved a bit of the juniper sauce. Why have today's youth ceased to give it their Attention (equal measures gin, Pernod, dry vermouth, crème de violette, dash of orange bitters)?

Popular music is, of course, responsible. You get goat-bearded C&W hillbillies warbling about how the whiskey bottle let them down. You get long-haired thugs from New Jersey and Los Angeles ramroddin' with 'chicks' and chucking down the rock 'n' roll mouth-wash, Jack Daniel's. You get the new breed of model drinking nothing more important than Perrier or carrot juice. Worse yet, you get reformed 'wild-ass' rockers singing about the pleasures of abstinence. For those such as myself, this is a Nightmare (equal parts gin and Dubonnet, dash of cherry brandy and orange juice).

I rang up a 'spokesperson' at the British headquarters of Gordon's gin. Gordon's is desperate to recapture the lovely youth market. These days, every time you go to the cinema in London you are assaulted by a Gordon's advertisement. What happens is the screen goes completely green and a voice says something amusing, like 'Here is a frog in a field drinking Gordon's gin'. Gin isn't green, but a Gordon's bottle *is*, you see. I don't think this campaign is working. But the spokesperson insisted. He talked about 'penetration' into the youth market, about 'desirability', 'profile' and 'targeting'.' I didn't understand a word (I was sipping a Dog's Nose at the time). He tried to baffle me with statistics. Did you know, he asked triumphantly, that four bottles of Gordon's gin are consumed every second of the day and night? Well, that's Elizabeth Taylor for you, I replied. The spokesperson didn't seem to find this funny. Never trust a gin drinker.

*Tom Hibbert lives in London and enjoys the occasional gimlet (three parts gin, one part lime juice).*

# ABBA ever after: Whither rock 'n' roll?

*Mail on Sunday*, **26 December 1993**

As a 'top' pop critic, I am forever being asked: 'Tell me, whither rock 'n' roll?' My response is always the same: 'I'm not altogether sure, I'm distressed to say.' But a series of alarming episodes in the last few days has left me fretting somewhat about the future, if any, of rock and pop.

1. Despite having been dead for twenty-three years, Jimi Hendrix was in the news again. Somebody thought it would be 'cool' to resume investigations into the guitarist's death. Unless those crashing bores – the conspiracy theorists – are right and Jimi was murdered by the Black Power movement on a grassy knoll or something, what is the point of this? To sell a few more copies of the J.M. Hendrix back catalogue, presumably.

2. I was watching *A Woman's Guide to Adultery*, surely the worst television 'drama' since *The Onedin Line*, and all these dreary people were blathering away in the kitchen while, in the background, a Tasmin Archer CD was playing. Now, I really quite like Tasmin Archer, but this rather put me off.

3. I had the misfortune to hear Cilla Black and Barry Manilow's attempt at an 'Xmas' hit, 'You'll Never Walk Alone'. It really

302

is frightful. Barry is normally so professional, but here we find him performing a harmony whole-tone run on the chorus, beneath Cilla's nasal stridency, and when he reaches the final syllable ('You'll never walk a-LONE'), it collapses in an unlovely dissonance. If Baz and 'our' Cilla are heavily influenced by the oeuvre of Edgard Varèse, they could have had the decency to inform us beforehand.

4. Mr Blobby's intensely annoying single (it's called 'Mr Blobby') went to number one in the hit parade despite the fact that Radio 1 (not often noted for sensible artistic decisions) hardly played it at all. It's sold over half a million copies. Oh, dear. I am convinced that Mr Blobby, wobbling nincompoop of a 'character' as seen in TV's *Noel's House Party* (in case you didn't know), is a feeble plot hatched to disguise the fact that there are, in these shabby times, no proper stars any more.

5. I was reading the *Melody Maker* when I noticed that something was different about Britain's most aged musical publication. It hasn't got staples in any more! I don't know what this says about our modern society, but I'm sure it's nothing good.

6. La Toya Jackson popped up on the telly with her silly hair and her angst-ridden 'sincerity' in a live-from-Israel press conference situation. 'I cannot and will not be a silent collaborator of his (i.e. her brother's) crimes against small innocent children,' she sobbed. 'My mother always said, "Michael, he's a faggot. That damned faggot, I can't stand him."' Charming. It's all very sordid. And little Michael's new single, 'Gone Too Soon', upon which he coos 'like a rainbow fading in the twinkling of an eye . . .' in grotesque 'child-like' manner, does nothing to cheer up the squalid situation.

7. And worst of all. In a recent survey, I have learned, students were asked to nominate their favourite live act of 1993. Who should come out on top but Björn Again, the Australian buffoons whose gimmick is pretending to be ABBA. I have said it before and I'll say it again: what, pray, is the point of forming a group if you're

simply going to pretend to be someone else? Is it 'art'? I don't think so. And yet, 1993 has seen a proliferation of these sound-alike, look-alike entertainments all doing briskish business. There's the Australian Doors (as if the real Doors weren't ghastly enough the first time round) and there's the Australian Pink Floyd. And there's Elton Jack, who bills himself as 'Australia's Number One Elton John Impersonator'. What? Is Australia riddled with the things? Is there an Elton Reg, an Elton Bruce, an Elton Sydney Opera House? And why does Britain fall for these phoney nostalgia-vendors every time?

So whither rock 'n' roll? The only conclusion I can draw from all of the above is that to make it in the giddy world of pop these days, your best bet is to a) be a fake; b) be dead; or c) like Mr Blobby be totally non-existent. Don't, whatever you do, be original or anything like that; I mean, think of the effort . . .

# Got the T-shirt

*Mail on Sunday*, 30 January 1994

Rummaging about in the recesses of my wardrobe in search of a lively pair of socks, I came across a selection of pop-orientated garments I had quite forgotten I possessed. Item: One Ozzy Osbourne T-shirt featuring hideous horror-style representation of the celebrated singer as a prowling werewolf; Item: One Beat T-shirt (circa 1980, slightly soiled) featuring an inept cartoon of the defunct 2 Tone troupe; Item: Two Mr. Mister T-shirts featuring swirling logos that would drive Brian Sewell to distraction and the depths of despair.

'What have I got all these horrible T-shirts for?' I asked myself. 'I can't even remember who Mr. Mister were!' I could only think that I had once imagined that if I hung on to these togs for long enough they might one day be worth a fortune at the auction houses where daft people pay daft prices for daft pop memorabilia. These days, T-shirts with pop acts emblazoned on their fronts often outsell the recordings of the pop acts in question. Bands on tour make more money from merchandising (i.e. foyer sales of their ghastly shirts that fade after one go in the non-fast colours cycle than they do from ticket sales).

Yes, the T-shirt is big business, and in recognition of this fact, *Music Week*, the trade publication that publishes the hit parade, has taken to printing a T-Shirt Chart. 'Fashion, ooh-ooh-ooh-ooh, wah-wah,' as David Bowie so cleverly put it; the T-shirt will never go out of style. But what does the shirt chart tell us sociology buffs about the pop fans of today? Well . . .

1. *Red Dwarf* (not a pop group at all but a sci-fi comedy series on BBC2 which isn't very funny at all)
2. Take That (charmless pop group for the teeny-tinies)
3. Reg Holdsworth (a comical bloke in spectacles who lives in a supermarket in *Coronation Street* and gets into scrapes in the tinned meats aisle)
4. Björk (Icelandic popstress who squeals a lot and eats puffins but is quite pretty)
5. Meat Loaf (tawdry, portly rock screamer)
6. Victor Meldrew (a grumpy bloke in an overrated BBC sitcom)
7. Nirvana (American group that used to take millions of drugs and are the 'Godfathers' of grunge – allegedly)
8. Cypress Hill (got me there, mates)
9. Mr Blobby (this is definitely the last time the foam-filled hit-making buffoon appears in this column, I promise)
10. The Wonder Stuff (long-haired rock group who are not unamusing in their own way).

So what does it all signify? I'll let you be the judge of that.

Which brings me to this: where has my ZZ Top T-shirt (circa 1985) gone? It had a pair of female-fashioned legs on the front and was enormous. No matter, I don't think I could bear to wear it again now that ZZ Top, with their new LP, *Antenna* (RCA 74321 182602), have proved themselves to be so useless.

Status Quo have been churning out the same heads-down-no-nonsense-mindless-boogie for years and are widely derided for this. ZZ Top, who do exactly the same thing, remain fashionable. I cannot understand it.

I give you, here, a chart of The Most Interesting Things About ZZ Top . . .

1. In their early days, they would have buffalo and rattlesnakes on stage with them because they come from Texas and, surprisingly, are proud of it
2. Guitarist Billy Gibbons coined the phrase 'spanking the plank' which, translated into English, means 'playing the electric guitar'
3. One of them once forgot he had a small firearm secreted in his cowboy boot and shot himself in the foot (the clot!)
4. Two of them have beards and one of them hasn't and the one who hasn't is called Frank Beard. Ho ho
5. I once asked the two of them who have beards whether they sleep with said beards on the outside or the inside of the sheets. They were stumped for an answer
6. There is no '6'.

# Ad it up to here

*Mail on Sunday*, 13 February 1994

'Do you know me?' The cove in the wellington boots, the smart raincoat and the flat cap, swaggering across a trout farm on the telly, was attempting quite clearly to pass himself off as a country squire. But something – was it the artifice of his ageing curls? – gave him away.

'Do you know me?' he asked. And we, the viewers, shouted back at the small screen: 'Yes, of course we know you. Alas, alack. Because you're the fellow who was in the Who and sang "Hope I die before I get old". But you didn't die at all because here you are with your fish, advertising American Express of all things.'

Shortly after this sad spectacle of a commercial, all of Roger Daltrey's trout died in a bizarre accident. Hope I die before I get old? Hope I die before I get poor and can't afford a new Barbour, more like. For many, this credit card ad of some ten years ago marked the end of what is popularly called 'The Sixties', the era of holding hands, admiring flowers and not caring about money ('bread') very much.

Some say the '60s ended in December 1969, when at a Rolling Stones concert in Altamont, California, a man was stabbed to death by Hells Angels; others argue that they drew to a close in the summer of 1972 when Gary Glitter, tottering on his lofty heels, first appeared on *Top of the Pops* 'singing' his terrible hit, 'Rock & Roll (Parts I & II)', on the same day, incidentally, that Israeli athletes were murdered in the Olympic Village.

Apparently, however, according to *TIME* magazine, which knows about these things, the death of the '60s took place only the other day. 'Just In Case You Hadn't Heard – The Sixties Are Over', the organ announced. The proof of this awful fact? Bob Dylan, '60s sage and mouth-organ-puffing old goat, has finally allowed his music to be used on a TV commercial. Oh, crass commercialism, from the prince of protest music! The song in question? 'The Times They Are A-Changin'', the one they used to sing at civil rights rallies thirty years ago. The product being advertised? Coopers & Lybrand, a firm of accountants. Horror! Bob's 'sold out', so the '60s are over . . . But hold your horses – there's nothing exactly novel about classic songs of the '60s being used to puff fabulous products of the '80s and '90s, is there? You remember that youth who went to the laundrette and took off all his clothes (save his gleaming underpants) to the sound of 'I Heard It Through the Grapevine', don't you? Tunes by the Beach Boys have been used to shift power drill attachments and Steppenwolf's 'Born to Be Wild' – which accompanied that fabled pair of hippie bikers, Dennis Hopper and Peter Fonda, across America in the film *Easy Rider* many years ago – has been heard on the small screen in recent times piping up on behalf of posh cars for thrusting executives. 'Like a true nature's child' goes the song, as a gent with too much hair gel adjusts his smart tie and whirls down the road, looking quite smug.

The Beatles' 'Revolution' has been pressed into service to sell Nike trainers, Crosby, Stills, Nash & Young's 'Teach Your Children' has done sterling work for Fruit of the Loom undergarments, and the Byrds' 'Turn, Turn, Turn' has been used by, ahem, *TIME* magazine. (What happens when you read a magazine? You turn the pages. Turn, Turn, Turn. Get it?) And currently playing on televisions across America is a singularly annoying commercial for

the Red Cross, in which the elderly songbird Ms Carly Simon pretends, most unconvincingly, to be a paramedic to musical accompaniment from the Rolling Stones and 'Gimme Shelter' (which
has already been used in Britain to make the RAC look 'groovy').

So what does all this mean? It means that, gosh, yes, the '60s
really are over. It also means that Mick Jagger and Keith Richards
must be very rich indeed, for not only have they managed to flog
'Gimme Shelter' twice, but when their old chestnut 'Satisfaction'
was used to sell Snickers, the makers of that delightful confection
coughed up $ 2.8 million to the composers.

# Denver booted: John Denver's autobiography

*Mail on Sunday*, 20 November 1994

In a previous life, John Denver was a mountain lion. Don't laugh, it is true! Well, I'm sure it isn't true, actually, but that's not the point. The point is that he, Denver, believes it to be true. Yes, here again we have an American whose sense of reality has been drummed away, by celebrity and too much money, unto nothing.

John Denver was the man in pebble specs who, during the '70s, made US folk music and country and western so alarmingly respectable and polite with rather weedy songs such as 'Mountain High' and 'Country Roads' and prissy appearances on *The Muppets* and other telly shows. In his self-serving autobiography, we learn that he was a genius and a terribly caring person all along (it wasn't his fault that his first marriage failed: he was only unfaithful when away from home on tour because a man has needs like those of a mountain lion, after all).

This is a book jam-packed with hippie/New Age nonsense. 'Capricorns have a hard time coping when they're young,' the author tells us (I suppose that all people born under other star signs cope admirably). He keeps trying to get in touch with his 'inner child' (EST courses, macrobiotics and masses of Chinese proverbs seem

311

to aid him not much in his quest). Then, when his records stop selling, he discovers world hunger. 'I kept asking myself why hunger is allowed to exist,' he goes. He comes to a conclusion: 'Hunger is a truly environmental issue.' Cripes!

*Take Me Home* is an hilarious (unintentionally so) thing, what with its folksy style – 'Holy, Moly!' is Denver's favoured and most flavoured expletive – its proliferation of retrograde 'far out's and the bit where he loses his virginity . . . 'oh, the rapture of a girl's body!' To save you the trouble of reading it, I herewith present the most 'exciting' bits of the 250 pages:

He once went to see the film *Doctor Zhivago* and 'wept inconsolably for hours'.

He once lost two of his toes in a lawnmower accident.

He once changed the tyres on a car and screwed the bolts on backwards.

He once thought about committing suicide but, noticing that it was a 'beautiful' day, decided against it. That's it.

John Denver says he's 'got his head together' now. He is a 'dedicated golfer'. Thank goodness for that.

*Tom Hibbert once contemplated suicide while watching John Denver dancing with Pan's People on BBC Two. That's true.*

# Reality bytes: The Internet

*Mail on Sunday*, 26 March 1995

I was first introduced to the 'delights' of the future by a mad Grateful Dead fan bloke in California some seven years ago. He was furiously proud of his 'super-information-highway' computer 'web' thingie via which he could communicate with other members of the hippie 'Deadhead' community at the touch of several million buttons.

'Watch!' he said. I watched. Click. And clack. There popped up on the screen a new technology-styled missive from someone called Moonchild Rainforest Sun Patio Jacuzzi Cactus Smith, or something like that, which read: 'Phil Lesh. Morning Dew at Jones Beach. Bitching bass. 11/11/88. Thoughts?' 'Amazing, isn't it?' said the Grateful Dead fan bloke. 'Absolutely (hem hem)!' I agreed. 'But in my country we can communicate with one another in an even more impressive way. What happens is you get something that we call a PEN and another thing called PAPER and a STAMP and an ENVELOPE and you stick these all together. Hey presto! A fellow called a POSTMAN does the rest. It's as easy as A-B-C . . . And, failing that, there's a Scottish invention we call the TELEPHONE. What happens in this case is . . .'

My Deadhead authority looked crestfallen. Battered to bits by Anglo snootiness and superiority, not to mention sarcasm, which

Americans still aren't very good at. But he had the last laugh, didn't he? This super-information so-called flipping highway is about to take over the world of popular music and we old Luddites who scoffed, who still wear our 'Back to Mono' badges with pride (because we thought, and still do, that stereo was a rubbish invention . . . who cares which side of the room a guitar solo is coming from so long as it's a good one? . . .), have our faces covered in egg, so to speak. I am sorry to say that Internet stuff and CD-ROM tosh and interactive virtual reality guff seem to be here to stay. More is the pity. A) You need lots of money to join in with the 'fun'. B) You have to spend time on learning 'skills' that would be better put to other purposes. C) Oh, what a major disappointment when you've got the hang of it all and begin to embrace the pop music of the next decades . . . Observe . . .

Pop personages who reckon that all this swindly new technology is the way ahead and absolutely fabulous include:

- Todd Rundgren. Twenty-five years ago he used to write sublime three-minute pop songs. Then he discovered computers and went bonkers. At his recent London concerts, he invited members of the audience on to the stage to take over the machines and make an infernal din. Modern pop democracy sounds horrible. You have been warned.

- Peter Gabriel. He does lots of spiffing things with the CD-ROM wheeze, apparently. Buy his stuff and not only can you listen to it but you can go boating in a bathysphere underneath a Cumbrian lake with the great man and a lawnmower on your head. Or something. In stunning colour. Virtual 'reality' never sounded so dull . . .

- The Artist Formerly Known As Tiny. Pooh! says 'Prince' to his record company; in the future, everybody around the globe will be tapping into the Internet to hear my latest great musical masterworks. Um . . . how does this work, exactly, financially speaking? How many Artist-Future-ly-Known-As-Idiotic fans in Guinea-Bissau are privy to the necessary hardware? Etcetera?

- Bob Dylan. Unlikely as it seems, the ancient mouth-organ-puffing goat is also the subject of a forthcoming CD-ROM affair on which the user will, probably, be able to stumble around a bit, have a perm, hide from the press, mumble, go to bed, write a forbiddingly awful poem about a spider, snooze – just like the real thing!!!
- Bobby Crush. On the ivory-tickling gleamer's latest interactive CD-ROM, YOU, the user, can become either one of Bobby's sparkling teeth or a piano-tuner's guide dog ... the choice is yours! And so what if I made this last bit up? Such novel 'attractions' are only a matter of time ...

Oh, come along, people, face it. The greatest invention of the twentieth century has nowt to do with this computerised nonsense: it is the simple electric guitar. If you do not believe me, just listen to Teenage Fanclub's LP, *Deep Fried Fanclub* (Paperhouse/Fire), which is covered in the lovely and elderly things with no futurama hogwash to baffle or batter you. You can't 'strum' a computer keyboard like you can a wonky old tennis racket in front of your bedroom mirror, now, can you, kids? Luddites of the world unite. Super 'information' highway? Just say NO!

# Track records: *Desert Island Discs*

## *Mail on Sunday*, 6 August 1995

'. . . And after my second solo crossing of the Pacific in a modified cardboard box, I published my third volume of memoirs, which I dedicated to my dear old mum.' Sue Lawley crosses her alluring legs, leans into the microphone and purrs, 'Your next record?' 'Well, Sue,' I purr back . . . and then I wake up.

It is a recurring dream – me on *Desert Island Discs*. Is it not everyone's loftiest ambition to be the guest on this most esteemed of wireless programmes? It is certainly mine. For what more fun is there to be had in life than compiling lists of one's favourite records of all time and then arguing about it with some other list-compiler down the boozer? In preparation for the day, Sue 'inevitably' calls me up. I have whittled my favourite songs of all time down to a shortlist of 2,000, with Freda Payne's 'Band of Gold', the Byrds' 'Eight Miles High' and Blur's 'Parklife' in a dead heat for the coveted number-one spot.

Making musical lists is enormous fun, I am sure you will agree. Everyone's at it. Last week the nominees for the Mercury Music Prize's Album of the Year were announced; ten top platters by the likes of Oasis, Portishead, Leftfield, PJ Harvey, Supergrass, Tricky, Elastica, Van Morrison, Guy Barker (token jazz personage, or is he the classical one?) and James MacMillan (token classical personage, or is it the other way around?). If there were any justice in this world, Supergrass would win the award for their splendid bratpop (with Oasis worthy runners-up for being the band most like the Beatles) – but there isn't. Look at last year: the judges got involved in a spot of argy bargy (grown-up version of arguing about lists of favourite songs down the boozer) and so in the end what happened was the gong went to an LP that no one particularly liked but no one particularly hated, i.e. M People. Another triumph for mediocrity.

Then there is the list of the one hundred so-called Greatest Albums Ever Made, as seen in the last edition of *Mojo* magazine (and on sale in HMV shops everywhere). Strangely enough, I was invited to vote for these things; unfortunately, so were several hundred other writers and so my brilliant selections scarcely got a mention (though I'm rather proud of the fact that Moby Grape's first LP, something hardly anyone in the world has ever actually heard, climbed into the chart at the fabulous notch of 50). The Beach Boys' *Pet Sounds* was votest Greatest Album Ever, which is just about acceptable, but at number two was *Astral Weeks* by that grumpy growler Van Morrison. Poo. If *Astral Weeks* is the second-best LP ever made then I am . . . Sue Lawley. Lists. Pah. They really get one's blood boiling, don't they, because everyone else is always WRONG. Sue crosses her legs again and asks me to nominate my 'luxury' for that fabled desert island. A boozer and a bloke with awful taste in music to argue with unto eternity, I reply. Sue titters winningly. 'Thank you, *Tom Hibbert*, for sharing your *Desert Island Discs* with us.' 'No, thank YOU, Sue.'

# Tents atmosphere: Rock festivals then and now

*Mail on Sunday*, 3 September 1995

Tom at a Bob Dylan show in London's Hyde Park, July 1996, with (*left to right*) Andy Gill, Andy Kershaw and Mark and Clare Ellen (courtesy of Allyce Hibbert).

In the *Loaded* Comedy Tent, a charmless fellow was cracking obvious and entirely unfunny 'jokes' about pizza delivery men (they are all spotty and they always turn up late, ho ho ho, plus a lot of unnecessary swear words). In the *Melody Maker* Tent, some hapless

318

group featuring several trillion guitarists were performing a 'song' that would go on for several trillion centuries. Out in the cold distance, people who knew no better were bungee-jumping from a high crane. In the Carlsberg Tent, people who knew no better were quaffing a kind of pink cider (whatever will they think of next?) that can only be described as 'not very nice'.

All around one wafted the unlovely scent of fast-ish food – burgers, kebabs, hot dogs, cold dogs, dogs from Japan and, for the very daring, 'alternative noodles' (whatever they might be) – and from the many stalls that lit up the place like a fairground. And then there were the shops – hundreds of 'em offering everything from nasty T-shirts guaranteed to fall apart in the launderette through badly drawn posters of Stonehenge to 'legal highs' (i.e. herbal-style pills which are supposed to make the purchaser/ swallower's head go all awry but which, undoubtedly, have no effect on the body whatsoever). Oh, and on the main stage the so-called 'grunge' group Soundgarden were churning out the weediest heavy metal ever heard unto eternity. Dear me, never a dull moment at last weekend's Reading Festival. And as I never tired of telling my companions, much to their annoyance, 'Eh, oop, festivals weren't like this in my day, laddie. Oh, no. None of yer namby-pamby food outlets and sideshows in my day. In my day we made our own fun. Blah blah drone.' When my wife went to the lavatory and came back to report that – gasp – it actually had lavatory paper therein, I almost had a funny turn. Lavatory paper? At a pop festival?

Goodness gracious, kids today, eh? They don't know they're born, etc. etc. Why, in my day you were lucky to find a lavatory at all, and if you did it would be a latrine like something out of a Wilfred Owen poem, and then you quite often slipped into the unseemly quagmire. In short, everything was rather disgusting – to misquote Joseph Conrad: 'The squalor! The squalor!' – but . . . THAT'S HOW WE LIKED IT!

By a strange coincidence, a documentary about the Isle of Wight Festival of 1970 (the one featuring Jimi Hendrix playing our National Anthem rather badly and lots of stupid would-be 'anarchists' tearing down the corrugated fence and beating people up in the names of peace and freedom) was showing on the TV while the 1995 Reading Festival squiggled on. Just observe the difference betwixt then and now . . .

THEN. All one had was a huge field and one stage upon which the performers, er, performed. Sometimes – as at the Bath Festival of 1970 – this was palatable. Jefferson Airplane, the Byrds, Steppenwolf, Led Zeppelin – there was a line-up to conjure with. Mostly, it wasn't. The folk-singing pixie-person Donovan would, invariably, turn up uninvited and bore the hordes for hours with prissy songs about how lovely trees are and the like. But at least it was all LOUD.

NOW. Massive TV screens on either side of the main stage but you can't hear a thing. The sole 'residents' for miles around the Reading Festival site are an industrial estate and a Kwik-Fit Fitter – unoccupied on a Bank Holiday weekend, but even so we can't disturb the neighbours, now, can we?

THEN. In my day, we made our own fun, blah blah drone. Whenever we got listless (quite often, because Donovan or, yet worse, the Keef Hartley Big Band were usually up there being dreary), we would devise amusing-type festive games of our own making, i.e. Hunt the Latrine, Try to Buy a Piece of Cheese off Somebody Because There's No Food On Site and We're a Bit Hungry, Laugh at the Stupid Hippie Juggler Who is Standing at the Front and Blocking Everybody's View and even Sod This for a Lark Can We Go Home Now (Where Did We Park the Car? Duh, We Haven't GOT a Car Man, Remember?).

NOW. Boredom, supposedly, a thing of the past. Bungee-jumping and other treats (see above).

Headlining the Reading Festival (he came on long after Hole (Courtney Love seemed a trifle tipsy) and Björk (trying as hard as she could to be annoyingly bonkers) and Teenage Fanclub (sadly, I missed them, thanks to a prior engagement with my television set on the Friday night)) was Neil Young. Fascinating enough, Neil played at the first ever of these pop festival affairs – Monterey in 1967 (he was a member of Buffalo Springfield) – and here he was at the latest. Late on Sunday night, up there before a dwindling crowd, he looked older than Hell but he played like a mad angel. Some things, one is conservatively glad to say, never change.

# One in a million

*Mail on Sunday*, 22 October 1995

Free the Sting Accountant One. This is the name of my newly established action group, our one noble aim: to get Keith Moore, fifty-one, released from prison into which he has been so cruelly incarcerated by our unmerciful legal system. Yes, just the other day the so-called 'trial of the century' came to its conclusion in an astonishing 'guilty' verdict for the man at the adding (or subtracting) machine and six years' hard labour (so to speak). A nation was rocked to its very foundations. What, exactly, was Moore, the Martyr, 'guilty' of? Of robbing the piggy bank of a top rock star (but this is an ancient pop tradition – examine the cases of Noel Redding out of the Jimi Hendrix Experience, the Small Faces, the diminutive songstrel *avec* 'beauty spot' Ms Lynsey de Paul, who all sold lots of records but found that when they put their cashcards into the hole in the wall, the dreaded words 'Insufficient Funds' were upon the screen in harsh, green letters because they had been, in hippie terminology, 'ripped off', man). And just look to what purpose Mr Moore put Mr Sting's (or Mr Gordon Sumner's, to use his more sensible name) loose change of millions. He invested in a chain of Indian restaurants; what could be more environment friendly in this *fin de siècle* age when McDonald's and Burger Kings and 'theme eateries' 'inspired' by Arnold Schwarzerperson and/or 'supermodels' with no discernible bodies (or brains) are threatening to colonise the entire Western world? Then he had this brilliant wheeze to convert former Russian military aircraft for civilian use, i.e. change weapons of death into useful things in which passengers put too much luggage in the overhead lockers and then get plastered on free vodka.

Such a scheme could put an end to all war as we know it. Isn't that what Sting, the earnest protest singer, wants? Anyway, thus far the Free the Sting Accountant One fighting fund has collected the princely sum of 36 pence (plus a second-class stamp – all contributions exceedingly welcome); and there's a benefit LP in the offing: lots of top pop groups playing their favourite old Police songs for the worthy cause (Blur, Oasis, ZZ Top and Big Country do not seem to be returning my calls, for some strange reason, but it can only be a matter of time, surely?). The thing is, readers, this man MUST walk free. Why, it's not his fault that Sting grew so grotesquely rich that he (Sting) didn't even notice that some millions of quid had gone missing until tipped off by an anonymous letter that arrived at his (Sting's) Californian abode. No, it is the fault of all the people who were silly enough to buy Sting's dreadful records. Hence: WE ARE ALL GUILTY.

And here's another thing to make yer average pop music fan slightly hopping mad. Apparently, according to the meeja, 'poetry is the new rock 'n' roll'. A few months ago it was comedy that was the 'new rock 'n' roll' but, apparently, everybody got bored with that unlikely chestnut. So now it's poetry. Bah, humbug. Whatever will they think of next . . . 'soap opera is the new rock 'n' roll' – a selection of not very good actors out of *Emmerdale* join Lemmy from Motörhead and the bass player of the Smashing Pumpkins for a pointless discussion chaired by TV's 'Mr Rock' Robert Sandall (as seen on VH-1, the satellite rock thing for old fogies)? . . . Or 'Grouting the tiles in one's bathroom is the new rock 'n' roll: Sarah Dunant meets a plumber and Justine from Elastica'? . . . 'Capital punishment is the new rock 'n' roll: heated debate from the House of Commons featuring Tony Blair and His Rolling Stones'? Give us, as they say, a break. Rock 'n' roll, as every fule kno, is the new synchronised swimming and poetry is, as ever, simply irksome.

In a recent poll, conducted by BBC Radio, a paltry 7,000 listeners voted for their favourite poem of all time and the winner was the rather ridiculous 'If' by Rudyard Kipling (as you know, the one that goes 'If you can be a real man shouting at foreigners but still be kind to foreigners serving them kippers for breakfast and ask them if there's still jam for tea because there's a jackdaw sitting on the cardinal's chair', or something (not much) like that). Is this any relation to 'If', the song which whittled its way to number one when breathed by Telly 'Kojak' Savalas in 1975? I rather fear it is. Which proves my point, doesn't it?

# Sleep talk

*Observer*, **9 March 1997**

Insomnia is not a very nice condition. Until I turned about twenty-five it did not, for me, exist. I slept like a baby. But then God, all-night sweats thinking what a useless item of humanity I was and trying to go to sleep by naming the members of Herman's Hermits or pretending that I was Clive Lloyd scoring a brilliant century, that sort of thing. Nothing worked.

But recently, the proliferation of all-night radio stations has been a boon to persons suffering from the unable-to-slumber scenario. Good book? Mug of cocoa? Pah. Here is my recipe for your sleepless night. Start off on the World Service. John Tidmarsh is talking about fireflies in Angola. This is the stuff! Except that then Tidmarsh's Outlook ends and some ghastly jazz programme comes on so you turn yer knob to Radio 5 Live, upon which there's a raging debate about the future of rugby league, and so you turn your dial a bit more to Talk Radio, upon which Mike Dicken is trying to be 'controversial' by saying that women drivers are useless. So it's down the dial again to LBC (heard only in the London region, unfortunately) for Clive Bull. This man is a genius. There you are, trying to fall asleep, having tuned in to 'obviously boring', when Bull comes on saying, 'And tonight's topics are "What happens when you are cremated?" and "Which cast members of *Crossroads* are dead?" Bull has a certain dry wit that keeps one from going mad in the wee hours. I rang a late-night phone-in once. I told Pete Murray that cockroaches were not the disease-ridden characters he was saying they were. I was cut off. I never went back to sleep. Ever.

# Supertramp: Is this really the most fun you can have with a washing-up glove?

*Observer*, 22 June 1997

The Albert Hall programme sellers are doing brisk business. 'Six pounds,' I cry in disbelief. 'Six quid for a booklet with a picture of a kettle in Outer Space (typical Supertramp 'imagery', this) on the front. That seems a trifle exorbitant, don't you think?' The programme-seller shrugs her shoulders. If I don't buy, there's plenty more that will.

The average Supertramp fan, of which there are surprisingly many after all these years (it is ten years since this distinctly unfashionable rock troupe last toured), is a well-heeled soul, it would appear; middle-aged and mobile of telephone, with the William Hague hair look for the gentlemen, fluffy minor royalty for the ladies; polite suits for the gentlemen, a retro Laura Ashley-styled look for the gels.

'Boldly, better than ever, they're back,' boasts the glossy brochure. 'Supertramp, one of the truly defining bands in pop music history . . .' Then, for your six quid, you get a) a picture of a dog biscuit on the surface of the moon (v. 'meaningful'); b) enormous photographs of a load of sensibly dressed and often bearded men playing musical instruments; c) some further guff about 'the return of the magic . . . the reprise of irresistible memories and of lyrics, poignant, witty and wise . . . fresh but familiar, ever surprising in their musical audacity . . .' etc. Er, can I have my money back? The stage is dark, the hall is packed, crowd hushed in anticipation and then roar, hurrah, flashing lights flash and they are **THERE**, all dressed in smart, dark suits, gathered around their keyboards and various other things, playing some rather complicated jazz-rock-oriented arrangement with grand accomplishment. Supertramp, the band that time forgot, the group more derided by the hip 'n' groovy than almost any other (though Emerson, Lake & Palmer and Yes might run them a close race) are back and doing what they do best, which is showing off their technical prowess.

You never get a dud note with Supertramp. You get dizzying displays of keyboard/guitar/ saxophone wizardry . . . and, of course, absolutely no passion at all. Supertramp are for those who like their hi-fis shiny and spanky and have absolutely no objection whatsoever to drum solos and 'songs' that go on forever. Or as the programme would have it: 'The sound of quality . . . a smile . . . a melody . . . a memory.' Supertramp . . . yes, they may be very dull but, by golly, are they **WORTHY**! There are thousands of them up there on the stage (well, eight, at any rate) and they all look like celebrity hairdressers (except for John Helliwell, on woodwinds and unamusing jokes, who resembles a jolly geography teacher). They are not the most exciting band to observe – they don't do anything except play and the static nature of their performance is hardly enlivened by the gigantic screen at the back which, if this were Pink Floyd or U2 or somebody, would be showing eye-dazzling footage of cosmic doings and mushroom clouds and icons of history and that sort of caper, but, as this is Supertramp, is very much more feeble. Throughout the evening this screen seems to show nothing more thrilling than what looks like an orange washing-up glove.

But the crowd are faithful and satisfied, impressed by endless solos and rather weedy lyrics about skies and birds. On more than one occasion there even threatens to be an outbreak of gasp DANCING down there among the stalls. This, you must recall, is the band that no less a personage than Princess Diana once declared to be among her very favourites. Supertramp played a Prince's Trust concert in 1986 and, as Helliwell told *Mojo* magazine earlier this year, 'I think Prince Charles had his ear-plugs, and I know he nodded off because my son was sitting in a box with them. But Di was on the front of her seat, really digging it.' *Some Things Never Change* is the title of Supertramp's new LP (its cover features, naturally enough, an elderly couple at a table taking tea on, you guessed it, the moon) but that title is somewhat misleading, for Roger Hodgson is no longer a member of the combo.

This, for the layman, is a great pity, as Hodgson was the one who wrote the group's more acceptable, poppy songs, things like 'Dreamer' and that frankly rather GOOD one about school whose name I can't remember. Stripped of Hodgson's melodies, the Supertramp 'sound' becomes more than a little wearying, song turning into interminable song. All one can do of a positive nature is admire the professional execution.

As the washing-up glove pops up upon the screen once more, I find myself drifting off. Well, what's wrong with that? I am in good company. Supertramp – the group that sent Prince Charles to sleep.

# Ministry of Sounds

*Mail on Sunday*, 22 May 1994

Not one of the many recent newspaper profiles of Tony Blair failed to mention one important – nay vital – fact: the fact that many years ago while at university, this probable future Labour leader and possible future prime minister was in a rock band with Mark Ellen (who went on to present *Whistle Test* on the telly and to edit *Smash Hits*, *Q* and *Mojo* magazines). Said group were called Ugly Rumours and were, by all accounts, thoroughly dreadful. Blair was the singer. He laboured under the delusion that he was somehow 'Jagger-esque'. This fact, that Tony Blair used to be in a band with Mark Ellen and may be our next PM, is made yet more interesting by the insertion of a further fact: astonishingly enough, I, your humble pop correspondent, am today, in 1994, in a rock band with Mark Ellen. I do the 'singing' and I play the guitar (something which Blair, contrary to certain reports, could never quite manage) and this can mean, surely, only one thing: it is I, not Blair, who is destined to be the next leader of our once-proud island nation. The signs cannot be ignored. And when I am swept to power, as I clearly shall be, by the popular vote, there will be some sweeping changes round here, I can tell you, particularly in the field of pop music.

- Item: Deportation to Australia to be brought back for certain crimes, i.e. being a member of Take That or simply being a person whose music I take a personal dislike to, i.e. Sting.
- Item: Diplomatic relations with America to be cut off until Bill Clinton learns to puff the saxophone properly and stops playing ghastly old Fleetwood Mac records at his gala affairs.
- Item: All charity discs to be referred to the Minister for Charity Records (me) before being granted a release licence. (Under this new law we would be spared having to listen to 'Absolutely Fabulous', the new Comic Relief single by the Pet Shop Boys, which is absolutely terrible. I know this record is in a good cause, but under my dictatorship . . . er, sorry, administration, there will be no need for 'good causes' because everyone in need throughout the world will be properly cared for (apart from Huey Lewis & the News).
- Item: The Monkees will reform, and I'll change the curtains in 10 Downing Street.
- Item: On second thoughts, I've decided that I may not accept high office after all, because it's so much more fun just sitting here listening to the latest pop releases and telling you how fantastic (or not) they are . . .

Releases such as Roger Taylor's (he's the drummer out of Queen) 'Nazis 1994' single. Not a charity disc, this, but what used to be called a 'protest' record, upon which Taylor rails against the fact that certain hideous people of the neo-Fascist persuasion – it's the craze that's sweeping Europe! – have suggested, ridiculously, that the Holocaust never actually happened. 'So they're saying now it never happened,' fumes Roger over and over again above pumping drums and squiggling guitars.

Apart from the subject matter – very worthy – the record has nothing to recommend it, it is so dull. But R. Taylor has been complaining about the fact his song has not been played very much on the radio, as if there were some Nazi broadcasting conspiracy afoot to suppress his works. This is all very well but anybody can make a 'right on' record, can't they? If it doesn't sound any good, why should radio be duty-bound to spin it? I once witnessed in a pub an acoustic ensemble strumming their instruments and looking earnest as they warbled a 'self-penned' song which went something like 'Homeless people, it's all very sad/Homeless children, it makes you mad'. The bearded group's heart was in the right place, certainly, but their music (and their lyric) was fearful. Should they (I think they were called Righteous Bliss) be broadcast just because they are 'nice'? Shoot the messenger.

And what, if I were to become PM, would I do about Traffic? Here we have one of the very original English 'psychedelic' bands. Hundreds of years ago (1968), they bunked off to 'get their heads together', as the old hippie saying went, in a cottage in the Berkshire countryside and recorded lots of singles all about being borne on the wings of gigantic albatrosses across fluffy clouds of marshmallow. Or something. They were quite good, in a flitty 'Swinging Sixties' sort of way. Alas, they have reformed (although one of the original members, Dave Mason, is notable by his absence, and another, Chris Wood, is dead, which leaves only Steve Winwood and Jim Capaldi . . . so it's a bit like Paul McCartney and Ringo Starr making a record and calling themselves the Beatles). Traffic's new LP, *Far From Home* (Virgin CDV 2727), doesn't sound like proper Traffic at all; rather, it sounds like an extension of the last Steve Winwood polished and MTV-friendly album, plush and boring. Traffic? They used to wear flared trousers and tea cosies upon their heads. Now they wear Armani suits. Something should be done. Who on earth shall I appoint as my first minister of pop? Suggestions, please.

# Tony Blairing error

*Mail on Sunday*, **12 August 1995**

'Maggie, Maggie, Maggie, Out Out Out!' That was the rather uninspired chant we used to, er, chant back in the glory days of the '80s when there was Poll Tax in the air and a closed-down miner on every street corner. What will we rabble rousers be shouting after the next General Election, I wonder. I rather fear it will be something like this: 'Oh dear, oh dear, oh dear, oh dear, it's Tony, Tony, Tony, Tony Blair.' The man's an absolute shocker.

I am not referring here to his 'New Labour' policies (whatever they might be) but to the manner in which he clambers aboard the good ship pop (music) at every eventuality, imagining he might ingratiate himself to the 'yoof' of the nation by so doing. He was at it again just the other day. He delivered what one newspaper described as a 'rousing speech' to 200 of the pop biz's leading executives at the BPI (that's the British Phonographic Industry to you) annual general meeting.

That 'rousing speech' not in full: 'Music is not just about glitz and glamour, it's about industry,' he spouted. Hurrah. Let's work, as Mick Jagger once 'sang'. He went on to praise the music industry, declaring it as important to the UK as the coal and steel industries. Uh oh. Excuse me, Tone, what coal and steel industries? Is the subtext here that when you are swept to power by the popular vote

333

and your tooth-packed smile, you are going to close down the music industry? Putting me and millions of people like me and millions of pop stars out of a job? Oh dear, it's Tony Blair. And after he had made his silly, self-serving speech he was presented with an Eric Clapton edition Fender Stratocaster guitar. Which is a bit stupid because he can't play the guitar and I jolly well hope he has written it – the gift – down in the Register of Members' Interests because if he hasn't – as he failed to do about that Concorde trip to America in 1986 – I shall personally make sure that he goes to prison for a very long time . . . Failing that, I shall confiscate his Eric Clapton edition Fender Stratocaster guitar – because I, unlike him, am, at least, able to squeeze a note or two of the introduction to 'Layla' out of such things. 'Diddle-diddle-diddle-dee': that's how it goes. Virgin Records' managing director Paul Conroy had this to say about Tony Blur's speech: 'It was like when Kennedy dawned on the politics of America.' Oh, sure. Is this a joke or something? 'Here was a person of our generation who understands us and the music industry. He knew what a Fender guitar was.' Bully. 'And he knows the difference between Motörhead and Enya.' For goodness' sake, I've got the hippy hippy shake, EVERYBODY knows the difference between Motörhead – crashingly boring heavy metal exercise, very loud – and Enya – stupendously dull New Age style waftings, very soft – even my dear old mum. If this is the best that our putative prime minister can do – tell the difference between a noisy racket and a smoothie snooze – then he'd be better off taking his snout from out of the trough that is pop music. I have said it before and I will say it again: it ill behoves a politician to have any opinion whatsoever about pop music. Alec Douglas-Home calls the Beatles his 'secret weapon', Tipper Gore (wife of the Vice-President of the US) says quite a lot of rock lyrics are rather too saucy for her liking and something must be done about it (and then jigs the night away to the fearful sounds of Fleetwood Mac). Such political people just end up looking extremely SILLY. Don't they?

## TONY BLAIRING ERROR

If Tony Blair had been given some sensible advice before that ridiculous speech of his, he might have said something like this: 'Hello, voters. I'm a bit of a groover, me. When I was at school we all used to argue about who was better – the Beatles or the Rolling Stones. So it gives me immense pleasure to announce that on 14 August, a similar argument will be raging in the playgrounds of our many schools, which though run down by previous Conservative governments will be really fab again when I come to power. Hem hem. The argument is this: Who is better? Blur or Oasis?' Wild applause. 'Thank you, thank you.'

Tomorrow, both Oasis' 'Roll With It' single and Blur's 'Country House' are released. Which will get to number one first? This is the question engaging a nation. The smart money is on Oasis. Tony Blair has bet 50p each way on Whitney Houston.

Tom and Mark Ellen practising in Chiswick, circa 1997
(courtesy of Allyce Hibbert).

# Part Seven

## The new rock 'n' roll

Taking up the mantle of the *Observer*'s diarist character
Pendennis, Tom is free to comment on political matters,
a lifelong fascination. Going a step further, he decides to
stand for parliament in his native Henley-on-Thames.

Tom's Pendennis column in the *Observer*.

# Pendennis: Tarzan the AHP man[1]

## *Observer*, 2 March 1997

I don't like aeroplane pilots very much. Do you? No. They are awful. They are riddled to the gills with unseemly japery, i.e. every time you have finished your so-called 'meal' (in which the only edible items were the plastic fork and the 'towelette'), they turn the Fasten Your Seat Belt signs on because of some 'turbulence'. Therefore you can't go to the so-called 'toilet' to throw up said plastic fork and have to utilise the sick bag provided in the so-called 'pocket' of your so-called 'seat' in front of you, thus making the fat religious maniac who has been laughing throughout the film starring Dudley Moore very irate indeed.

Then, THEN, when you have been stabbed almost to death with a plastic fork, which the fat person next to you forgot to eat, the voice of the pilot comes oozing into your ears. You are trying to sleep, listening to *The Best of the Goodies* on the in-flight pleasure network. But the pilot cuts in with his reserved middle-class accent, 'We're flying at 36,000 ft,' he purrs, 'and if you look out of your left windows, you'll be able to see the westerly coast of Ireland.' So

---

[1] Note that some of the Pendennis columns in this chapter have been abridged in order to focus on the principal theme of Tom's election campaign.

339

THAT's what we're going to crash into, that's where we'll die a horrible death.

I mention this only because Norman 'on your bike' Tebbit, the goody Lord, has been having a bit of a go at my dear friend Michael Heseltine. Outrageous. Now, finally, I can reveal that I, Pendennis, am about to sling my hat (slightly soiled) in the ring and take Michael Heseltine to task. Yes. I, Pendennis, can confess that he (Pendennis) is to put himself up for candidature at the forthcoming General Election on behalf of the Alternative Heseltine Party. You see, the thing is that Tarzan Brilliantine, for that is his name, has a slender majority of only several trillion and I greatly fear that on the grand day stupid persons, of which there are many, might put their pencilled voting-booth ticks in the wrong bit. The Alternative Heseltine Party (stupid acronym: AHP) will see that justice is done. Somehow.

# Pendennis

# Election '97: Repeal the Corn Laws! Suffrage for ladies!! Vote Tom Hibbert!!!

*Observer*, 6 April 1997

### Thursday 3 April

And so, Easter behind us, my campaign for election to the Mother of all Parliaments begins in earnest and the Hibbert household is in a state of no little turmoil! Even Trusty, our pedigree Golden Retriever (or is it a Labrador? Celia, my fragrant and supportive wife of many a happy year, and a stern believer in Family Values, is the dog expert in these parts!) seems excited by coming events! Celia (who keeps joking that she wouldn't vote for me in a million years and intends to put her X by the name of Heseltine, Michael Ray Dibdin (Con)) is being most, er, supportive, although somewhat sniffy about the constant intrusions of my Election Agent. The boys Benjy and Coriolanus are being absolute bricks also, suggesting, 'Pater, why don't you dress up as a chicken like everybody else in the newspapers? That would be absolutely def and WICKED!' 'Hah!' huffs little Griselda (three years old or is it five? Time passes so quickly in the giddy world of politics. What was it that that rather common fellow in the raincoat, Harold Wilson, used to say? 'A week in politics is as good as a rest', something like that). 'Hah! How could anybody possibly tell the difference betwixt Papa and a chicken, anyway?' Oh, how we all roar as I, a stern believer in Family Values, tan their mischievous hides with my fountain pen!

## Friday 4 April

My Election Agent comes barging into the house uninvited as per usual and is roundly bitten on the ankle by Trusty.

He has finally found me a soapbox (a wooden Sandeman's Port crate with a silhouette of Orson Welles on the side) upon which to stand in Falaise Square, Henley-on-Thames, as I amaze the huddled masses with my sturdy oratory. Good for him. We quarrel for some time about what colour my campaign rosettes should be. I am all for something calm and dignified, such as off-puce, but my Election Agent favours something Day-Glo with spangles on, which spins round due to battery operation.

My Election Agent then suggests that I dress up as a chicken when I go canvassing. Sometimes I think he is not taking this campaign entirely seriously. I tell him so in no uncertain terms, but all he says is, 'Celia, I fear your husband is becoming a trifle pompous, haw haw! Pass the dry sherry, there's a dear.' Celia, so supportive, snaps back: 'Look, if you are really going to make a thrust of this General Election caper, don't you think it is time to think about the issues?' I stare at my beloved in some amazement. What can she mean? 'A manifesto. Don't you think your party should have a man-i-fest-o?' Oh, good point.

## Saturday 5 April

Have been up all night working on my manifesto. It is, I think I can say without fear of contradiction, quite splendid. I am a stern believer in Family Values and think that Capital Punishment should be reintroduced for people who shoot policemen, child-molesters and the entire cast of the film *Evita*. Yes, there's votes aplenty in this. My Election Agent barges in, is assaulted by Trusty, and then says in an overly cross tone, 'Manifestos are all very well, but don't you think we should choose a name for your so-called "party"?' Hmm. Good point.

My Election Agent wants us to be called the Stout Party because 'when nobody votes for you, we can quip "Collapse of Stout Party"! Haw haw!' I fail to detect the humour in this and plump for a party name more calm and dignified: Whig. I shall be the representative of the Whig Party for the constituency of Henley-on-Thames on Thursday 1 May, and I won't dress up as a chicken. Much rejoicing.

## Sunday 6 April

Have been up all night working on my manifesto (again). I really think I have cracked it this time. This should give Michael Ray Dibdin Heseltine (Con) something to think about and no mistake. Here we go: 'Good day. May I introduce myself. My name is Tom Hibbert and, as a stern believer in Family Values and capital punishment for sundry crimes, as are my supportive wife Celia and our three polite children, Benjy, Coriolanus and Griselda, I, your Whig Party candidate in the forthcoming General Election, hope and trust that I can depend on your support at the, er, forthcoming General Election. My message is plain. My message is simple. My message is vital for taking this country into the forthcoming millennium, proud and prosperous. The main issues at stake, I believe, and I am sure you do too, are these:

- Repeal of the Corn Laws.
- Local issues: That newsagent's on the corner of Bell Street is an absolute eyesore, inside and out. Something must be done.
- Abolition of Slavery.
- Local issues: The Thames river at the bottom of Henley only adds to traffic congestion. Should we fill it in or relocate it up Friday Street? We shall be having a referendum re this one.

- Votes for Women over thirty.
- Capital Punishment.
- Family Values.
- Corporal Punishment.
- Local issues: Henley deserves a proper Post Office, not something apologetic tucked away in the corner of that ghastly newsagent's in Bell Street. Eh?
- Britain Deserves Better!
- You Can Only Be Sure With The Whigs!
- Vote For Me! (Unless you have already made your mind up and are voting for M.R.D. Heseltine (Con), which is fair enough, it's a free country after all.) (NB Celia thinks this last bit is 'wimpy'. I shall delete it.)

## Monday 7 April

It's off on the stump with soapbox, twirling rosette and 'attractive' children in tow. Celia is 'far too busy' to accompany me. Most annoying. I shall let you know of my progress next week. In the meantime, Vote Whig!

Pendennis

# On the Stump: Vote for me!

*Observer*, 20 April 1997

## Monday 14 April

'Pater, Papa!' The supportive boys come rushing in from the games room where they have been watching the televisual device. 'A journalist has thrown his hat into the ring to stand against someone jolly important! Come and look!' My excitement knows few bounds. This can only be a reference to me, and my stance against Michael Ray Dibdin Heseltine. Imagine, then, my alarm when all I see on the screen is somebody called Martin Bell. Benjy and Coriolanus have a jolly good laugh at my red-faced expense. At this point my election agent appears and 'quips': 'Well, why don't you buy a white suit?' I have a white suit, actually, but alas my daughter Griselda drew all over it in coloured crayons for a school project and I have no intention of looking like a leftover member of untimely beat combo Jethro Tull. 'Why ever not?' asks my supportive wife, Celia. 'You couldn't possibly look any sillier than you do.'

## Tuesday 15 April

The candidates have been announced and there are only seven of us which, for my money, gives me a one in seven chance of (inevitable) victory. The Referendum candidate's Christian name is Sebastian. I ask you, who would ever vote for somebody called Sebastian? Ha! Then there is the Natural Law candidate, whose names are Nigel Vivien Peers. Poo. As for Michael Ray Dibdin . . . I scent victory, until my agent calls my attention to the Statement of Persons Nominated and Notice of Poll. 'Hibbert, Thomas Roderick,' it somewhat embarrassingly declares. 'Roderick?' he roars. 'You don't stand a chance!'

## Wednesday 16 April

To breakfast, where I spy my agent enjoying a bowl of Coco Pops, upon which my supportive wife Celia (stern believer in Family Values) is pouring dry sherry from a decanter. I always believed that cereals were supposed to be laced with semi-skimmed milk – but times change, I suppose. And I, as your Whig candidate, must change with them. Nonetheless, I find this scenario unseemly and make the biggest decision of my campaign so far. I sack my agent. He is crestfallen, managing only the noisiest of laughs as he says: 'Well, I was going to vote for Heseltine, anyway, just like everyone else!'

## Thursday 17 April

Celia confronts me with a letter. 'Ah, another keen voter, I suppose,' I gleam. 'No,' she replies, somewhat snootily. 'This is what is called Divorce Papers!' What on earth can she, a stern believer in Family Values, mean by this? Never mind. I have been advised to hire a 'spin doctor'. So immediately I ask my old chum Alan 'Fluff' Freeman if he will serve. 'Not 'arf!' he replies in his ribald fashion. Hurrah.

## Friday 18 April

I expect you have read that my children, Coriolanus, Benjy and Griselda, do not exist and I simply found three suitable-looking kiddiwinks at the off-licence, bribed them with 'Alcopops' and kidnapped them for 'photo-ops'. There is not a scintilla of truth in these allegations. Except there is. But I remain and shall always remain a stern believer in Family Values.

# Pendennis

## Election '97: Vote for me!

*Observer*, 27 April 1997

### Monday 21 April

It is with no little reluctance that I have had to 'let go' of the services of my new spin doctor, Alan 'Fluff' Freeman. His ideas seemed less than plentiful – i.e. for us to drive around the Henley-on-Thames constituency in an ostentatious 'stretch limo' while 'Fluff' plays his favourite records (*Tales From Topographic Oceans* by some beat combo called Yes) at great volume while barking his catchphrases ('Not 'arf') from the window. 'Where are the votes to be gained in that kind of caper?' I enquire. 'Listen, mate,' he replies. 'Didn't you know? Politics is the new rock and roll! Tony Blair used to be in the Rolling Stones, or something like that. Get with it, me old mucker! Not 'arf!' Is that a tear in the eye of the man of the Australian persuasion I spy as I issue his marching orders? I rather imagine it might not be. Politics is a serious business and it is high time everyone realised this. Especially, my soon-to-be-defeated rival Michael Ray Dibdin Heseltine, who appears to imagine . . . er, memo to self: must get round to reading Heseltine's election 'literature'.

## Tuesday 22 April

It is with a certain reluctance that I drop round to my erstwhile election agent's 'bachelor pad' to invite him back aboard my campaign (everyone else feeling far too humble to undertake such a vital and difficult quest). I find him in the kitchenette enjoying a cup of coffee (Nescafé Gold Blend, I rather suspect) with my supportive wife Celia, stern supporter of Family Values. 'Oh, Gawd, it's you,' says Celia, in a tone which seems, for her, surprisingly non-welcoming. My agent, however, seems delighted to rejoin the fight – so much so that he slips me a shiny pound coin to pop down to the corner shop for a further jar of coffee.

## Wednesday 23 April

To the fine offices of the *Thames Gazette*, an august journal in my constituency with a circulation rumoured to be in the low hundreds. 'So what are your policies, then, Tim?' asks the editor, who has an amusing way of getting my name wrong for reasons best known to himself. 'Well, as a Whig,' I reply, in my most pompous, er, I mean 'severe' manner, 'I am very much in favour of' – 'Yes, can I interrupt you there,' says my interrogator. 'We're very pushed for time. And indeed space. So just a photograph will suffice.' I hand him a snapshot of myself playing crazy golf with a couple of lads I met in an off-licence in Kent. 'As a stern believer in Family Values,' I say, 'I think it important to introduce youngsters to outdoor pursuits at an early age – and here you see my sons, Coriolanus and Benjy, tackling the long eighth at the Maidstone Leisure Centre.'

'Look, everybody knows you made your children up for the purposes of your campaign and don't actually have any kids at all!' he snaps. Blast! News travels fast in the constituency of Henley! Still, the *Reading Evening Post* has done me justice. In a six-page spread about the election, I am pleased to see that, at the bottom of the last page, under 'Other Candidates' it says: 'THOMAS HIBBERT Whig'. A proud moment, indeed.

## Thursday 24 April

On the 'stump' in Henley, passing out leaflets to the goodly citizens of this lovely regatta-styled haven (lovely, so long as you don't count that ghastly newsagent's on the corner of Bell Street). 'Hello, I am your Whig candidate and trust that I can count on your vote at the general election?' I beam to a gentleman who is, on closer inspection, entirely bald. 'Wig? You taking the piss or something? Think baldies are figures of fun?' My agent calms this (clearly) non-voting-for-me personage by explaining that I have just been released into the 'care of the community' and am entirely mad due to insufficient medication. This seems to appease the balding gent and he and my agent waltz into the nearest hostelry for a 'swift half'. They are gone some time. I give up 'stumping' and return home. To, I have to say, an empty house.

# Pendennis

## Why the Whig's a wag

*Observer*, 11 May 1997

And so Pendennis's quest for ultimate power has ended for another five years, anyway. If I understand **PR** (proportional representation) properly (which it is possible that I do not), my massive minority-lost-deposit 160 votes would have got my Whig Party about 56 seats. Which may have proved embarrassing because I've only got four chairs in my house. Ho, ho! Pendennis has just won his own Unfunny Joke competition (dream date with Chelsea Clinton, set of steak knives, the usual rubbish). But seriously, folks, as the late (blub) Sir Hughford of Green used to say, I think that my campaign to oust Michael Ray Dibdin Heseltine has paid dividends. All right, he got about a trillion more votes than me, but he seemed ill-at-ease when he heard **MY** result. And what happened the very next day? He was rushed to hospital. Gave up all thoughts of Conservative leadership. I feel rather guilty about all this. But it is nice to know that the 'little man' CAN make a difference. Get better soon, Mr Heseltine. Pendennis means that most sincerely.

# 313 Henley

Electorate 66,424        Boundary change

*+MICHAEL HESELTINE (C) ......... 23,908

Timothy Horton (LD) .................. 12,741

Duncan Enright (Lab)................ 11,700

Sebastian Sainsbury (Ref).......... 2,299

Mrs Sue Miles (Green) ............... 514

Nigel Barlow (NLP)..................... 221

Thomas Hibbert (Whig).............. 160

Poll 77.60%        **C Maj 11,167**

**No Change**     Swing 7.21% C to LD

General election results for Henley constituency, May 1997.

# Politics: When girl bands fancy Dennis Skinner, you know politics really is the new rock 'n' roll

*Observer*, 18 May 1997

From the esteemed newspaper, the *Henley Standard*, dateline 9 May 1997, came this report on the exit from government of Michael Ray Dibdin Heseltine. 'There was a dazed look about the departing Deputy Prime Minister. More like a wounded lion than the King of the Jungle. At least Tom Hibbert, candidate for the Whig Party, managed to raise a smile from Heseltine at the end of a long evening. "Michael Heseltine's my hero!" Hibbert proclaimed to the weary audience, with more than a hint of irony.'

What the paper forgot to mention is that Mr Hibbert went on to declare: 'And politics is the new rock 'n' roll!' And how very true this is. Heseltine, despite his hair loosely based on an original idea by Status Quo and his mace-throwing antics so reminiscent of the guitar-trashing capers of Pete Townshend of the Who, was never rock 'n' roll. Nor was J. Major. But Tony Blair can crank out a mean lick or two on his trusty Fender Stratocaster, while impersonating his hero Paul Rodgers. Gordon Brown can frug like nobody's business once the Foo Fighters hit the CD player. When Tory chairman Kenneth Baker appeared at the BRIT Awards some years ago, he was roundly booed (much to the annoyance of 'Sir' Cliff Richard).

Can you imagine such a thing happening to John Prescott now? Of course not. 'I'm from the rock 'n' roll generation,' declared Call-Me-Tony Blair. And look what happened next. Swept to power, crying, in ancient stadium-rock tradition, 'Britain, I lurve ya!' Yes, Mr Hibbert was definitely correct – but what do the rock 'n' rollers think?

'I went to the Labour Party party at the Festival Hall. All the people were in their twenties and it was very exciting – feeling political while listening to very loud electronic music until the sun came up. We've got a prime minister who goes home and – like a lot of us – plugs in a Stratocaster and rocks. That's terribly exciting and I think a lot of people are responding to it.'

*Mark Ellen, once in the band Ugly Rumours with Tony Blair and now publisher of Q magazine*

'The lead singer of Kenickie said she fancied Dennis Skinner. Another of them fancies John Prescott. It's hip.'

*Paddy Davis of Bad Moon PR*

'Years ago, you wouldn't get a model talking politics; now they'll hang, have a Marlboro Light and seem quite proud to have little discussions. When Gordon Brown made his decision over Bank of England interest rate formulation, there was a lot of interest from the girls – everyone was talking about it.'

*Paula Karaiskos of Storm Model Management*

'Tony Blair is undoubtedly the first pop-star prime minister. You only have to look at him being mobbed on Downing Street. He inspires adulation. Get him with Noel Gallagher and he'd make the cover. He's the most powerful man in the land and he's shaken his hair to Zeppelin. He's not exactly cool but his taste is pretty zeitgeist-friendly.'

Melody Maker *editor Mark Sutherland*

# Coda

## 'We shall not see his like again'

Tom and Robyn Hitchcock, 'jamming' in Chiswick, circa 1997
(courtesy of Allyce Hibbert).

# Hibbert and I

# 'Haunting the plains of west London'

## Robyn Hitchcock

Oh, what a vision is Tom Hibbert. Thin with dark ruffled hair, a scarf, John Lennon spectacles, cigarette permanently in his blue-veined talons, the delight of irony on his humorous lips. I remember Tom drinking double Scotches at lunchtime in a cloud of fresh-lit Marlboro smoke. I remember him coming to my house for a wake the night Lennon died. I remember listening to 'New Age' with him on New Year's Eve, 1999, drinking to the undoubted horrors of the forthcoming century. I remember his support for our music; his love of the Byrds; 'Eight Miles High' playing his coffin into the incinerator at his funeral.

There was no Tom without alcohol. The booze may have killed him, but he was never himself without it. After his pancreatitis, after months in intensive care, after months of solicitude from his anxious wife and friends, they were delivered a dried-up Tom who wasn't there. He was a ghost who yet haunted the plains of west London. 'You must never drink alcohol again' was the mantra given him on his recovery. But the doctors were addressing his body, not his nature.

Several times I visited his house, where he sat like an inmate at a day-care centre, parked in front of a television with his cigarettes, watching vintage football matches. There was no smile on his face, no light in his eyes: he was polite but dead, almost as if he'd been stuffed for the benefit of those who loved him.

Occasionally I'd pass the old Tom on Chiswick High Road; his walk was confident and his grin broad. But even before I smelled his breath, I could tell he'd been at the spirits.

'Well, then – how are you? Shall we get together for something soon?'

Alas, we couldn't, officially, get together for anything Tom would have enjoyed: for his own sake – medically – every rendezvous with him had to be a sober one.

In the end, the booze claimed him. He disappeared from his wife and his friends; briefly returned to the chilly parental matrix that was perhaps the root of his malaise; then into solitude, petrol-station sandwiches, little glass bottles. I was sad but unsurprised. At least on the way out he could be himself.

I'm grateful for Tom and for what he was to all of us who knew him as his maximum self. It cost him – and Allyce – a lot to keep him here, but I'm so glad that he was, when he was. Love on ya, Hibbs.

# Tom Hibbert, 1952–2011

## Mark Ellen, *Guardian*, 2 September 2011

**Journalist known for his softly ruthless interview technique**

Tom Hibbert, a former *Observer* columnist and mainstay of both *Smash Hits* and *Q* magazines, has died aged fifty-nine, from complications brought about by diabetes. His cavalier humour and softly ruthless interview technique earned him a wide following in the pop-culture publications of the 1980s and '90s, as well as the affection and respect of his colleagues.

The son of the historian Christopher Hibbert, Tom was born in Henley-on-Thames, Oxfordshire, and went to Leighton Park Quaker school in Reading and then the local grammar, but dropped out of Leeds University after a term to play in various uncelebrated rock bands and chance his arm as a journalist.

Tom was unsuited to the home-improvement periodicals for which he wrote in the late '70s, but in 1980 his droll and quizzical reviews began to appear in *New Music News*, an underground rock weekly launched by Felix Dennis to fill the vacuum left by the strike-bound *NME* and *Melody Maker*. Tom admired very few musicians beyond Iggy Pop, Ray Davies and Jerry Garcia, but filed fond, waspish and lightly mocking deconstructions of many others. Asked by another staff member why he made up all the entries in the short-lived publication's letters column, his response was flatly logical: 'Because we don't have any readers.'

At *Smash Hits* in the mid-'80s, he helped invent a cartoon fantasy world in which everyone interviewed seemed to exhibit the same slapstick characteristics. All his subjects – Paul McCartney, David Bowie, Bucks Fizz, John Lydon – were delightfully over-exaggerated, as mischievous and eccentric as their interrogator. The magazine was so successful that even the prime minister, seeking re-election in 1987, believed she could speak to the entire nation's teenage youth by allowing Hibbert and his ancient tape-recorder through the door at Downing Street.

Margaret Thatcher's undoing was to attempt to prove that she, too, was a pop-music enthusiast. Tom took great delight in revealing that her favourite singer was Cliff Richard, whom she admired for being professional, and that her favourite record – on-message for the cost-conscious curator of an economic boom – was the fearful 1953 novelty hit '(How Much Is) That Doggie in the Window?'

Tom was unafraid of silence. He would give his subjects the impression that, despite their obvious successes, they were still somehow shameful underachievers and then sit back quietly with a cigarette to enjoy the panicked response. Both in work and life, he refused to take anything seriously. When given the job of writing the 'trail' to flag up the contents of the next *Smash Hits*, he would advertise groups that existed only in his fertile imagination – such as the failed pop idol Reg 'Reg' Snipton or an intriguing electronic duo, the Human Saucepans of the Orinoco.

Hibbert was transferred in 1986 to the new rock monthly *Q*, where a long-running feature known as 'Who the hell . . . ?' was devised especially for his withering humour and his extraordinary ability to get pompous public figures to make buffoons of themselves.

Month after month, the gullible and self-important celebrities of the day – Jeremy Beadle, Jeffrey Archer, Robert Maxwell, Samantha Fox, Keith Floyd, Bernard Manning, David Mellor, Sir Jimmy

Savile – would find their pearls of wisdom gently lampooned and their carefully constructed profiles vigorously barbecued. Tom flew to Brazil and tracked down the train robber Ronnie Biggs (whom, inevitably, he both liked and rather admired). He puffed his way across the Alps, pointing his microphone at the charity-walking Ian Botham and his elephant. The health minister Edwina Currie once advised him that his fondness for nicotine might lower his sperm count.

The *Observer* hired Tom to write its Pendennis column in the mid-'90s – witty and bone-dry conceits from the perspective of a smoke-fugged barstool – but in 1997 he developed pneumonia and acute pancreatitis, and spent three months in the intensive care unit of his local hospital in Hammersmith, west London. In his characteristic resigned and shrugging manner, he spent the last fourteen years of his life unable to work and living with the after-effects of an illness from which he never fully recovered.

Tom is survived by his wife, Allyce.

Tom Hibbert, journalist, born 28 May 1952; died 28 August 2011.

Tom with his father Christopher and sister Kate, Henley, circa 2000
(courtesy of Allyce Hibbert).

# Acknowledgements

### Fanx Ta-Ra (with a polite nod to Sad Café)

*The editors would like to express their deepest gratitude to the following:*
Allyce Hibbert for her memories and her photos; Mark Ellen and Mat Snow for helping to get the ball rolling; Caroline Grimshaw for her dinner-party images and her design for the cover; Chris Heath for going above 'n' beyond with some obscure Hibbert scans; Paul Rider for his priceless *Smash Hits* and *Q* photographs; Kipper Williams for his splendid Hibbs-assisted cartoons.

And to all the book's wonderful contributors: Mark Williams, Mark Ellen, William Shaw, Caroline Grimshaw, Sylvia Patterson, Paul Rider, Tom Doyle, Kipper Williams, Paul Du Noyer, Chris Heath, Bob Stanley and Robyn Hitchcock.

Also to Paul Gorman, who allowed us to quote from the 2001 interview he did with Tom. Plus of course to Nine Eight's Pete Selby, whose idea the book was in the first place; our agent Matthew Hamilton, who thrashed out the deal; James Lilford, who cleaned it all up in the edit; and to the Rock's Backpages team who supported us both through the work.

*B.H. and J.M-B.*